The A to Z of the New Testament

The A to Z of the New Testament

Things Experts Know That
Everyone Else Should Too

James F. McGrath

WILLIAM B. EERDMANS PUBLISHING COMPANY

GRAND RAPIDS, MICHIGAN

Wm. B. Eerdmans Publishing Co.
4035 Park East Court SE, Grand Rapids, Michigan 49546
www.eerdmans.com

29 28 27 26 25 24 23   1 2 3 4 5 6 7

ISBN 978-0-8028-8230-1

Library of Congress Cataloging-in-Publication Data

A catalog record for this book is available from the Library of
Congress.

Scripture quotations, unless otherwise indicated, are from the
New Revised Standard Version Updated Edition (NRSVUE).

Dedicated to the memory of Kelly Lewis-Walls Porter,
student and friend extraordinaire

Contents

CONTENTS

A

ABCs and Beyond

I still vividly remember when I was invited, while working on my doctorate at Durham University in England, to present on my subject area at a Sixth Form Study Day. As an American studying in the United Kingdom, I had no idea what that meant. With hindsight I can explain, for those who are as unfamiliar as I had been, that it is something universities in the UK offer to students who are doing A Levels (roughly equivalent to Advanced Placement exams in the United States) to help them with that as well as give them some exposure to what university study entails.

Being clueless when I was asked to participate, I requested a copy of the curriculum so I could get a sense of what students covered if they did New Testament, which was my area. Most of the key things one learns in any introductory course were on there: the authorship of the Gospels; the order in which they were written and how they relate to one another; the differences among them. It struck me profoundly that one could spend an entire lifetime in a church and yet never be introduced to these subjects, and even if one was, it would most likely be in an extremely cursory fashion. The disconnect between the emphatic proclamations of the Bible's importance I encountered in every church I attended or visited

1

and the lack of any detailed attention to the kinds of things these students were already learning in British high schools left me with the distinct feeling that something was wrong. Yet I knew that sermons that covered these topics would bore all but a small number of Bible nerds like me. I also knew that most Sunday school classes had no interest in tackling such subjects or were not equipped to do so.

Although I did not know at that time that I would get the opportunity to address the issue through a book, this volume essentially offers what I instinctively felt was missing and sorely needed. The book you are reading seeks to introduce the ABCs of New Testament study—the things taught in an introductory course at a university—to anyone interested, and to get you up to speed on all of the most crucial topics, from A to Z. While it covers the basics and is accessible to absolute beginners, it will take you—whether a beginner or someone who already knows quite a bit about the Bible— much further than you probably expect that a book this size could. For those who actually are taking a university course, all the technical terminology and stuff like that is covered. But for the benefit of everyone else, the book doesn't go through those things in a highly systematized but potentially boring order. If you want that, there are plenty of books that offer it.

In this book I try to keep things fun. Each chapter picks one topic that can be understood easily and then brings in the necessary information to explore it. While keeping things lighthearted and interesting, the book does offer all the kinds of introductory information a student is expected to cover in an advanced high school or introductory university course. I am convinced that if British teenagers can be expected to understand these things, then the vast majority of people in churches also can—and should be given the opportunity to do so.

Digging Deeper

For those who want simple answers to simple questions about the New Testament, those are available in abundance in books or online. The problem is that not only are there often many different answers, offered with equally absolute confidence, but very often the questions themselves are not as simple and straightforward as one might assume. Take this, for example: When did Paul write his first letter to the Corinthians? Wikipedia or Britannica will tell you (with a cautionary "probably") that the date of 1 Corinthians is around AD 53-54. It is a good answer, but it is important to understand how it is arrived at, which involves piecing together details from Paul's letters, the Acts of the Apostles, and historical sources outside the New Testament.

But that's not all. Unless you dig deeper still, you might miss a hidden assumption in the question itself—namely, the assumption that 1 Corinthians is Paul's first letter to that church. Surely, you may object, that is obvious and needs no discussion, since otherwise why would they call it 1 Corinthians? Well, it is the first of Paul's letters to that community in Corinth that is extant—that is, that we still have. But in the letter we call 1 Corinthians, Paul mentions having written to them *previously* (1 Cor 5:9). Most scholars conclude from what Paul says in 1 and 2 Corinthians about his correspondence with the church that he wrote to them at least four times (see 2 Cor 2:3-4 for the evidence that we are missing his third letter as well). If we had all the letters, our 1 and 2 Corinthians might be known as 2 and 4 Corinthians.

This isn't just trivia. Understanding Paul's relationship with the Corinthian church, and deducing what they wrote to him, is crucially important to understanding what Paul wrote. If you hear in a sermon that certain things were happening in the church in Corinth, you may not ask how the preacher knows that. What biblical scholars do is read Paul's letters and figure out from them what issues in the church he may have been responding to. As we explore in more detail later in the book, Paul's letters to churches were part of a conversation about things known to both him and his readers. We are missing the context and the rest of the conversation. That makes it challenging to understand why Paul wrote what he did and what he meant by it. Sermons try to make things easy for the listener, jumping straight to the application of what Paul wrote to a contemporary audience. A good sermon will be grounded in what scholars have written, including not only deductions from Paul's letters but also extensive research into what we know about places like Corinth, Thessaloniki, and Philippi in that time. If you've ever heard a sermon, there's a reasonable chance that you've been exposed to some of the results of that research in a diluted and simplified form. This book pulls back the curtain so you can learn not only what preachers have drawn on in crafting their sermons but also the methods and processes that have allowed researchers to draw their conclusions. In at least some cases, you may discover that you've also heard preachers who ignore or depart from what experts have to say about the very texts they quote in their sermons.

In any decent university course about the New Testament, you won't receive a list of pat answers, although key bits of information will be presented, such as that the letters of Paul in the New Testament are arranged by size rather than chronologically (i.e., in the order in which they were written). The focus will be on learning what the key issues are, what hidden assumptions and biases influence the conclusions drawn by interpreters, and how scholars figure out the answers to questions—and what degree of confidence they have in those answers. The focus, then, is not on learning answers but on learning how scholars come up with answers. Some churches teach people to expect clear and simple statements in response to questions about the Bible. Academic study of the Bible will help you understand why we sometimes have clear answers, at others we simply don't know, and in between there is a range of degrees of certainty. It will also introduce you to the methods and processes whereby scholars seek to find better answers to the things that puzzle us.

Everybody's a Critic

In New Testament studies, the term "criticism" is used in a technical way that is prone to being misunderstood. "Critic" comes from the Greek word for judgment. Film critics certainly may point out weaknesses in a movie, but what we expect from them (if they are good at their job) is not negativity for the sake of it but careful analysis. Criticism involves not just watching a movie or reading a piece of literature but studying and analyzing it, noticing not just the story it tells but how it tells it, and then offering an assessment. There are various critical approaches to the New Testament. Literary criticism of the New Testament is the application of the tools and methods developed by literary critics. Redaction criticism means the same kind of careful study with a focus on the editing process. Historical criticism is the same thing but for history. The list of such approaches is quite long.

I just mentioned redaction criticism. "Redaction" isn't an everyday word unless you work in a field that involves a lot of editing. There are lots of technical terms of this sort that are liable either to be misunderstood or to lead to incomprehension. I'm not going to bombard you with them here in the introduction. The approach of this book is to look at key themes, issues, and passages and introduce the terminology and less familiar concepts gradually and gently, in a context in which they are clearly relevant. A lot of technical terms are misunderstood not so much because they are unfamiliar but because they are not explained when you encounter them. If a word has an everyday usage that is different from the technical usage, there's no surprise if confusion results. For example, I distinctly remember a student asking me as I talked about my first book, *John's Apologetic Christology*, "What makes you think John was being apologetic?" I meant that John was defending his view of Jesus, but the student assumed I meant that he was saying he was sorry. Another example is someone taking computer science and being confused by references to "strings." Students can look up unfamiliar words, but terms like these aren't unfamiliar—they are just being used in a technical sense. Looking up "apologetic" or "strings" won't necessarily tell you which possible meaning is intended. The technical sense of those words must be explained.

When I titled this section "Everybody's a Critic," I really meant it. Many people read books, watch movies and plays, and attend concerts. Some who do so can tell you whether or not they liked it but cannot tell you why. A good critic, regardless of whether they work as a professional one, can tell you why they liked or disliked something and in the process help you appreciate it better. In this book you will not only learn what the tools of New Testament criticism are but experience them in use, so that you can cultivate the same skills. You may already have a favorite gospel or letter in the New Testament. By the end of this book you should be able to explain more clearly why it is your favorite. As you get a closer look at the New Testament, you may even find a new favorite among the texts as you learn to appreciate them in new ways, analyze them through new lenses and approaches, and in the process notice things about them you hadn't before.

Alphabet Soup

While the book does take the letters of the alphabet as its overarching theme, that doesn't at all mean the chapters cover New Testament topics in alphabetical order. Key words are introduced when they come up, and sidebars throughout the book highlight the definitions of important terms. The book is not organized around terminology and concepts but integrates those into the exploration of themes, topics, and questions that readers will find relevant and meaningful. This isn't just a way to make otherwise boring content seem interesting. All content, even really useful stuff, will seem boring if you don't already know what it is good for or how to apply and use it. Think of the YouTube video that you'd find completely uninteresting any other time but you watch with rapt attention when the plumbing issue it addresses has come up in your own life. That is the reason for the approach adopted in this book. It is better to introduce a problem and then offer a tool that can help solve it than to offer a systematic presentation of tools and only at some later point learn to apply them. Computer science students regularly have an aha moment when they discover how practically useful the things they learned in linear algebra turn out to be. Sadly, in every course of study some students simply give up, convinced that they aren't good at math or languages or whatever, because of the way it is taught.

By the end of this book, I hope that you will not only understand the New Testament better but also understand *how* to understand the New Testament. Even more than that, I hope you'll be convinced that this is something that you can be good at, and that you will want to further explore the details of the New Testament and perhaps even make your own contribution to the study of them.

B

Born in a Barn?

When I was growing up as a city boy, I don't think I encountered the expression "Were you born in a barn?" The first time I heard it, I didn't immediately understand that the person was noticing I had left a door open and telling me I should close it. The expression probably comes from a context in which people have enough contact with barns that they have a sense of what someone might behave like, or neglect to pay attention to, if they were born in one. I don't know how many readers of this book will be in the "I know barns" category and how many will be as clueless about them as I am. But many readers of this book will share one assumption about barns—namely, that Jesus was born in one.

If you look closely at the New Testament stories about the birth of Jesus, you'll find the word "barn" doesn't appear in them. Although I can't say that I have checked every single English translation ever made, I am nonetheless confident about this. So why is it that people think they *know* that Jesus was born in a barn? The answer would likely come as a question: Where else would one find a manger? That, it turns out, is precisely the right question to ask. Mangers aren't familiar to city people either, so much so that you may hear someone refer to Jesus having been "born in a manger." They clearly don't know what a manger is if they say that. No one who did would envisage Mary trying to awkwardly give birth to her son directly *into* a feeding trough for animals. A barn is uncomfortable enough, and childbirth is painful enough. No need to add to Mary's suffering!

Let's leave that painful misunderstanding to one side and return to the question we raised: Where might one find a manger if not in a barn or stable, and why should we even consider other possibilities? First, we should say that barns do get a mention in the New Testament, if modern English translations are anything to go by (Matt 3:12; 6:26; 13:30; Luke 3:17; 12:18, 24). It is not as though there was no such thing in the ancient world. The Greek word *apothēkē* denotes a storehouse of any sort, whether for grain or other things. We are still not dealing with the modern barn that might be full of hay and an animal enclosure or stable, but it is not entirely different. Most readers of the Gospel of Luke don't envisage Jesus having been born in a place that was exclusively or primarily a storehouse for grain (or for anything else), or even a barn that houses a stable, but (if the crèches and paintings are anything to go by) in a little lean-to in a back alley. However, since the text doesn't mention a barn or even a stable, the key question is not what one of these is like but why modern readers insert one into their mental picture of the birth of Jesus when such words do not occur in the text. The answer is because we think it is obvious where a manger would be found. But what is obvious in one culture or one era may be completely alien and unknown in another. Likewise, what may have seemed obvious to an ancient author and their first readers, so obvious that it did not require mentioning, may never occur to us when reading today—unless we take the time and effort to learn about ancient ways of doing things.

More than anything else, digging into the cultural background of the account of Jesus's birth story in the Gospel of

Luke makes us aware of the huge *economic* gulf that separates us from the author and earliest readers of that story, and also from Jesus and his family. Barns may be unfamiliar to some readers, things seen only on television and in movies or on occasional drives through the countryside. Other readers will know them inside and out from firsthand experience. In both instances, however, we read the New Testament through a lens of economic privilege beyond the imagination of ordinary people in Jesus's time. Most people, whether they were agriculturalists or raised animals, did not have extensive properties with large structures to shelter grain or livestock. An ordinary individual in Jesus's time and context would have brought their few animals into their home at night throughout most of the year. If there was something that we might call a "stable," it was *within* the structure of the home. Feeding troughs would be located within that structure as well. If Jesus was laid in a manger after he was born, the assumption most ancient Mediterranean readers would make is that it was located inside a home.

Some readers are already objecting in their minds. Sure, animals in the home might be the norm, but in this case we're dealing with an *inn*, and so surely if it had a manger, it would have been in a stable, right? It does indeed seem likely that a commercial inn would have had a stable where animals ridden by guests could be tied up and kept safe during the night. That still isn't what most people envisage when the Christmas story is read, a place where travelers might be coming and going and where there were mainly horses and donkeys. However, a more important point is that the story in the Gospel of Luke does not use the word that means a commercial inn.

This may surprise you but would not have surprised Luke's earliest readers. In the ancient Mediterranean world, inns were not where most people stayed when traveling. Think about the apostle Paul in Acts, traveling around the

Mediterranean world both by sea and by land. How many times does he check into a hotel? Not once. When we imagine ancient people doing so, we are reading cultures of the modern English-speaking world into the text. We envisage Joseph and Mary zooming down the ancient freeway on their donkey, passing neon sign after neon sign that flashes No Vacancy. That wasn't what happened in the ancient cultural context in which the story was set. Even today, in cultures with similar values to those of the New Testament context, if someone with connections of any sort were to arrive in town without sending advance word and check into a hotel, their local connections would be deeply offended. As we see Jesus doing, and later Paul and others, people relied on hospitality. You stayed with someone you knew, or someone who knew someone you knew. If necessary, if the connection was more distant, you brought a letter of introduction. The only case in which a commercial inn would be used was when one could not rely on any such network of connections. That was sometimes true of traders and of foreigners.

It is thus unsurprising that the word for a commercial inn does appear at one point in the Gospel of Luke: in the parable of the good Samaritan. The Samaritan is an outsider in Judea and not especially welcome. So he takes the man he rescued to an inn. The rescued man, being unconscious and naked, might belong to any people, and there was no way of knowing what local connections he had if any. The very reason the story has the man's clothes stolen is not that this was typical but that it robbed the man of anything that might have indicated that he belonged to the same people as the passersby. The Samaritan helps him nevertheless. He doesn't know whether the man is a Jew or a Samaritan or something else. He has mercy on him as a fellow human being.

The word that is translated as "inn" in Luke's infancy story in most modern English translations occurs elsewhere in the gospel, when reference is made to the "guest room" where the disciples are to prepare the Passover and where the Last Supper occurs (Luke 22:11; also Mark 14:14). This is an extra room in a home, one that might function normally as a guest room but could also provide a place for hosting a meal with guests. If we read the infancy story in Luke with this meaning in mind, we get a different impression than we will from typical modern retellings of the Christmas story. The home where Joseph and Mary have arrived is crowded. They are relying on hospitality from whomever showed it to them. They place Jesus in a feeding trough at the edge of the living space adjacent to where animals were brought into the home at night. Why are they not in a spare room or some other better accommodations? Luke doesn't tell readers explicitly because the answer would have seemed obvious: it is because other people who were deemed more important guests were already occupying whatever guest room the home might have had.

One point thus remains the same as in the modern Western idea of what happened. The family relies on hospitality and does not find a welcome on arrival. Indeed, if anything, that meaning is made clearer by shifting to a more culturally and historically plausible reconstruction of what occurred. In the modern world, hotels being full just means one is unlucky, or there's a convention in town. The story as Luke's early readers would have understood it conveys something more than a lack of good fortune and available space. It conveys that Joseph and Mary were not the most important guests in the home of a relative in the birthplace of Joseph's illustrious ancestor David. They were shown the minimum of hospitality that was required by the culture and the sense of obligation felt by their hosts. Others were apparently deemed worthy of a better space, while Joseph and Mary (and eventually Jesus) made do with what was left.

Will New Testament Study Ruin Your Christmas Pageant?

Biblical scholars sometimes get a reputation for being party poopers and spoilsports. We cast doubt on things people assumed were clear, raise questions about things that never occurred to them, and in other ways make things confusing—or at least complicated—that previously seemed simple. Having read the opening of this chapter, you can now probably see that what people have is the *illusion* of simplicity and clarity. Sometimes the biblical text is translated into English in a way that is clear, and yet a footnote says that the meaning is uncertain. Pastors through sermons, translators through translations, and various others by other means try to make things clear and simple whenever they can. If you took that to mean that things really are consistently always simple, and scholars come along and make things unnecessarily complicated, then hopefully I can challenge that impression. You most certainly were riding a bicycle with relative ease when it had training wheels on it, and when they were taken off, you could be forgiven for thinking that your parents were just being mean. In fact, they were helping you to transition to full-fledged bike riding. That's the aim of this book: reading the New Testament without training wheels. As with bike riding, it is more difficult to begin with, but once you get the hang of it, you'll find it profoundly rewarding.

So what is complicated about Christmas? In the section heading I mention Christmas pageants, those events in churches when children put towels on their heads and pretend they are Middle Eastern shepherds. Angels, shepherds, magi, and a host of other characters all jostle for room in a crowded manger scene. Some of those characters don't appear in the same gospel, and while sometimes combining details from different versions of the same story can lead to a single richer story, in this case it isn't clear we are dealing with different version of the same story as opposed to two different and perhaps incompatible stories of the infancy of Jesus. Trace the geographic movements of the family with me and judge for yourself. If you really want to see it clearly, don't just look at a map of the Eastern Mediterranean online. Print a map off the internet, and then use different colored pencils or pens to number the stops and trace the journey according to each gospel in visual form. It will help you see the differences even more clearly than you will just by reading the text.

In the Gospel of Matthew the first specific place we find Joseph and Mary is in Bethlehem (Matt 2:1). The magi find them in a house (Matt 2:11). Since Herod the Great inquires when the star appeared and then proceeds to slaughter the boys who are two years old and younger, we are given to understand that the star appeared two years earlier and thus that Jesus was around two years old at that time. From there Joseph, Mary, and Jesus flee to Egypt and remain there until Herod dies. Based on information from other sources, in particular the historian Flavius Josephus, we know that Herod died in or around the year 4 BC. (As an aside, I prefer to use BC and AD because this calendar is not a common one but a Christian one, and so rebranding it using "Common Era" seems disrespectful to those who use other calendars. On the other hand, I find it very odd to have to tell people that, according to Matthew's Gospel, Jesus was born roughly six years "Before Christ.") We don't know how long Joseph, Mary, and Jesus are supposed to have remained in Egypt, but when they learn that Herod is dead, they seek to return whence they had fled. Matthew is very clear on that last point: they would have naturally returned to the place they left, namely Bethlehem. The only reason they do not is due to their concern that Herod's son Archelaus, who succeeded him as ruler of Judea, might have orders or simply an inclination to continue his father's efforts to eliminate Jesus as a rival king of the Jews.

They thus go to Galilee, also ruled over by one of Herod's sons, Herod Antipas, but presumably he was not likely to be on the lookout for people who fled a massacre in Bethlehem.

When we read Luke's Gospel on its own terms, we get a very different impression. Mary and Joseph are from Nazareth. They go to Bethlehem only because a census requires them to. If we understand Luke to mean that a census of the Roman Empire was carried out that required everyone to return to a place their distant ancestors were from, then we should take the extra step to ask why any ruler or government would ever do that. What would the point be? Taxes are collected where you live, not where your ancestors happen to have been from. It is extremely unlikely that this kind of unprecedented event occurred and no one wrote about it other than one gospel author. In fact, we know about the census under Quirinius from other sources. It was a Roman census of Judea carried out when the region was transferred to direct Roman rule. This happened when Archelaus was deposed. The populace of Judea actually petitioned the Romans to remove him, such was his unpopularity. It has been suggested that Jesus's parable in Luke 19 is patterned on these events. Archelaus was deposed in 6 AD, and the census took place the same year. No matter how one tries to adjust things, there is no way for Jesus to have been born before the death of Herod the Great and after the removal of his son who reigned in his stead in Jerusalem. Apologists will sometimes claim otherwise. While there are gaps in our knowledge about the legates of Syria and the life and career of Quirinius, there isn't a period when there are gaps in both in which we could posit an otherwise unknown stint of Quirinius as governor of Syria while Herod the Great was king. At some point it is appropriate to stop trying to force the Bible to tell the story we think it should and instead listen to the story it actually tells.

Luke's Gospel has Joseph and Mary go to Bethlehem for Quirinius's census, and that's not inherently improbable.

During the era of the Hasmoneans, the dynasty that ruled in Jerusalem before Herod, there was a concerted effort to extend their rule over Galilee, and as a result many Judeans settled there. It is plausible that Joseph, a descendant of David, had a claim on property in Judea and might have needed to be included in the census to safeguard that claim. This would not have required that his wife go there with him, since, unlike modern censuses that are interested in everyone in a household, ancient ones and indeed most before the modern era were concerned only with heads of household, property ownership, tax responsibilities, and other such practical matters. According to Luke, when Joseph and Mary are in Bethlehem, they don't have a home of their own to stay in and aren't even the first or most honored guests in the home they do stay in. They make do, squeezing into the main living area, and when Jesus is born, he is placed in a manger in that space.

We asked how long they stayed in Egypt in Matthew's telling of the story, and there was no clear answer. If we ask how soon after Jesus's birth in Luke's version they move on to their next destination, Jerusalem, we have a clear answer. Luke says they went to offer the sacrifice required by Jewish law for the mother's purification. Leviticus 12 specifies that a mother must wait thirty-three days after the birth of a son (or perhaps after the circumcision on the eighth day) and then offer the required sacrifice. So after Jesus was born, within two months he was in Jerusalem, according to Luke, who says that once they had done all that was required, they returned to Nazareth, which in Luke is their hometown. There is no room for a

Circumcision in Judaism is the removal of the foreskin from the penis of a male child on the eighth day after he is born. The significance of this as a sign of God's covenant with Abraham (Gen 17) will be important later in the book.

relocation to Bethlehem for Jesus to be there at age two, as depicted in Matthew. Luke's story is simply a different one, with a different timeline from Matthew's.

Those who have been told they should expect all the historical details to line up and everything to agree among the gospels, as well as between them and external sources, may be very troubled at this point (or may have turned to apologists who offer them simplistic and frankly dubious solutions to the problems they perceive). But ancient readers would not necessarily have had the issues that modern readers do. They expected an important person to have their significance emphasized in any biographical account by angels, signs, and the like. What worries us would have reassured many ancient readers.

How Can One Man Have Two Genealogies?

The first time I tried reading the Bible all the way through, it was a King James Version that I inherited from my grandfather. I got stuck in Chronicles for a long time because of the genealogies. I did eventually make it all the way through, in case you were wondering. Many modern Bibles actually format genealogies differently so that you can spot them and skim them. There's a famous saying that even if someone believes the entire Bible to be equally *inspired*, that doesn't mean it is equally *inspiring*. Nonetheless, there can be interesting and even inspiring things in genealogies if we know what to look for. Paying attention to Matthew's genealogy provides another example of how misunderstandings arise as a result of disconnects between Matthew's aims as an ancient author and our own assumptions as readers.

According to Matthew 1:17 there were fourteen generations from Abraham to David, fourteen from David to the exile, and fourteen from the exile to Christ. Have you ever counted them? Go ahead and do so now—I'll wait. When you come back, assuming you did not count any name more than once, you'll be aware that Matthew does not in fact list forty-two names or generations. In the last group there are only thirteen. If you look up Matthew's source material, you will further discover that in the middle group he has had to leave out some of the names of kings found in 1 Chronicles 3 in order to end up with fourteen. Once again we might be tempted to think Matthew is being tricky—or bad at math. Yet this view is problematic. Did the author of this gospel not think his readers could count? Did he not think that anyone would look at 1 Chronicles? The fact that you likely never checked his math or looked up his source material doesn't mean that no one would ever be likely to do so. Why would Matthew introduce a numerical scheme only to have to play fast and loose with the numbers and names in order to get it to almost fit, and even then not quite? The answer is that numbers had a symbolic significance for ancient Jews. Indeed, they could have more than one kind of significance.

Later we'll see how the number forty created a resonance between Matthew's Gospel and an earlier story. The number seven (twice which is fourteen) also has biblical resonances. More importantly, ancient Jews used letters as numbers. Let me explain. Puns seem to be something that human beings make no matter what language they speak. We find them in Greek, Hebrew, Aramaic, and English. But there is a way of playing on words that exists in those ancient languages that English doesn't have. All the letters in each of those ancient languages had a numeric equivalent, meaning that you could add up the numerical value of every word or name. It was similar to Roman numerals except that instead of just using a subset of the letters of the alphabet as numbers, every letter in Greek, Hebrew, and Aramaic did double duty. As a result, you could treat the letters in any word or name as their numerical equivalents, add them up, and tally the result. Hence the graffiti that was found at Pompeii in which someone declared their love for a girl whose "number is 545": that wasn't her phone number or address but what the numerical values of the letters in her name added up to. (I'm not sure why he didn't just write her name, unless he actually loved more than one woman whose name had this numerical value and wanted to profess his love to both without either finding out about the other.)

In rabbinic tradition, finding significance in the numerical value of words and names, and making connections between passages on that basis, became an established part of the toolbox for biblical interpretation. This came to be known as gematria. Matthew appears to be doing something similar. The name David has the numerical value of fourteen, and his name is the fourteenth one in Matthew's genealogy. That is likely the significance of his arrangement around the number fourteen. For us, numbers are about mathematical precision. For ancient people, they often had a different significance. (Another famous number, 666, is explored in another chapter in this book.) Ancient authors and readers had shared knowledge and assumptions that facilitated communication between them. We lack those things and as a result misunderstand. This is one major reason why just reading the Bible and nothing else is simply not enough. Texts taken out of context become pretexts. That is true not only of small snippets quoted outside their original literary context but of whole books read detached from their historical and cultural context.

Gematria means calculating the numerical value of words in the text of the Bible to find hidden or deeper significance in the text. It is sometimes suggested that the word derives from the Greek geometria (from which English gets the word "geometry"), and while this is doubtful, the similarity may help you remember gematria.

Matthew's genealogy has other interesting features that you'll miss if you skip over it or skim it. It contains names that it did not strictly need when judged by the standards of its time. Ancient genealogies, especially royal genealogies, were patrilineal, meaning they traced descent on the father's side. It was the eldest son who inherited the throne under normal circumstances. Matthew's genealogy, however, includes several women: Rahab, Tamar, Ruth, and Bathsheba (simply called the wife of Uriah). These women have something in common. Either explicitly or implicitly they were understood to all be gentiles, non-Israelites. Rahab was a Canaanite. Tamar was often assumed to be, although that is less explicit. Ruth was from Moab. And Bathsheba, being married to a foreigner, was assumed to be one as well (2 Sam 11:3 tells us Uriah was a Hittite). Through the inclusion of these women, just like the arrival of the worshiping magi, Matthew depicts gentiles as having a place in the story of the Messiah. That makes for a nice bookend with the gospel's ending, where the apostles are commissioned to make disciples of all nations (Matt 28:18–20). The word "nations" in Greek is the same one that is translated in other places as "gentiles." In Hebrew as in Greek, the word "nations" was used by Jews to denote the *other* nations—that is, everyone else.

Gentiles denotes those who are not Jews, just as "barbarians" originally denoted those who did not speak Greek. The Greek word ethnē *(like the Hebrew word* goyim) *literally means "nations." It was used by Jews to refer to the nations other than themselves, hence the translation in some places as "gentiles."*

Luke's Gospel contains a very different genealogy from that in Matthew. I say this not only because Luke's goes all the way back to Adam as son of God, whereas Matthew's goes back to Abraham. The genealogies diverge between David and Joseph, giving a different string of names and "begats." Why might that be the case? Sometimes you'll hear that one of the genealogies is Mary's, but both Matthew and Luke are explicit that they are tracing Jesus's lineage via Joseph even if, owing to a miraculous conception, he is not Jesus's biological father (as we would put it today). More likely, the reason Luke's genealogy is different has to do with a curse uttered by Jeremiah the prophet. Jeremiah 22:24-30 says that no descendant of Jeconiah (sometimes called Coniah or Jehoiachin) will ever sit on the throne of his ancestors. Matthew 1:12 says that Jesus was descended from Jeconiah. Does that disqualify him from being the Messiah? If you presume that God never changes his mind, then it would have to, I suppose. That might well have led the author of Luke to provide a different lineage for Jesus. For most people in that era, the fact that Jesus had been crucified by the Romans rather than instituting the expected renewed Davidic kingdom was probably the bigger concern. If that didn't disqualify Jesus, nothing would. God was full of surprises and consistently willing to forgive and welcome even when prior statements had seemed to leave no room for that. What was a problematic issue for one gospel author may not have been for another, just as what is troubling for some readers because of their assumptions about the New Testament texts can be incredibly helpful to other readers, who will be relieved that the problems and difficulties they noticed are not all in their head and be grateful for helpful ways to think about the texts in light of these characteristics.

Before proceeding, let me point out one irony about people trying to avoid having Matthew and Luke offer contradictory genealogies by saying one is Mary's. As we've already seen, both Matthew and Luke claim to offer genealogies through Joseph. The names in the genealogies diverge between Joseph and David, and claiming that one is Mary's doesn't work as an attempt to make the problem go away. If you are inclined to insist that all the details in the Bible must agree without contradiction, then grabbing hold of solutions like this may seem attractive. However, if the only way to claim that the Bible is inerrant and doesn't provide contradictory genealogies of Joseph is to pretend that Luke doesn't say that he is offering Joseph's genealogy, then you are denying what the Bible says in order to defend your doctrine about the Bible. As with Matthew's approach to interpretation (which we will make the focus of a later chapter), many other things in these ancient texts will not fit our expectations of how they should be. The problem is not with the texts but with readers. It does not show respect to the Bible to force it into our cultural or other interpretive framework. It is possible to honor the Bible with one's words, praising it and emphasizing its authority, while insulting and mistreating it by how one interprets it.

From Matthew to Math

There are a lot of other points related to numbers, math, and dates that deserve mention here. For instance, exactly why is it that Jesus wasn't born in the year zero? The calendar doesn't have a year zero, but we would at least have expected Jesus to be born in the first year of our Lord (which is what Anno Domini, AD, stands for). A monk named Dionysius Exiguus living in what is today Constanța, Romania, calculated the date in the sixth century, creating our modern dating system. He was off by several years, as already noted, but we should not be too quick to criticize him. Much of the confusion of historians about ancient figures' lives and dates is a result of the lack of a standardized system of years. Only mentioning what year in the reign of a particular king it was meant that later historians were going to have a *lot* of work to do to correlate and calculate. It is impressive that a standard way of calculating years caught on and got as close as it did.

So if it wasn't the year zero or the year 1, now you're worried that I'm going to tell you that it wasn't December 25 either. Well, if you're someone who prioritizes the Bible over church tradition, you're probably already well aware that the date for celebrating Christmas doesn't appear in the Bible (and indeed there's nothing about celebrating Christmas as a holiday either, whenever it might have occurred). The dates for churches' celebrations of the birth of Christ were chosen later. I say "dates" because the Eastern Orthodox celebrate Christmas on a different day than Catholics and Protestants do. Even that these things happened "in the bleak midwinter" is an assumption, one that the stories themselves do not support. Some argue that the celebration of Christmas in December or January is a result of an attempt to date the birth of Jesus in relation to his death. Others have pointed out that, if shepherds were watching their flocks by night as Luke says, then it was likely lambing season, which is in the spring. The truth is that we aren't told, and this is not surprising. Ancient people, and most people until very recently, didn't focus a lot of attention on record keeping and precise dates, not yet even having a calendar system that would make it an easy matter to do so. Perhaps it is ironic that the impact of Jesus was so profound that it led people to develop a standard calendar and dating system, and that in relation to that system it is hard to date the birth of Jesus precisely. Those who inspire something new often stand apart in awkward ways from the new systems and realities they inspire. The celebration of the birth of Jesus in the English-speaking world in the present day in all its aspects—the date, the combination of details from Matthew and Luke, and so on—reframes the birth of Jesus in a radical way. When he was born, presumably few if any suspected that within a matter of centuries there would be an effort to date all events in relation to him. The effort of New Testament scholars is to glimpse Jesus as he was before people came to think of history as centered on him, precisely so that we can understand the life that inspired this change and so much else.

If you take a look at a map of Bethlehem and its surroundings, you'll see that it's even more unlikely that anyone "saw three ships come sailing in." Songs, like paintings, inevitably reflect the culture and assumptions of the creative artist as well as details in an ancient story they are seeking or purporting to depict. The celebration of Christmas has never been about getting the date right but about commemorating the event itself. As you've seen in this chapter, that may be the point of the stories themselves that are at the heart of this discussion. If their aim was to honor Jesus rather than to provide historical information, then there's no reason to reject songs, artwork, or children's pageants merely because they don't line up with the accounts in Matthew and Luke, especially when the accounts in those two gospels don't line up with each other.

For Further Reading

Bailey, Kenneth E. "The Manger and the Inn: A Middle Eastern View of the Birth Story of Jesus." *The Presbyterian Outlook*, December 21, 2006, https://pres-outlook.org/2006/12/the-manger-and-the-inn-a-middle-eastern-view-of-the-birth-story-of-jesus/.

Barnes, Timothy D. "The Date of Herod's Death." *Journal of Theological Studies* 19, no. 1 (1968): 204–9.

Brown, Raymond E. *The Birth of the Messiah: A Commentary on the Infancy Narratives in the Gospels of Matthew and Luke*. New York: Doubleday, 1993.

Carlson, Stephen C. "The Accommodations of Joseph and Mary in Bethlehem: Κατάλυμα in Luke 2.7." *New Testament Studies* 56, no. 3 (2010): 326–42.

Gaventa, Beverly. *Mary: Glimpses of the Mother of Jesus*. Minneapolis: Fortress, 1999.

C

Camels, Critters, and Calculations

Jesus seems to have had a thing about camels, and to have particularly enjoyed plays on words about them. He condemns Pharisees for many things, including that they "strain out a gnat but swallow a camel" (Matt 23:24). There is background knowledge that is crucial to understanding what he meant. But first there is a linguistic point, a play on words that you won't pick up on reading an English translation. The Aramaic word for a louse, weevil, and other insects that are considered vermin is *galma*, while a camel is *gamla* (Aramaic was Jesus's mother tongue—more on that later). The words are the same except for the order of the consonants. Neither small insects nor camels were kosher, and thus if one ingests either, it violates Torah. (*Kosher* denotes food that is permissible to eat according to Jewish law as historically interpreted by the rabbis. It is often misleadingly translated as "clean" in English Bibles.) Moreover, if something falls into your drink and drowns, there is the additional issue of corpse impurity. There is in fact rabbinic discussion of whether a very tiny insect conveys impurity. It was a highly practical matter, and in places where water was scarce, if a tiny gnat rendered your drink impure, it might be a matter of life and death. The consensus of the rabbis was that very tiny insects did not convey impurity. Jesus is thus caricaturing his opponents as going to one extreme—unnecessarily straining out a tiny bug—while simultaneously going to another. The reference to swallowing a camel is obviously not literal. Jesus's point was to represent in a hyperbolic image how his opponents, in his view, were ignoring much bigger and more important issues.

The **Mishnah** is one of the oldest and most authoritative rabbinic texts, putting in writing their oral tradition that discusses the application of the Jewish law. The two **Talmudim** (plural of **Talmud**), from Jerusalem and Babylonia, compile still more oral tradition, expanding and commenting further on the law as well as the Mishnah itself.

Midrash is often misrepresented by Christians. Its most basic sense is simply interpretation, but it sometimes denotes the exploration of gaps and puzzles in scriptural stories through imaginative retelling. The latter is referred to as "haggadah," while discussion of how to interpret and apply law is called "halakah."

Camels were the largest animal commonly encountered in that region and served the same symbolic function as elephants do in places where those are familiar. Later rabbis referred to elephants in this context, and in the Babylonian Talmud (b. Berakhot 55b; see also Baba Metzi'a 38b) there is a reference to an elephant passing through the eye of a needle as an example of something people do not dream about since dreams draw on our lived experience. Today we would use a similar image and say that Jesus was accusing his opponents of ignoring the elephant in the room. Aramaic also had an adjective derived from "camel" that was used to indicate something's large size. The adjective was particularly used to describe insects. In the rabbinic midrash Genesis Rabbah (5:9; 20:8) a camel is added after a list of insects that are brought into the world as a result of the curse on the ground. As far back as we can trace, the mention of a camel here has puzzled interpreters. Perhaps because of the potential for puns, camels and insects were associated by many Jewish teachers and not only Jesus.

Another saying of Jesus involving a camel refers to the impossibility of one passing through the eye of a needle (Mark 10:25 and parallels). For today's readers who don't sew, the eye of a needle is the little hole at the top that the thread goes through. If you've never sewn, you won't know just how difficult it is to get a thread, never mind something larger, through that tiny opening. At some point while listening to a sermon about this passage, you may have heard a preacher confidently tell their congregation that there was a tiny gate in the wall of Jerusalem called "the eye

Aramaic was the language of ancient Babylonia. It became the lingua franca across a wide area, including in Palestine, and so was the native language of Jesus and his earliest followers. The dialect of Aramaic used by Eastern Christians is often referred to as "Syriac."

of the needle" and that a camel could in fact pass through it on its knees as long as it wasn't carrying anything. This is another example of something that circulates as truth even though there is no evidence for it. Gates in cities are the kinds of things that ancient sources tend to mention. If such a gate existed, we would expect it to be mentioned. The absence of any hint of its existence means we should assume that it did not exist. It is easy to understand why this was made up. Most of the readers of this book are rich by global standards. Wouldn't you prefer for Jesus to mean that it is possible for you to enter the kingdom of God as long as you get rid of all your baggage and get down on your knees, rather than that it is impossible?

So, sorry, there was no gate called "the eye of the needle." That wasn't what Jesus was talking about. Yet there are a couple of Christian sources that suggest that the word for camel in Aramaic also meant a large rope. We do not have any instances of the word being used in writing with that sense, and so it is possible that this represents not information about the Aramaic language but an early example of

Christian preachers seeking to tone down the saying. Even if there was such a usage, it seems to have been rare. In view of that, we should reject the claim that Jesus meant rope rather than camel. It remains possible, yet unproven, that Jesus may have used a word with more than one meaning in order to make a pun and make his hearers think. Interestingly, there are Greek words for camel and rope that sound similar, so the wordplay would have worked in Greek if not in Aramaic. Depending on whether one envisages a rope or a camel, the object that one is attempting to pass through the eye of the needle might be a hundred or a thousand times larger than the opening. In both scenarios the effort will be equally futile, and that is the point.

Dessert in the Desert?

The Gospels say that John the Baptist ate locusts and wild honey (Mark 1:6 and parallels). Discussing this topic here will allow us to give the chapter a unifying theme, even if that theme is "ingesting bugs." For those readers who are not intimately acquainted with Leviticus 11:20–23 and are wondering how John's food preference relates to the subject of swallowing gnats, it's important to know that locusts (unlike most insects) are kosher. We are not told why John ate locusts and wild honey, nor that that was all he ever ate. What the two foodstuffs seem to have in common is that both are available even to those with no money, crops, or livestock; both are potentially available to someone in a remote location; and neither requires another human as intermediary in the process. Whether it was poverty, purity, or preference that led John to eat these things is not stated. To get beyond his culinary habits to their significance, the best we can do is try to correlate this information with other things we are told about him. At one point Jesus said that John came "neither eating nor drinking" (Matt 11:18). Luke realized this could not be literally true or John would have died, and so adds that John neither ate *bread* nor drank *wine*. Here too there is ambiguity. Was Jesus a rowdy partier, while John was an ascetic? If so, how in the world did they work closely together? Did Jesus accept hospitality and dinner invitations from people, whereas John did not? Were both of these characterizations caricatures by the opponents of John and Jesus that made them seem more different than they were? The Gospels tell us much less about John than we wish we knew.

Because there has been puzzlement about what John ate, some have suggested that a word may have been misunderstood, miscopied, or mistranslated, much like the case of the camel in the previous section. Some ancient sources understood John to have eaten pancakes rather than locusts. For many in the English-speaking world, that will seem inherently likely, but the idea of eating locusts was neither as surprising nor as distasteful for people in Jesus's time as it likely is for you (unless you're one of the few readers who've developed a liking for chocolate-covered grasshoppers). How could anyone mix up locusts and pancakes, you ask? The Greek words *akris* and *enkris* sound similar, and that may be how confusion arose. According to Epiphanius of Salamis, a fourth-century bishop in Cyprus, there were Jewish Christians (sometimes referred to as Ebionites) who had a version of the Gospel of Matthew that read "cakes dipped in honey" where the Greek gospels have "locusts" (Epiphanius, *Panarion* 30.13.4–5). Here too we must be cautious. Just as modern interpreters may look at similar words and guess that at some point a misunderstanding or copying error crept in, ancient interpreters and scribes were capable of doing the same thing. Moreover, some Jewish Christians espoused vegetarianism, and that may have motivated them to seek a way to avoid having John the Baptist eat locusts.

I could not resist making as many puns as possible in a chapter that has plays on words as one of its unifying themes. Yet the depiction of John in the *desert* provides an example of how the modern English sense of a word in a translation of the Bible may not correspond to the meaning of the underlying word in the Greek New Testament. The word for wilderness in Greek is the one from which the English word "hermit" derives. It denotes being away from densely populated areas, somewhere remote, but it does not indicate that the place was arid. There are certainly traditions about John being active in the Judean wilderness, which can be called a desert, albeit a rocky rather than a sandy one. Yet he is also associated with places like Aenon near Salim, where he baptized his followers precisely because "there was an abundance of water there" (John 3:23). The immediate vicinity of the Jordan River is consistently covered with vegetation (although it dwindles as one gets almost to the Dead Sea). Between this and the fact that we do not know whether the Roman custom of eating dessert had caught on in Judea, we should probably avoid saying that John's consumption of honey means he ate dessert in the desert.

*A **lexicon** is a dictionary of an ancient language. Whereas modern languages have dictionaries describing current usage, ancient languages for the most part lacked such lists of words and definitions. This makes it necessary to deduce ancient word meaning from the way words are used in texts.*

The general principle to take away from this is that questions about the meaning of ancient words must be answered by consulting one or more lexicons, rather than merely Googling it. Sometimes you'll get a confident answer online that has no linguistic basis. Many of these urban legends have circulated so widely and are included in so many sermons that you might assume that it is common knowledge and thus true. Never be satisfied that something is repeated often, whether on the internet or in print. Demand sources and evidence.

We will save most of our discussion of John's clothing for a later chapter, but I had to at least mention it here. After all, we are told John wore clothing made from camel-hair fabric, and any excuse will do to mention camels one more time. Just as one may make plays on words, creating additional layers of meaning by using a word that sounds like another, John's clothing called to mind the stories about Elijah (2 Kgs 1:8). John's clothing made a statement, and the statement was this: "I'm like Elijah, an uncompromising prophet here to shake things up, ready and able to challenge the religious and political leadership."

Beastie, Don't Lose My Number

Earlier in the book we introduced gematria, the system in which every letter of the Greek, Hebrew, and Aramaic alphabets had a numerical value, which meant that one could make connections between words, names, and numbers in ways not possible in English. The most famous New Testament example is in Revelation 13:18. That is the only place in the New Testament where the number 666 appears, and the author of Revelation expects those in the churches in Asia Minor, the original recipients of what he wrote, to know how to calculate the number of a name and, more than that, to be able to do so for the number 666. The number thus refers to someone in the original readers' time, using Greek or Hebrew/Aramaic letters and their numerical equivalents. Can we do the same?

To deduce the correct answer, we will want to do more than just calculate the number of every possible name and combination of names. There are other places in Revelation where the author provides clues and asks those with wisdom to do some calculating. The references in the book will narrow the range of possibilities when we seek to correlate his beast with possible figures that would have been familiar and meaningful to the book's original readers. (If you take the view that the book is primarily about our own future, long after the time of the original readers, you turn the book into a mean prank on the churches in Asia Minor to whom it was sent. The original recipients were the first to read the author's instruction to the reader to calculate and understand the meaning of 666. Yet if the solution is some figure from our time or still in the future, the original recipients were being asked to do something that had no chance of success.)

In chapter 17 the beast with seven heads reappears. It is said to represent a city with seven hills—that is, Rome. It is ridden by a woman called Babylon the prostitute, and many interpreters understand this to refer to Rome as well. The heads also represent seven kings, of whom five have fallen and one is king now, with one more still to come. That should make things easy, shouldn't it? Five were prior to the time of the readers, and one is contemporary with them. If you start with Julius Caesar as the first in the series, then the sixth who reigns in the time of the readers would be Nero. The challenge is that the book seems to be aware of the death of Nero and the belief, which developed soon after, that he was not really dead and would return. Some therefore begin with Augustus rather than Julius Caesar. A good commentary on Revelation, as well as many studies more specifically focused on these passages, will provide an abundance of information on the possibilities and the arguments for and against each. Here we can simply note that the number 666 fits Nero particularly well. If you take the name and title in Greek, Neron Kaisar (Caesar Nero), spell it with Hebrew/Aramaic letters, and tally the result, you get 666. Moreover, if you leave off the final *n* and spell it the Latin way as Nero Kaisar, the result is 616. That is important because we have a manuscript of Revelation that reads 616 rather than 666. The variant suggests that a scribe understood to whom reference was being made, did the math, and, because they were assuming the Latin spelling, "fixed" the text so that the numerical calculation worked.

People often assume that we know by some independent means when the works in the New Testament were written. It is a frequent mistake of students to look up what a source like Wikipedia, or even a study Bible, says about when something was written and then work from there. That is putting the cart before the horse (or the beast or camel, if you prefer something that ties in more directly to this chapter). We cannot say that the emperor in view in Revelation must have been Nero because Revelation was written in the 60s. The reasoning is rather that Revelation would most likely have been written in the 60s if we think its references to one king who currently is reigning (or had recently died and was expected to return) have Nero in view. The dates of writing are not explicitly given in any New Testament texts, and we deduce their likely date or a range of possible dates from what is in them, rather than vice versa.

Before moving on, I should not neglect to mention that the number 666 appears in 1 Kings 10:14 // 2 Chronicles 9:13 (the two slashes mean the texts are parallel). There it refers to the weight of gold that Solomon received each year as measured in talents. This is relevant not just because some think there is a connection between these passages and Revelation because of the number 666. It's also relevant because Jesus told a parable about talents (Matt 25:14-30 // Luke 19:11-27). Many who read it wrongly assume that he was referring to talents in the modern English sense of the word (i.e., abilities). The parable probably influenced the meaning of the English word. A talent in ancient Greek, on the other hand, was a measure of weight. The exact measure varied but never by so much that a talent was anything other than a *huge* amount of money. You could perhaps consider it to represent a bucket

full of silver coins. The precise value of silver may fluctu-
ate, and buckets may differ slightly in their capacity, yet the
overall point does not change. Matthew typically increases
the amounts mentioned in parables, which is why in Luke's
version each receives a mina, which was one-sixtieth of a
talent. Not an insignificant amount, but smaller nonetheless.
This information may help you understand the parable of
the unforgiving debtor in Matthew 18:21–35 better. The first
debtor in the parable owes 10,000 talents. The image is comical. No one person could rack up such a debt. It is as though
the story starts with a man whose personal debt is the size of
the national debt. He is forgiven, which probably seemed just
as implausible to the original hearers. The man whose debt
was canceled then fails to forgive a debt owed to him in the
value of 100 denarii. That's about a hundred days' wages and
more than a quarter of a year's salary—not an insignificant
sum by any means, unless measured against the unforgiving
man's much larger debt. It is, in modern terms, roughly the
difference between a debt of perhaps around $10,000 and
debt of billions of dollars. The point of the parable is that
the things you are asked to forgive that other people do to
you are significant—but nothing compared to what has been
forgiven you.

We started with animals and have ended with numbers
and money. Can we connect the (camel hair) threads running
through the chapter and tie them all together? I think so. No
amount of talent will enable you to pass a camel through the
eye of a needle. And the number of talents you have (in the
ancient sense of a measure of weight in silver) may make
it as hard for you to enter the kingdom of God as it is for
a camel to pass through the eye of a needle. If this saying
is too challenging, feel free to substitute a rope in place of
the camel. If you can pass it through the eye of a (standard-
sized) needle, let me know.

For Further Reading

Bauckham, Richard. *Climax of Prophecy: Studies on the Book of Revelation.* London: Bloomsbury, 1998.

Kelhoffer, James A. *The Diet of John the Baptist: "Locusts and Wild Honey" in Synoptic and Patristic Interpretation.* Tübingen: Mohr Siebeck, 2005.

Koester, Craig R. "The Number of the Beast in Revelation 13 in Light of Papyri, Graffiti, and Inscriptions." *Journal of Early Christian History* 6, no. 3 (2016): 1–21.

Kooten, George H. van. "The Jewish War and the Roman Civil War of 68–69 C.E.: Jewish, Pagan, and Christian Perspectives." Pages 419–50 in *The Jewish Revolt against Rome: Interdisciplinary Perspectives.* Edited by Mladen Popović. Supplements to the Journal for the Study of Judaism 154. Leiden: Brill, 2011.

Macchia, Frank D., and John Christopher Thomas. *Revelation.* Grand Rapids: Eerdmans, 2016.

Marcus, Joel. *John the Baptist in History and Theology.* Columbia: University of South Carolina Press, 2018.

Rojas-Flores, Gonzalo. "The Book of Revelation and the First Years of Nero's Reign." *Biblica* 85 (2004): 375–92.

Williams, Benjamin. "Gnats, Fleas, Flies, and a Camel: A Case Study in the Reception of Genesis Rabbah." *Jewish Quarterly Review* 107, no. 2 (2017): 157–81.

Witherington, Ben, III. *Revelation.* New Cambridge Bible Commentary. New York: Cambridge University Press, 2003.

D

Dead Men Walking

Christians who recite the Apostles' or Nicene Creed mention the resurrection twice whenever they do so. The first occurrence in both is about the resurrection of Jesus. The second is about something related but distinct—resurrection as the form afterlife will take *for everyone*. I suspect that many wrongly assume that in the Apostles' Creed the second reference is synonymous with the first, the resurrection of Jesus being so important that it gets mentioned twice. In most English translations, the Nicene Creed makes it clearer that the reference is to something else, something still hoped for in the future: the resurrection as afterlife for the one reciting the creed and not just something that happened to Jesus in the past.

I will say more about ideas of afterlife in general in a later chapter. Here our focus is on the fact that references to being "raised from the dead" in the New Testament do not all have the same thing in mind. Most of the time when we are told that someone was raised from the dead in the New Testament, it envisages them returning to life in the same sense they were alive before. We might want to call this "resuscitation" to distinguish it. When Paul talks about the resurrection of Jesus, a resurrection in which those who are "in Christ" have begun to participate and will eventually experience fully, he does not mean having been brought back to life only to die again. He means that Jesus has entered into eternal life, what might be called "the life of the age to come." That is why Paul says in Romans 6:9 that Christ has been raised never to die again. The same could not be said about individuals who are said in the Gospels to have been restored to life as a result of miraculous healing by Jesus or his apostles.

Judaism in this era had a concept of two ages. The present age is characterized by imperfection. Death comes to all. Sin abounds. Evil sometimes seems to prevail. The hope arose that God would eventually bring history, as it had been up until that point, to a close and institute a new manner of existence, what some called the kingdom of God or the age to come. The dead would be raised, judgment would be carried out, and paradise would be restored. There was no expectation that one lone individual would be raised from the dead in this sense ahead of the general resurrection of all the dead at the end of the age. Paul's conviction that Jesus had been raised in *that* sense required a significant reconfiguration of the idea of two ages.

Where previously the assumption had been that the end of one age would mark the beginning of the other, Paul became convinced that he was now living in a period of overlap of the two ages. On the one hand, the resurrection of Jesus meant that the general resurrection had begun. When Paul refers to Jesus as the *first fruits* from among the dead (1 Cor 15:20, 23), this is what he means. Jesus is like the very early crops that mark the beginning of the overall harvest. Those first fruits were to be offered to God (see, e.g., Lev 23:9-14), making the image all the more meaningful. On the other hand, while Paul says that Christians have been rescued from the present evil age (Gal 1:4), they continue to live within it.

One reason why scholars doubt that Paul wrote Ephesians and Colossians is that those letters say what Paul otherwise carefully avoids saying. In 2 Corinthians 4:14 he says that the God who raised Jesus *will also raise* us (so too 1 Cor 6:14). In Colossians 3:1 and Ephesians 2:6, however, the recipients are told that they *have been raised* with Christ, and Ephesians even adds that they have been seated in heaven along with him. In the letters whose authenticity is largely undisputed, Paul *does* say that Christians are united with Jesus in his death and resurrection. In Romans, Paul presents baptism as uniting those who undergo it with Christ. But while he is happy to speak of being in Christ, crucified with Christ, and buried with Christ, he is consistent in using the future tense to refer to the resurrection of those who are in Christ.

The way Paul puts it is that those who are in Christ have already begun to "walk in newness of life" (Rom 6:4). Paul considered himself and his contemporaries to be living in a time of overlap of the two ages. Jesus's resurrection meant the age to come had begun, but the defeat of death and full arrival of God's kingdom in which all experience resurrection life had yet to arrive. You may sometimes encounter terms like "realized eschatology" or "inaugurated eschatology" in this context. Eschatology is the study of or one's view about the last things, how history will end. Saying that it is partially realized or inaugurated means that some of the things expected to happen at the end of time have already come about. Paul, however, is adamant that not everything that was expected in the age to come should characterize life in the present. In the kingdom of God there may not be marriage and sex, but that did not mean for Paul that Christians should forgo those things. Some might be called to be celibate, but not all were. Paul was particularly adamant that those who were married should not try to live now as though they were already like the angels and thus no longer engage

Eschatology refers to what a person or group believes about the "end times," the end of history and events leading up to it.

in sexual intercourse (1 Cor 7). Some scholars think that the Corinthians had what Paul considered an "over-realized eschatology." If a realized eschatology maintains a tension between the already fulfilled and the not yet fulfilled, one that is over-realized moves too many of the things expected at the end into the present and treats them as already fulfilled.

When Christians came to believe that Jesus had been raised into the life of the age to come, and yet not as part of the final resurrection and judgment of all human beings, there were no instructions already in existence that could serve as a guide to how to make sense of this situation. They were figuring things out as they went along, and different Christians drew different conclusions. While Paul in his correspondence with the church in Corinth speaks against universal celibacy, in some churches that was exactly what was taught. We see this not only in works like the Acts of Paul and Thecla and the Acts of Thomas outside the New Testament but also in 1 Timothy 4:3. The condemnation of those who forbid marriage and meat provides evidence that some must have been doing precisely that.

In Jewish understanding of the future God had in store, there was a long-standing expectation that it would involve a second exodus, this time with God bringing the scattered exiles back home. In the second part of the book of Isaiah, this imagery features prominently. In the Persian era some had returned from exile in Babylon to rebuild the temple and the city of Jerusalem and settle once more in their historic homeland, but many did not. There continued to be an enormous diaspora of Jews and Samaritans. Moreover, tensions between Jews and Samaritans made it seem extremely unlikely there could be a united Israel once more. The Davidic royal line no longer ruled even over Judah (from this point on, more often referred to as the province or region of Judea). Many living in Jesus's time considered the exile to be an ongoing situation. The book of Daniel famously reinterpreted Jeremiah's prediction of seventy years of exile as seventy weeks of years—that is, 70 × 7 = 490 years (Jer 25:8-14; Dan 9). The author of Daniel, writing in the midst of the crisis prompted by the persecution of the Jews during the reign of the Syrian king Antiochus IV, hoped that the fulfillment would happen soon and lead to the restoration of God's people. In other works that tell the story of that persecution, in particular 2 and 4 Maccabees, the hope is expressed that the deaths of martyrs, who refuse to deny their God whatever the cost, may be like a sacrifice and turn away God's anger from his people.

Both the hopes and the specific connection with martyrdom provided material to help the early followers of Jesus make sense of his death. They seem to have connected all these things and, as a result, to have envisaged Jesus as leading a new exodus out of the present age, out from under slavery to sin and death, and into the age to come with its new life. Baptism resonated with the passing through water that featured prominently in the first exodus and yet could also be connected with Jesus's death and resurrection.

What Kind of Bodies?

In 1 Corinthians 15, Paul responds to questions the Corinthians had about the nature of resurrection bodies. Many in the church in Corinth were not from a Jewish background and found the notion of resurrection, of an afterlife that involved a body, quite bizarre. Within the framework of Greek thought, it was desirable to escape the body and exist in a purely spiritual form. Paul, in contrast, emphatically states that he doesn't desire to be unclothed (without his body) but to be clothed differently (2 Cor 5:3-4). For those within the Pharisaic strand of Judaism, God had made human beings as a whole. One might be able to distinguish between body and soul, flesh and mind, but these were aspects of human beings who would be incomplete if any of these were lacking. In English we have a relevant term that derives from Greek words that Paul used when writing about this topic. Human beings are psychosomatic unities. *Psychē* in Greek means "soul," and *sōma* means "body." The terms, and other words derived from them, are still used in medicine to refer to mind and body. A disembodied human being, from the perspective of the Pharisees, is not a "free spirit" in the literal sense but rather deficient. To be disembodied is to be missing an aspect of what makes us whole, the way God created humans to be from the beginning. We see in the Gospels that Jesus subscribed to the Pharisaic view on this subject, debating with Sadducees about the resurrection (Mark 12:18–27; Matt 22:23–32; Luke 20:27–38).

Even among those who subscribed to this view, however, there was disagreement about the nature of the resurrection body. We see this clearly if we compare Luke 24:39 with 1 Corinthians 15:50. Luke depicts the risen Jesus as emphasizing that he is still flesh and bone and not a ghost. Paul says that flesh and blood will not inherit the kingdom of God. We should not downplay their disagreement, although neither should we exaggerate it. Paul used "flesh" with decidedly negative connotations, and so it is unsurprising that he would disassociate it from resurrection life. He is nevertheless emphatic that resurrection is bodily. Luke's Jesus may be flesh and bone, but he can appear in a locked room. Luke may have assumed that Jesus's body would undergo further transformation as it ascended through the heavens. In ancient Jewish and early Christian accounts of heavenly ascents, there is sometimes a transformation step by step as someone moves through the successive heavens, each with its own degree of glory. The idea of seven heavens reflects the cosmology of that time, in which the sun, moon, and five visible planets were each thought to exist on spheres that surrounded the earth. The celestial realm was thought to be filled with angelic beings who oversaw various aspects of the workings of the cosmos.

Hebrews 7:26 emphasizes Jesus's status exalted higher than the heavens, into the very presence of God. Hebrews was not unique in envisaging the heavenly realm as the prototype for the earthly tabernacle, with its concentric courtyards of increasing holiness as one moved closer to the divine throne. On the Day of Atonement (Yom Kippur) the high priest brought blood into that most holy place to purify it from contamination by the sin of the people, allowing God to continue to dwell in their midst. In the same way the author of Hebrews envisages Jesus purifying the heavenly sanctuary so that he can bring us with him into the very presence of God. This imagery becomes problematic if taken as anything other than symbolic, however. Jesus's blood was shed on earth. In what sense could he have been thought to take that blood into the celestial realm? If we take the imagery in Hebrews literally, we will be confused by the order of events. If Jesus offered his sacrifice on earth by dying on the cross, and then the very body he sacrificed was restored to life, what would it mean to say that he ascended into the heavens bodily and offered his sacrifice in the heavenly sanctuary there? Presumably all of this is an elaborate symbolic reading of the Levitical text to emphasize that Jesus's obedience was accepted by God as like an atoning sacrifice and was counted not only in Jesus's own favor but for all those he represents in his priestly role. Hebrews is the only text that draws these kinds of detailed parallels between Leviticus and Jesus (departing from Leviticus whenever necessary because Jesus doesn't fit—for example, by making him a priest according to the order of Melchizedek since Jesus was not of priestly, much less high priestly, descent). Despite offering a perspective that is unique among the New Testament writing, it has had a disproportionate influence as many theologians have read the rest of early Christian literature through the lens of this work.

Other Early Risers

Among the most puzzling texts related to resurrection in the New Testament is Matthew 27:52-53, which says that at the moment Jesus died, not only did the earth quake but tombs opened and many bodies of saints came out. Apparently, however, they did not appear to anyone until after Jesus's resurrection. While Paul depicts Jesus as the first fruit of the resurrection, Matthew has an unspecified number of others beat him to it! If these individuals were resurrected in the same sense as Jesus, entering the eternal life of the age to come, then where would they do so? If they were to dwell on a new earth, then they must still be waiting even now. If they were raised in the sense of resuscitation, then one wonders what the point was of bringing them back to life, only for them to die again. None of these saints, even if they were incredibly famous, would have been recognizable for who they were by people in Jesus's time, and it is hard to imagine that many people would believe them if they claimed to be scriptural personages returned to life. The experience seems as though it would be traumatic for all involved—both for the dead who were raised and for those who encountered them. Most commentators remain puzzled by the story. Like the imagery in Hebrews and Revelation regarding topics like resurrection and heavenly existence, we can grasp the point even if we find the way it was made strange. Matthew presumably wanted to convey that Jesus's death and resurrection were connected with the general resurrection of the dead, in which not only his contemporary followers but also those who lived in earlier times would participate. As so often, when we turn symbols into stories and take the details of the latter literally, the result is confusing and awkward.

Finally, for those two or three readers who have been hoping I would address the topic explicitly, none of the New Testament authors has in mind anyone becoming zombies or the arrival of a zombie apocalypse. Apocalypse? Yes, most definitely. In fact, that English word is derived from the New Testament. Zombies? Sorry, no.

For Further Reading

Allison, Dale. *The End of the Ages Has Come: An Early Interpretation of the Passion and Resurrection of Jesus*. Eugene, OR: Wipf & Stock, 2013.

Elledge, Casey Deryl. *Resurrection of the Dead in Early Judaism, 200 BCE–CE 200*. Oxford: Oxford University Press, 2017.

Nickelsburg, George W. E. *Resurrection, Immortality, and Eternal Life in Intertestamental Judaism and Early Christianity*. Cambridge, MA: Harvard University Press, 2006.

Setzer, Claudia. *Resurrection of the Body in Early Judaism and Early Christianity: Doctrine, Community, and Self-Definition*. Leiden: Brill, 2004.

Williams, Jarvis J. *Maccabean Martyr Traditions in Paul's Theology of Atonement: Did Martyr Theology Shape Paul's Conception of Jesus's Death?* Eugene, OR: Wipf & Stock, 2010.

E

Eat Whatever Is Set before You

Jesus was from the inland village of Nazareth not far from
Sepphoris, which had been the capital of Galilee until Herod
Antipas built Tiberias and moved his capital there. These
changes happened while Jesus was growing up. The New
Testament gospels do not report that he visited either city.
When he began his public activity in Galilee, he did so with
a focus on the towns along Lake Tiberias, also known as Lake
Kinneret (and dubbed by Mark and probably known to you
as the Sea of Galilee even though it isn't a sea). Jesus had followers who were connected with the fishing industry there.
If your assumption about people who fish is that they are
either poor people struggling to feed themselves or wealthy
retirees relaxing, neither fits these people or their historical
context. The city of Tarichaea on Lake Tiberias (possibly the
same city as Migdal or Magdala, which means "Tower") was
the hub of a fish-salting industry that shipped its product all
over the Roman world. The Romans were famous for many
things, and while roads may top the list, garum definitely
ranks high. If you've never heard of garum, it is simply the
ancient Roman equivalent of the fish sauce you use when
making Chinese food (You don't? You should!) or the Worces-
tershire sauce you use when making beef stroganoff. (Make

sure you pronounce it as the British do: "Woostuh sauce.") As the salted fish ferments, it naturally produces glutamate, forms of which (such as monosodium glutamate or MSG for short) are used to this day to enhance flavor.

Mary Magdalene may be nicknamed for the city of Migdal or Magdala. In an era when women were rarely if ever designated in this way that it was common to nickname men, this would have indicated her status in Jesus's estimation. The fact that she financially supported the Jesus movement (Luke 8:1-3) also indicates her relative wealth and status. (Jesus may also have given her a nickname that highlighted her as a "tower," as he did with Simon when calling him Peter, which means "the Rock"—or "Rocky" if you prefer. Jesus enjoyed wordplay, and so the nicknames he bestowed may have had multiple significances.) In Mark 1:16-20 the brothers Simon and Andrew leave their nets, and then we are told that James and John leave their father Zebedee with the servants. This indicates that they too were people of means involved in the fishing industry. As you can see, food in the time of the New Testament is not just trivia or vaguely interesting background information. What people ate, how they ate it and with whom they ate, and many other aspects of eating tell us about these ancient people's values, the economic realities that impacted them on a daily basis, and much more. Paying close attention to food will also help us understand some of the things that Christians emphasized that set them apart from their contemporaries.

Luke's Fascination with Food

For a long time now, whenever I list the themes of Luke-Acts, I mention eating as one of them. Luke mentions a lot of meals in his two-volume work. Of course, when you write two volumes you have room to include twice as many stories.

Even so, there seems to be a distinctive interest in this topic compared with other gospels. Some of the stories Luke tells about meals are found in other gospels, but quite a few are unique to him. In Luke 5:29 Levi holds a banquet for Jesus at his house. In 7:36 Jesus is invited to dinner at a Pharisee's house. In 14:1-24 Jesus attends a banquet and points out how the guests choose places of honor at the table. In 19:5 Jesus invites himself over to Zacchaeus's house to stay with him, which would have included the provision of a meal (or "tea" as per the British children's song about the story). Turning to Luke's sequel volume, in Acts 2:42, 46, one of the key things that the early Christians do is eat ("break bread") together. In chapters 10-11 the major focus is on Peter going and having a meal with someone who isn't Jewish. In 16:34 Paul and Silas have a meal with the Philippian jailer. Still more examples could be added to the list. I'm convinced that the reason Luke tells so many stories about people eating is not merely that he was hungry when he wrote. (Just as you shouldn't shop for groceries while hungry, you shouldn't write a two-volume account of Jesus and his earliest followers while hungry either.) So what other reason is there? Understanding the significance of meals in the Greco-Roman world will help us answer that question.

Meals were one of the places where differences in social status were starkly visible. There is a famous letter that Pliny the Younger wrote to Avitus (Pliny, *Letters* 2.6), in which he comments on a meal he attended. On that occasion the host had different qualities of food and wine prepared and served his most important friends the best, other friends and acquaintances something not quite as good, with the worst for the freedmen. Yes, not only did the Romans practice slavery, but they also had a special social category for former slaves. They might be free, but there was no question of their being equal, either formally or in the estimation of others. They were granted citizenship (not everyone in the Roman Empire had that privileged status) when they were freed, but they were still considered ineligible for public office. (If you wish to read it for yourself, you can find the letter of Pliny that I've mentioned online in an older translation that is in the public domain, meaning it can be made freely available as it is not protected by copyright. In older editions, this particular letter may be numbered XIX, while in newer ones it is 2.6. When consulting older editions of primary texts, you'll often find that the way of numbering works and sections has changed, not only by replacing Roman numerals but by changing the numbering system entirely.)

Returning to the New Testament, you'll presumably have been struck by the contrast between the meal described in the letter from Pliny and the practice of at least some early Christians. The meals described in Luke-Acts are an example of one way in which Jesus and the early Christians sought not just to proclaim their message but to apply it. Paul writes that in Christ there is neither Jew nor Greek, slave nor free, male and female (Gal 3:28). These are precisely the sort of divisions that separated people at meals (and in other areas of life) in those days. In Luke-Acts we see the principle that Paul articulated in writing being lived out. Doing so would certainly have been considered a challenge to the status quo. Jesus ate with outcasts. His followers did the same, and some went further still, dining with gentiles (something that we see causing controversy in Gal 2:11–13). The lifestyle of the earliest Christians would have represented an important challenge to inequalities and divisions in the society of that time. Their proclamation and way of life went hand in hand and (in Luke's own words) "turned the world upside-down" (Acts 17:6). In what follows, we'll look more closely at some of the specific issues that would have come up when Christians tried to implement the practice of sharing meals across these divides.

Cooking with the Corinthians

Paul's letter we know as 1 Corinthians addresses a number of issues in the church in Corinth. Some are subjects that they had written to him to ask about. Others are things that he had heard, presumably from those who delivered the Corinthians' letter to him. Don't forget that there was nothing like a modern postal service in Paul's time. If he wrote a letter, he had to send someone to deliver it. If he received a letter, it was delivered to him by someone who brought it from the senders and could inform him about things where the letter originated, clarifying and supplementing the things that were written.

In 1 Corinthians 11:17–34, Paul talks about divisions among the Corinthians and how the divisions are turning their attempt to celebrate the Lord's Supper into something else entirely. The divisions may have been literal ones, in keeping with the meal practices in the Greco-Roman world we discussed above. Churches met in someone's home, and naturally a wealthier member would have had more room to accommodate such a gathering. When Christians came together there, they did not just pass around oyster crackers and the smallest juice cups ever invented. They gathered for a meal, with a ceremonial recollection of Jesus's final meal as just one part of it. It probably seemed natural for the host family to seat their social peers alongside them, with better-quality food and wine, and perhaps actually in different, if adjacent, parts of the house. The wealthier may also have had the freedom to arrive earlier. Sunday was not a holiday, and at this point in history no one confused it with the Jewish Sabbath, a day of rest. Sunday was the first day of the week and a working day. Sunday was not a day of rest for the early Christians or anyone else in that time. Christians met after the end of the workday, considering it the Lord's Day, the day of the week on which Jesus was raised from the dead. Sunday thus seemed the appropriate day for them to meet together and celebrate their faith in Jesus.

This is important background information when reading the New Testament and for understanding one story in particular. When Eutychus falls asleep and falls out the window to his death in Acts 20:7-12, it is not just the length of the sermon that is to blame. (You know the sort I mean, ones that might put someone to sleep on a Sunday morning even after they've had a good, long night's rest). Eutychus will have labored all day and then met with his fellow Christians. Paul then preached until midnight, and Eutychus couldn't manage to stay awake. Even with the background information we've provided, the story should probably still serve as a warning that sermons can be dangerous if they go on too long.

Returning to Paul's letter to the Corinthians, Paul warns his readers that if they eat in an unworthy manner, not recognizing the body of the Lord, they bring judgment on themselves. Note how Paul puts it. He does not say that they have failed to recognize the body *and blood* of the Lord, which might mean that they have failed to recognize the meaning or the transformed nature of the bread and wine they consume. What they have failed to recognize is the body. Paul emphasizes in chapter 12 of this same letter that the church is the body of Christ. When he warns about eating and drinking unworthily, he probably has in mind not some general sense in which a person might judge themselves unworthy, but specifically the manner in which they are behaving toward one another in the very act of celebrating this sacred communal meal. They are failing to be united, failing to esteem one another as fellow members of the body of Christ, and in so doing are harming their witness as well as one another.

If you attend a church that uses tiny individual-sized receptacles of grape juice and a small cracker for Communion, you may have been puzzled by 1 Corinthians 11:21. How could anyone not be hungry after such a tiny morsel of bread, and how could anyone get drunk from such a tiny cup? Now that you know that this was part of a meal, in a home, with full-sized portions of food and wine for at least some present, this hopefully makes more sense.

From Last Supper to Lord's Supper

Since Paul's letters were written before the gospels, 1 Corinthians 11 contains our earliest account of the Last Supper. Paul provides the information as something that he had received and in turn passed on to them, which he now reminds them of. This is one of the few places where Paul goes back over a story about Jesus that he had previously told the recipients of his letter. Here he provides a reminder because he has heard they are getting the Lord's Supper wrong. He makes a direct connection between Jesus's final meal with his disciples and the practice of Christians eating meals together. Paul's version is closest to Luke's among the gospels, not surprisingly given the close connection between Luke-Acts and Paul. The Gospel of John does not include the words of institution but does have Jesus speak about abiding in him like branches in a vine at that final meal (John 15). John also depicts Jesus in a separate earlier context as bread from heaven whose flesh and blood those who believe in him are to consume (John 6). One of our earliest Christian sources outside the New Testament is the Didache, the Greek word for teaching. (The word/name is pronounced in three syllables with the hard *ch* sound found in Scottish English, as in the word "loch." Pronouncing the last syllable as "kay" will do. Just don't pronounce the name as "did-ash" or "did-ache.") The Didache has instructions for a number of Christian practices, including the Lord's Supper. The words that it says to use for the Eucharist (from the Greek word for giving thanks) are not at all those found in the New Testament. This is another ancient primary text that you can and should explore online. It mentions the vine as well as the bread that was created by bringing together wheat from many fields, symbolizing the church coming together as one. Even with all the striking differences between these early Christian texts, there are common themes and threads, including some you might expect as well as others you might not. While Paul and the Synoptic Gospels (Matthew, Mark, and Luke) agree in focusing on the remembrance of Jesus's death, Paul, John, and the Didache emphasize unity in Christ. The origin and development of the Lord's Supper or Eucharist is a subject on which whole books have been written. Not everyone in the field of New Testament has researched that specific topic in depth, but anyone with interest in the New Testament should be aware of the key texts within and outside the New Testament and the questions that they raise.

One of the things that stands out in the accounts of the Last Supper in the New Testament is Jesus's vow, which appears to fall into the category of a Nazirite vow (Mark 14:25; Matt 26:29; Luke 22:18). While some people get Nazarene and Nazirite confused, they are different terms with different meanings. A Nazarene is someone from Nazareth. A Nazirite (as explained in Num 6) was someone who let their hair grow (remember Samson?) and refrained from all grape products until they fulfilled their vow, a vow being a solemn promise. Jesus said he will not touch the fruit of the vine again until the kingdom dawns. This isn't a typical vow because he isn't promising to give up grape products until he does something, but rather until God does something—namely, bring the kingdom, when Jesus and his disciples will be reunited and feast together. This promise by Jesus doesn't become part of the church's celebration of the Lord's Supper. Thus, while other details may be suspected of owing more to the later church's practice than to things Jesus himself said, the vow must be something that goes back to Jesus. It reflects his conviction that the end was near—whether in the sense of his impending death, the arrival of the kingdom of God, or both.

Food Sacrificed to Idols

Food sacrificed to idols is another subject that doesn't come up on a daily basis for most Christians in the English-speaking world today. Indeed, it may never come up. In ancient Corinth, though, it was a pressing issue. The question was not about whether to go and offer a sacrifice to a god other than the Father of Jesus and then partake of the meat thereafter. But meat that was sold in the marketplace and that was served in homes might well have been sacrificed. Banquets were held in rooms of temples. Individuals who invited you to dinner may have offered a sacrifice and then cooked their portion of the animal for the meal. Meat was a much scarcer commodity then than for most readers of this book. If you had an animal, you likely offered it to the gods before partaking of it. This is the background to the question asked by the Corinthians, and perhaps also to Paul's mention in Romans 14:2 of some Christians who eat only vegetables. Paul's advice to the Corinthians allowed them to eat anything without scruples unless it was explicitly pointed out that the meat came from sacrifice (1 Cor 10:27, perhaps echoing Jesus's teaching in Luke 10:8). Revelation 2:20 takes a harder line on this than Paul did. Acts 15:20 and 29 also prohibit that which is sacrificed to idols. According to Acts, Paul was present at a council in Jerusalem, the first of its kind, which aimed to address the question of whether gentile Christians needed to convert to Judaism and observe the law of Moses. If Paul agreed with this prohibition being imposed on gentile Christians, why does he never mention the council and its deci-sion? There's something puzzling there, and we will return to it in a later chapter.

Something Isn't Kosher

You might have expected the first big crisis in the earliest days of the Christian movement would be about a major point of doctrine. The divinity of Christ, the virgin birth, the mean-ing of the cross, or something else of that sort. Instead, the first major crisis related to things that Christians in the English-speaking world give little or no thought to, for the most part. Food was a biggie, and so was circumcision. We will discuss circumcision in a later chapter, and here will stick with our focus on food. The concept of kosher food is more widely familiar in some places in the English-speaking world than others. Unfortunately there are still many people who have the odd notion that for food to be kosher it needs to be "blessed by a rabbi." That is not even close to correct. Kosher food means food that follows the food laws in the Bible, as historically interpreted by the rabbis. Deuteronomy 14 is a key text on this topic. The rabbis added clarifications and decisions about less obvious matters. For instance, how do you make absolutely sure you haven't boiled a kid in its mother's milk? Separate meat and dairy altogether. That is why a cheeseburger isn't kosher: the possibility that the prin-ciple of the law, not to cook the baby animal in the milk of its mother, could unintentionally be infringed. (In case it wasn't clear, the reference in Exod 23:19 to a "kid" means a young goat and not a human child. I thought it important to mention that, lest you badly misunderstand what the passage is about!) In the first century as also today, there were different practices and different degrees of strictness. One of the

Kosher is the term for food that is permissible to eat according to Jewish law as historically in-terpreted by the rabbis.

things the New Testament tells us about the Pharisees is that they sought to be scrupulous about matters related to food, including purity but also the tithing of not just major crops but even herbs (Matt 23:23). Jesus doesn't criticize them for doing these things the law requires (see Deut 14:22–29). On the contrary, he explicitly affirms that these things should not be neglected. His criticism was that at least some of the Pharisees were scrupulous about these small details yet not as concerned about things that should be given greater priority such as mercy and justice. The same criticism applies to many religious individuals and movements, in every religious tradition and at every time in history.

The Torah requires payment of **tithes**, *10 percent of one's crops as a tax that supported the temple and helped the poor.*

When the Gospels say that Jesus ate with "sinners," it is unclear whether this means he ate with the vile and morally bankrupt or merely with people who were less observant in some areas than the most religious people of that era thought they should be. What is clear, however, is that he crossed boundaries with his dining habits. In the early church, those who allowed gentiles to become part of the Christian community and share in its meals were convinced that they were simply extending Jesus's principles and his approach to meals. Jesus's association with less observant Jews did not address the issue that arose later of whether gentile Christians had to keep kosher. Have you ever thought about what it would mean for Christian communities made up of Jews and non-Jews if some of them kept kosher and others did not, especially given the Christian practice of sharing meals together? If a gentile Christian hosted the church's meeting and served non-kosher food, Jewish Christians could not partake of it. Paul wanted Christians to be united. He also refused to impose the observance of the Jewish law on them. Yet he was not of the view that Jewish Christians should abandon observance of the law. He struggled to find a way to accomplish all these things. As we explore further in other parts of this book, not all early Christians agreed with his effort, and even among those who did, not everyone considered Paul's approach successful.

By now you can probably see why the earlier agreement of Paul and the Jerusalem apostles was bound to encounter problems. They agreed that the Jerusalem church would focus on proclaiming the gospel to Jews while Paul would go to the gentiles (Gal 2:7-9). In places like Corinth the church members were mostly non-Jews. In Jerusalem there may not have been any gentiles. The trouble arose, as they might well have anticipated, in Antioch, where there were significant Jewish and non-Jewish populations living side by side. We cannot here trace the history of how things developed beyond New Testament times, but it doesn't require a history lesson to realize that Christianity developed into a religion that today is practiced almost exclusively by non-Jews. It can thus be difficult for most of today's Christians to understand how these matters could have been such troubling and challenging issues for the early church. Viewed with hindsight, and with texts like the letters of Paul now authoritative scripture, the answers Paul gave may seem inevitable and obvious. In his own time they were anything but.

Let's Eat!

The title of this chapter comes from Paul's advice to the Corinthian church (1 Cor 10:27). It is also a fun, if dangerous, verse to take out of context. Someone has put food in front of you? Doesn't matter whether you're hungry or not—Paul has told you what you must do! This isn't the only phrase related to food where there is the potential for it to be interpreted and applied in interesting ways. Some have interpreted the phrase "drink ye all of it" in older English translations of

Matthew 26:27 to mean that no wine is to be left behind once the Communion service is done. In Greek it is clear that it means all of you should drink, and not that you should drink it all. You may also have encountered the saying "Eat, drink, and be merry, for tomorrow we die." The expression appears to combine the words and the sentiment expressed in Ecclesiastes 8:15 and Isaiah 22:13. In the former passage this is recommended, the reader being told that there is nothing better for one to do than to enjoy food and drink and be glad. Life is short, so enjoy it while it lasts. Yet 1 Corinthians 15:32 rejects the sentiment. Is this just another example of Paul rejecting what the Old Testament says? Ecclesiastes, like the overwhelming majority of texts in the Jewish scriptures, does not envisage an afterlife featuring rewards and punishments. Paul is thus right that the attitude that one might as well enjoy life reflects a view without the hope of resurrection. For Paul, there is something more important and more urgent that must take priority over the concerns of life in the present age, relegating matters of food and drink to secondary importance. As he puts it in Philippians 4:12 (the crucially ignored context of what may perhaps be the most misused verse in Paul's letters, Philippians 4:13), he is able to cope with hunger and with having food in abundance, with hardship and comfort, because he finds that Christ strengthens him.

For Further Reading

Burkert, Walter. *Greek Religion*. Cambridge, MA: Harvard University Press, 2006.

De Luco, Stephana, and Anna Lena. "Magdala/Taricheae." Pages 280–342 in *The Archaeological Record from Cities, Towns, and Villages*. Vol. 2 of *Galilee in the Late Second Temple and Mishnaic Periods*. Edited by David A. Fiensy and James Riley Strange. Minneapolis: Fortress, 2015.

Detienne, Marcel, and Jean Pierre Vernant. *The Cuisine of Sacrifice among the Greeks.* Chicago: University of Chicago Press, 1989.

Ekroth, Gunnel. "Meat in Ancient Greece: Sacrificial, Sacred or Secular?" *Food & History* 5 (2007): 249–72.

Gooch, Peter D. *Dangerous Food: 1 Corinthians 8–10 in Its Context.* Waterloo, ON: Wilfrid Laurier University Press, 2006.

Kim, Yung Suk. *A Theological Introduction to Paul's Letters: Exploring a Threefold Theology of Paul.* Eugene, OR: Cascade, 2011.

Mitchell, Margaret M. *Paul and the Rhetoric of Reconciliation: An Exegetical Investigation.* Louisville: Westminster John Knox, 1993.

Willis, Wendell. *Idol Meat in Corinth: The Pauline Argument in 1 Corinthians 8 and 10.* Eugene, OR: Wipf & Stock, 2004.

F

Fulfillment Fail?

If you take a class on how to interpret scripture at most universities or seminaries, you won't learn to interpret the Bible the way Matthew does. Indeed, you may be explicitly taught *not* to do the sorts of things Matthew did. (Other New Testament authors do the same kind of thing, but I'm going to pick on Matthew here because professors do that and life isn't fair). It thus seems natural to ask the question, If Matthew's Gospel were to be submitted as the final essay in a modern university or seminary course on biblical interpretation, as an assignment that aimed to demonstrate what its author had learned about the subject, what grade would it receive? Would the professor conclude that Matthew had not been paying attention in class? (Professors seem to want to assign grades to everything. The truth is that many of us really would rather not but haven't figured out another way to motivate students to do things that lead to learning. Who knows how Matthew's Gospel might look differently if he'd known it would be graded?)

You may not have taken such a class—indeed, that might be the very reason you're reading this book. So what exactly does Matthew do "wrong"? First, let me say that's probably not the right way to put things. We shouldn't judge ancient authors by modern standards that they didn't have in mind and so couldn't possibly live up to. By way of analogy, we could note that Matthew's Gospel doesn't include footnotes to indicate that the author had used the Gospel of Mark in composing his own gospel. Footnotes simply weren't a thing in that time, and so we should not fault ancient people for following norms of their time rather than our own. Today, however, we have easy ways of citing our sources to give them credit, and it is important to use them. Today Matthew would fail because of plagiarism. In his time he was simply doing what authors did. In the same way, Matthew's approach to interpreting scripture would not have been judged inappropriate or surprising in his time. What I am claiming in this chapter is that if someone today does what Matthew did way back then, we would consider it inappropriate. Let me explain why.

A Sign for a King

Earlier I quoted the saying that a text taken out of context becomes a pretext. (If you hadn't heard that before, it is a nice catchy way of remembering that context is important to understanding the Bible.) You may also have heard that Jesus fulfills countless predictions made by the prophets of ancient Israel. Put those two together and it can be a really unsettling experience the first time you go back and read the texts that the Gospel of Matthew includes in its story of Jesus, especially toward the beginning. Matthew's first two chapters (apart from the genealogy, which readers tend to skip) are very famous, being read in most churches at Christmas. In those chapters there are several quotations from the Jewish scriptures that are well known in Christian circles mostly because of Matthew's use of them. Among the most famous of those is Isaiah 7:14, traditionally rendered as something like "Behold, a virgin shall conceive and shall give birth to a son." You may have heard that the Hebrew text doesn't specifically say "virgin" but uses a word with a broader meaning, "young woman." Of course, a young woman might be expected or hoped to be a virgin in this context, so there may or may not be a significant difference. Matthew was using the Greek translation of Isaiah, however, and it uses a word that more specifically means "virgin."

That's not really where the big problem lies. No, the real issue is what Matthew leaves out, and what most Christmas pageants thus leave out. You can get through an entire Advent and Christmas season and never hear about Aram, Ephraim, Ahaz, or Assyria. Yet they are central to Isaiah 7. Is Matthew taking a verse out of context and twisting its meaning? Perhaps. Let's take a closer look. In Isaiah 7, King Ahaz of Judah, to whom Isaiah was a prophetic advisor, was worried about an alliance of kings to his north, in Israel and Syria. They were conspiring to oust Ahaz and arrange for him to be replaced by someone who would better serve their interests. It is in response to this that the sign of Immanuel is offered. Isaiah tells Ahaz that by the time the child can tell right from wrong, the kings he is worried about will be no more.

Think about that for a moment. If you were King Ahaz, living in the eighth century BC, would you be comforted by a message that said, "Don't worry, seven centuries or so from now a child will be born, in whose time the kings you are worried about will no longer be around?" I didn't think so. Ahaz wouldn't be around then either. No special sign is needed to demonstrate that the people alive today will not be alive more than half a millennium later. We can thus be certain that that wasn't the point. Once you think about it, it becomes obvious that something is amiss with the understanding that Isaiah 7:14 was about Jesus in its original context.

But is the problem with us, Matthew, or Isaiah? Let's pay close attention to what Isaiah 7 actually says. The significance of the child is that, within the short span between when

Isaiah was speaking and when a child soon to be conceived would reach an age of minimal moral discernment, the crisis would be over. The sign that is offered is not in fact that a virgin conceives. Even if the book of Isaiah used a word that unambiguously meant "virgin," that still wouldn't make the virgin's conception the point. If it were, the text would highlight the miraculous nature of the conception. That it doesn't suggests the virgin or young woman conceives in the normal manner. When you stop to think about it, you realize that everyone knows virgins who conceived. The process that led to them conceiving also led to them no longer being virgins. (If you don't understand what I'm referring to here, I'm afraid that an explanation lies beyond the scope of this book.) In its original context, Isaiah 7:14 refers to a child who could serve as a sign for King Ahaz. The next chapters of the book of Isaiah provide a likely identification for the child. Isaiah and a woman referred to as "the prophetess" have a child whom Isaiah names Mahershalalhashbaz (one of the most neglected biblical names, in case you are ever looking for one that will stand out and be distinctive). That child's role is to serve as a sign (Isa 8:3–4), for the same purpose as the child referred to in chapter 7. He even appears to be addressed as Immanuel in Isaiah 8:8. Now, you may be thinking, "But his actual name was Mahershalalhashbaz, not Immanuel." That is true—and the same may be said of Jesus, yet most Christians have no problem viewing him as the fulfillment of the Immanuel prediction nonetheless.

Is Matthew taking texts out of context, saying Jesus was predicted in them, and hoping no one will notice? That doesn't seem likely. But let's compare the other scriptures Matthew works into these chapters, because the more examples we look at, the more likely it is that the combined evidence will make clear what we ought to understand. Fulfillment of prophecy is a major theme throughout Matthew's

Gospel, where it is mentioned more frequently than in either Mark or Luke. If we can make sense of what is going on in these chapters, it will help us understand not just one story but the entirety of Matthew's Gospel.

God's Son Leaves Egypt

Another prophetic text that Jesus is said to fulfill is in Hosea 11: "Out of Egypt I called my son." If you read more than the small snippet Matthew quotes, you will see that it explicitly states in the context who is being talked about: "When Israel was a child, I loved him, and out of Egypt I called my son." God is depicted as talking about the people of Israel as God's beloved child, whom he called from slavery in Egypt. It then says that the son in question turned away and worshiped foreign gods—something that neither Matthew nor anyone since has claimed was fulfilled by Jesus. This appears to be another example of a text taken out of context. You could be forgiven for thinking that Matthew was trying to pull a fast one. The problem with that view is that Matthew's readers presumably knew the text in question. Matthew 2:15 doesn't even specify that the quotation is from the book of Hosea. Perhaps some readers and hearers would not have understood and would not have asked questions. But presumably some would, and if they did, they would find out what Hosea said. It also is very likely that at least some would immediately recognize the text that Matthew was referring to and know the whole section. If Matthew had been trying to deceive his contemporaries, he wouldn't have gotten away with it as easily as he might today when levels of biblical literacy are so much lower. It is more likely that we have misunderstood what Matthew means by fulfillment of prophecy.

Rather than it being a case of predictions that later come true, why not understand him to be referring to typology?

Typology involves noticing and finding significance in similarities between the stories of different individuals. When
Paul says that Adam was a type of Christ (Rom 5:14), he
doesn't mean that Adam living as he did was a prediction of
Jesus. He means that the similarities as well as the differences between the narrated lives of the two are significant,
encouraging readers to compare them.

Typology *looks for patterns of* Some translations render the word in
similarity and difference that other ways, as "pattern" or "prototype,"
connect individuals or events. for instance. When Matthew said Jesus
fulfilled Hosea 11, might he have meant
something along those lines, that Jesus's story as he tells it
fits the pattern of, or is modeled after, the story of the people
of Israel? We see Israel typology again in Matthew 4, when
Jesus is tempted in the wilderness. He faces the same tests
that Israel faced in the wilderness, in the same location, for
a period of forty days just as they faced them for forty years.
Jesus is said to have responded to the temptations by quoting
texts from Deuteronomy that in their original contexts were
about how Israel ought to have acted but failed to. Readers
are supposed to think in terms of comparison and contrast.
They are not supposed to think that the story of Israel's wilderness wanderings after the exodus were a prediction of
Jesus. Readers who knew the texts that Matthew was quoting
from would have understood his point. The issue is not with
what Matthew did but with how readers today tend to
misunderstand it.

Weeping and Wilderness

Let's apply this to another text that Matthew quotes and says
is fulfilled by events in Jesus's life, Jeremiah 31:15. The mention
of Ramah and Rachel points the reader immediately beyond
the gospel. Even if you do not get the references, you get that

a place and a person are being referred to that the gospel has not mentioned yet. As a reader, you are assumed to know the meaning and the context, or to ask about it if you do not. Turning to Jeremiah, you might still be puzzled, because in fact you would need to turn to Genesis to learn about Rachel, the wife of Jacob. Jacob was renamed Israel, and so Rachel is literally the mother of the children of Israel (or, to be more precise, of many rather than all of them, because Jacob had more than one wife). Jeremiah goes on to say that Rachel should stop weeping for her children because they will return to their own country. The reference is not to children slaughtered by a paranoid king but to Israelites carried off into exile. To make sense of Matthew's application of this to Jesus, we need to know not only what Jeremiah wrote but also that many in Matthew's time considered the exile to be an ongoing state of affairs. The people of Israel were still scattered and divided, and a foreign empire was still ultimately in control. The slaughter of the children of Bethlehem reflects this same experience. As if that were not enough, Matthew is also engaging in Moses typology here, echoing the story of the slaughter of the infants by Pharaoh. Through that allusion he is able to depict Jesus as a new Moses and contrast them by means of an ironic difference between the two individuals' stories. Where Moses had to flee *from* Egypt, Jesus and his parents will flee *to* Egypt. They will be on the run not from a hostile foreign king but from one who bears the title "king of the Jews." The contrasts between the two stories are as crucial to Matthew's point as the similarities.

Having mentioned the temptation in the wilderness, I ought to note that in that story the devil engages in proof-texting, leading to the famous saying "Even the devil can quote scripture." Jesus's response to the temptation points out that there is a context that is being neglected. In this case, it is not the immediate literary context of Psalm 91 but the wider context of the Bible as a whole. Many have constructed a theology of prosperity using texts that promise blessings and protections, ignoring other texts that describe or predict God's people facing hardships and suffering.

Double Donkey Ride

One more example of fulfillment of prophecy in Matthew's Gospel. Like Mark and Luke, Matthew talks about Jesus fulfilling prophecy by riding a donkey into Jerusalem. Only Matthew takes the statement as indicating that there were *two* donkeys present. The reference in Zechariah 9:9 is most likely poetic parallelism of a kind that is found all throughout the poetry in the Bible. Hebrew poetry typically offers groupings of two lines that relate to each other, most frequently by expressing the same meaning in a different way. This is called synonymous parallelism. There are other kinds of parallelism as well, but synonymous parallelism is the most common and the one that is relevant here. The repetition didn't mean that the king would ride two animals, but described the same animal in two ways. Once again we have to ask whether Matthew missed the original context and misunderstood the text, deliberately misrepresented it, or something else. It is hard to be certain, but here it is much harder to find an excuse or explanation for what Matthew did. If we consider all of these examples mentioned in this chapter, we see that they are not all exactly the same. On the whole, however, we can definitely say that Matthew interpreted the Jewish scriptures in ways that were perfectly acceptable in his time. I won't try to grade him on behalf of his ancient teachers, but they probably would have judged him quite skilled and perhaps highly adept at the methods they themselves taught and practiced. As for what he'd get if he took a class today that taught our modern approach, emphasizing the importance of understanding texts in their original context, he might well fail, depending on the precise assignment. I'd prefer to think he'd scrape by with a passing grade, because he clearly showed knowledge of and insight into relevant texts. Even though this chapter highlights the letter F, there is no reason to think Matthew would have received that letter grade.

Whenever I think about Matthew's reference to Jesus riding two donkeys at once, I think of a Volvo commercial from 2013 in which Jean-Claude Van Damme rides two trucks simultaneously. Look it up—you can definitely find it online. It may help you appreciate Matthew more if you imagine Jesus doing something similar with the two donkeys. Whatever you decide about Matthew as interpreter of scripture in his ancient context, it takes reading him in a modern one to find "daredevil Jesus" in his story.

For Further Reading

Allison, Dale C. *The New Moses: A Matthean Typology.* Eugene, OR: Wipf & Stock, 2013.

France, R. T. *Matthew: Evangelist and Teacher.* Eugene, OR: Wipf & Stock, 2004.

Hatina, Thomas, ed. *The Gospel of Matthew.* Vol. 2 of *Biblical Interpretation in Early Christian Gospels.* London: Bloomsbury, 2008.

Senior, Donald. *The Gospel of Matthew: Interpreting Biblical Texts Series.* Nashville: Abingdon, 2011.

Stovell, Beth, and Stanley E. Porter. *Biblical Hermeneutics: Five Views.* Downers Grove, IL: InterVarsity Press, 2012.

G

Greasy Jesus?

A range of words have come into English from Greek by way of the New Testament. A number of words in English Bibles are *transliterations* rather than *translations* of a Greek word. Examples include Christ (from *christos*, "anointed"), angel (from *angelos*, "messenger"), apostle (from *apostolos*, "emissary, one who is sent"), epistle (from *epistolē*, "letter"), deacon (from *diakonos*, "servant"), and synagogue (from *synagōgē*, "assembly, congregation"). We could list still other English words that are derived from Greek words found in the New Testament. Even though English Bibles translate the Greek word *ekklēsia* as "church," the English language has the word "ecclesiastical" (having to do with church), which derives from the Greek word. Word meanings evolve and change, sometimes expanding while at others narrowing. The Greek words that are rendered in English as "church" and "synagogue" both originally denoted an assembly, not necessarily a religious one, much less that of a particular religious community. The English words reflect a long process of development in which the reference came to be to Christian and Jewish assemblies and then to the buildings in which those groups meet.

Let's turn our attention to the first example mentioned above, Christ, which means "anointed." The same is true of another word that comes from Hebrew by way of transliteration: Messiah, from *mashiach*, likewise meaning "anointed."

The addition of the definite article before it (in English the word "the") turns the adjective into a title: the Anointed, or the anointed one. Yet even if English Bibles use "anointed one" or something of that sort, few readers will feel the meaning had been made clearer. Anointing is not something that we do terribly often, and if we encounter the actual practice at all, it is probably part of a religious ceremony. The Greek word referred more widely to the act of smearing oil on something or, more commonly, on someone.

Transliteration is when a word in one language is transformed into a word in another language, keeping close to the original sound. Examples from Greek in the New Testament include Christ (christos), epistle (epistolos), and apostle (apostolos).

The title of this chapter is intended to be more than a bad pun. To say someone is "greased" (or "oiled" if you prefer) wouldn't mean much today, unless of course you are speaking literally after a kitchen mishap. Using words like these may have more or less the same literal meaning as the Greek and Hebrew words in question, yet they do not convey anything like the sense intended by those who called Jesus "the Anointed" and eventually simply used "Christ" as a title. As it happens, this isn't a new problem. The Greek term was not self-explanatory to most who encountered it either. That is perhaps why those who talked about Jesus using this word came to be nicknamed Christians. Understanding what was meant by the term depended on familiarity with an ancient Israelite ritual, used in the installation of kings and high priests into their respective roles. It also depended on some knowledge of history and some expectations that arose as a result of those past events.

According to 2 Samuel 7:16, God promised King David, "Your house and your kingdom will endure forever before me; your throne shall be established forever." The character of that promise is made even more explicit in 1 Kings 9:5, which depicts God as reiterating his promise to David: "You shall never lack a successor on the throne of Israel." Jeremiah 33:17–18 says something similar, extending the point to the priesthood as well: "For thus says the Lord: David shall never lack a man to sit on the throne of the house of Israel, and the Levitical priests shall never lack a man in my presence to offer burnt offerings, to make grain offerings, and to make sacrifices for all time." The high priest, like the king, was anointed with oil as part of the ceremony installing them in that office.

At the time of the Babylonian exile, however, there was a disruption to the kingship and the priesthood. Not that the Davidic or Aaronic lines were wiped out. But the temple was destroyed and the rule of the house of David undone by the empire whose vassal the kingdom of Judah had been. As a result, expectations arose that God would restore the dynasty of David to the throne to rule a kingdom once again, and that the priesthood would resume its activity. The latter hope fared better in the short term than the former, with the temple being rebuilt as recounted in the book of Ezra. However, as Haggai 2:3 indicates, those who remembered the temple of the Judean monarchy were unimpressed with what a group of returned exiles were able to rebuild in its place.

The structure itself would not be the only problem some would have with the temple. As time passed, debates and conflicts would ensue about who should be high priest and about the proper way for things to be done in the temple. In the absence of a king, the high priest emerged as the de facto ruler and representative of the Jewish people during this period. The typical way one got appointed to such a role in most societies was by bribing a ruler. According to Jewish law, however, the role was hereditary, passing from father to eldest son. There was some back and forth that you can read about in 2 Maccabees 4, with various individuals vying for the role. Then the Syrian king Antiochus IV decided (for reasons that are not absolutely certain) to rededicate the temple in Jerusalem to the high god, whom Greeks called Zeus Olympus and Syrians called Ba'al Shamem (Lord of Heaven). When Antiochus rededicated the temple, he sacrificed a pig on the altar. From the perspective of a significant number of devout Jews, this was not merely an act in the spirit of the Hellenistic commonality that had identified the gods of Greece and Rome. This was desecration. It was blasphemy. But what should be done in response? Some fled cities and towns, hoping they could continue to observe their ancestral customs in remote places unmolested. Eventually some saw the need for an armed revolt to regain the freedom to practice their religion as they thought appropriate. The struggle to retake the temple eventually became more than that, a struggle for independence.

An individual named Judah Maccabee (sometimes rendered Judas Maccabeus) became a leader in that cause, together with other members of his family (who collectively came to be referred to as the Hasmoneans). Once they were successful in their effort to retake control of the sacred precincts of the temple in Jerusalem, they pushed on and sought appointment to a position that would allow them to safeguard the rights they fought for. Eventually Syrian rulers went from telling them how to worship to needing their support in dynastic struggles. The family came to be appointed as high priests and eventually also as kings—that is, into the two roles of leadership that were associated with ceremonies of anointing. The notion of leaders embodying kingship and priesthood rolled into one did not begin with Jesus or the first Christians. Just as objections to Antiochus's actions sparked resistance, the appointment of the Hasmoneans as high priests and kings met with criticism from those who noted they lacked the family background required for holders of either office. (As far as we can tell, many people did not have strong feelings about this innovation.) The group at Qumran articulated their expectation that God would restore both priesthood and kingship to the rightful families. This meant two anointed ones, two messiahs, one from Aaron and one from David. In the Dead Sea Scrolls they are often referred to as the anointed ones of Aaron and of Israel. These are important points in relation to the New Testament because it is common to hear people talk about Jesus fulfilling messianic expectations. He must have fulfilled some, or no one would have believed in him or taken claims about him seriously. He clearly did not fulfill everyone's expectations, not least because not everyone had the same expectations. Messianic hopes were not universal. The reality of ancient Jewish messianism is rather more . . . messy (and not just because of the ritual involving oil).

Messiah and *Christ* transliterate words in Hebrew and Greek, respectively, which both mean "anointed one." This reflects the practice of pouring oil on the heads of new kings and priests when they ascended to those roles.

When New Testament authors refer to Jesus as the Messiah/Christ/Anointed, it is often in connection with his descent from David. This means they saw him as a royal figure. It is really only the Letter to the Hebrews that asserts that Jesus was also high priest. In relation to the expectation of a royal figure, a restorer of the Davidic dynasty to the throne, however varied the hopes may have been, they surely all agreed on one thing. When God restored the line of David to the throne, it would involve a descendant of David actually becoming king, rather than being executed by the Roman authorities. The notion of a crucified royal messiah would have seemed self-contradictory. No wonder Paul says this was a stumbling block (1 Cor 1:23). Whether the king was envisaged as occupying an exalted celestial position of dominion over all humankind, or simply as an earthly ruler, there was agreement that he was supposed to ascend the throne in victory rather than be executed by imperial powers.

You will sometimes hear Christians blame the Jews of the first century (as well as since) for "misunderstanding" who and what the Messiah had to be. The truth is that they did not misunderstand. A king was supposed to rule in a manner that was visible on earth. It is such a basic point that it would not normally need to be emphasized. Because Jesus did not conform to these expectations, his followers who were persuaded that he was the Messiah turned to the scriptures and found or reinterpreted things that would allow them to make sense of this and assert that Jesus could be the Messiah even so. When Paul says that he is determined to know only Christ and him crucified, he is placing at the center of his entire life and ministry that which was the most difficult point to accept or even make sense of when it comes to early Christian beliefs. There was no way to avoid wrestling with this. Some undoubtedly lost their faith in Jesus after the crucifixion. Others had their worldview radically revised so that a victim of the most shameful form of Roman execution could be the expression of God's salvation.

When evaluating the historicity of the New Testament's contents, scholars have in the past delineated a variety of criteria that they considered useful for that purpose. Those criteria have been severely criticized, yet they have a certain usefulness nevertheless. None of them provides a guarantee of authenticity, but history is not about certainty. It is about assessing probability. One of the criteria of authenticity is known as the criterion of embarrassment. (Note that the singular of "criteria" is "criterion," and be sure to use that when refer-

Criteria of authenticity are principles that have been proposed to guide scholars in evaluating the historicity of information about Jesus in ancient sources.

ring to only one, lest you yourself be embarrassed by criteria.) The criterion of embarrassment highlights the fact that
people are less likely to make things up that reflect poorly on
them, their group, or another individual whom they hold in
high esteem. To use a completely hypothetical scenario, if
someone supports a particular presidential candidate and
after the election insists that the candidate did not really
lose, you can be pretty sure that they at least appear to have
lost. A supporter of the candidate would not invent their failure to win. In the same way the early Christians who claimed
that Jesus is the Davidic anointed one, the restorer of the
dynasty of David to the throne, would not have invented his
death by crucifixion. That Jesus had been crucified did not
support their claim but, on the contrary, seemed to under-
mine it. The reason the cross is so central to New Testament
authors is that it was the key difficulty that required attention and explanation.

Angels

"Angel" is another English word that is a result of transliteration. The Greek word *angelos* means "messenger." There is thus
room for ambiguity in some passages. The use of the Greek
word to denote celestial beings created by God can be traced
back at least to the Septuagint, the Greek translation of the
Jewish scriptures that was the Bible of
the earliest Greek-speaking Christians.
When New Testament authors quoted
scripture, it was often (but not always)
from the Septuagint. We can see the influence of the Septuagint, for instance,
when New Testament authors used the
word *angelos* to translate not only the Hebrew word *malakh*
(messenger) but also the Hebrew word *elohim* (God or gods),

*The **Septuagint** (usually ab-
breviated **LXX**) is the name
given to a Greek translation of
the Jewish scriptures that was
widely used in the first century.*

which they sometimes rendered as *angeloi* (the plural of *angelos*). An example is Psalm 8:5, which is quoted in Hebrews 2:7 where the specific meaning of "angels" is central to the author's point. Jesus had been made lower than the angels but, the author of the Letter to the Hebrews emphasizes, he is in fact superior to angels. Among the Dead Sea Scrolls we continue to see the Hebrew *elohim* used for the multitude of celestial beings and even in reference to Melchizedek in 11Q13.

There was an enormous amount of interest in angels in Judaism in the era in which Christianity arose. The concept of seven archangels or chief angels, as well as a host (pun intended) of others, developed and was explored in a great many literary works. The idea of seven top angels seems to be in view in Revelation 3:1, 4:5, and 5:6 (see also 1 Tim 5:21). In works like 1 Enoch the notion of fallen angels was explored in connection with the story in Genesis about sons of God who found daughters of men attractive and had children with them (Gen 6:4). Others connected a rebellion of angels with the Garden of Eden story in Genesis 3. All of this literature took things that were vague in Genesis and other texts and elaborated on them, filling in gaps in ways that created whole new systems of thought. Those ideas about angels were part of the worldview and assumptions shared by the first Christians.

Abba and Maranatha

Before it became more widely thought of as the name of a Swedish band, *abba* was most familiar as an Aramaic word that is transliterated in the New Testament. If you have heard that it means "daddy," that is simply not true. The Aramaic word means "father," and that is how it is used by Paul in Galatians 4:6 and Romans 8:15 (see also Mark 14:36, where *abba* also occurs). The mention of it in early Christian sources in Greek suggests the word was significant, but that significance was not because it was a term of cuddly intimacy. The concept of father across the Mediterranean world included a high level of authority and ownership, even if a child in the household had access to the father to an extent others outside the family did not. You will likely encounter the Latin term *paterfamilias* in reference to the Roman head of household, the patriarch of the family in this ancient patriarchal context. The significance of *abba* for the early church was first and foremost that Jesus used it. What made it distinctive and noteworthy was the fact that this was uttered in prayer in the vernacular language of ordinary people, whereas formal prayer tended to use Hebrew, the language of scripture and liturgy but no longer of everyday speech. Intriguingly, the longer form of the Aramaic prayer known as the Kaddish, still used today, speaks of God as heavenly Father but expresses its wishes in the third person rather than addressing God directly.

The early church preserved Aramaic expressions, including but not limited to ones spoken by Jesus, and often the precise reason they found it significant to do so is obscure. Think about how some English translations transliterated the Greek word *anathema* when Paul uses it in 1 Corinthians 16:22, turning it into a new English word in the process. That Greek word served as an equivalent for the Hebrew *herem*, which is often translated as "under the ban" when it occurs in the context of dedicating whole cities of Canaan to God and to total destruction. That Greek word appears alongside a transliterated Aramaic one in that passage—namely, *maranatha*. Actually, it is two words, and precisely which two words is a matter of debate. The options are "Our Lord, come!" (*marana tha*) and "Our Lord has come" (*maran atha*). To complicate things further, you need three or four words to express the meaning in English because Aramaic conveys through suffixes things that we convey through pronouns, and some English tenses require helping verbs, which are not used in Aramaic. The expression might have been popular precisely because it could serve as both creed and prayer, an expression of faith and hope for those living in the time between Jesus's activity in their midst and what Paul referred to as the *parousia*, Jesus's arrival in glory and honor, often referred to today as the "second coming." Our Lord has come and will come again.

Gethsemane and Golgotha

If we did any more transliterations that start with "A," we would probably have had to start this chapter's title with that letter as well, so let's end with a couple more transliterations that begin with "G" for the sake of balance. Place names tend to be transliterated too. Sometimes English translations obscure this by standardizing how names are spelled. There were no dictionaries or publishing style sheets in the first century, so the names of people and places could be written in different ways, especially if they were foreign names being rendered in another language. One example is Jerusalem, which is spelled differently in different places in the New Testament. The fact that the Gospel of John and Revelation spell this name differently is just one of the pieces of evidence that convinces scholars these works were not written by the same author.

Two Aramaic place names that occur in the New Testament are Gethsemane and Golgotha. Both appear in the passion narratives. Gethsemane occurs in Mark 14:32 and Matthew 26:36. Golgotha occurs in Mark 15:22, Matthew 27:33, and John 19:17. Luke does not preserve these transliterated names for his audience. Such details may clue us in to a particular author's style and perhaps also their aims, although just like the reason for including transliterations, the precise motive for omitting them is not always obvious. Sometimes we conflate things that multiple sources say but which are not found in any single one of them. "Garden of Gethsemane" combines the name from Mark and Matthew with the unnamed garden from John 18:1. Other times multiple sources say the same thing. John 19:17 agrees with Mark and Matthew on the name Golgotha and its meaning, "the place of the skull." We discuss where that place may have been in a later chapter in this book.

But What about *Ephphatha*, *Talitha Koum*, and Others?

In two instances the words that Jesus uttered when healing people were recalled, presumably under the assumption that the words themselves were significant and powerful. *Ephphatha*, "be opened" (Mark 7:34), and *talitha koum*, "little girl, get up" (Mark 5:41), both fall into this category. Some manuscripts transliterate the latter as *talitha koumi*, but *koum* reflects the pronunciation of Galileans in the time of Jesus and is more likely original. Some scribes who knew Aramaic but not Jesus's regional dialect would have fixed what they perceived to be an error. This means we have on this one occasion the very words of Jesus as he spoke them in his native language and exactly as he pronounced them. For the early church, the focus was on communicating widely in the lingua franca of the era, hence our sources being in Greek, with very few of the exact Aramaic words Jesus uttered being preserved. This rare example is thus noteworthy.

But why did they choose to preserve precisely the words that they did? In a few instances it is difficult even to make out what words stand behind the transliteration. For example, there are no obvious Aramaic words that could stand behind *boanērges* that would have meant "sons of thunder"

(Mark 3:17). Indeed, it has proven difficult to recognize meaningful words behind that at all, even if Mark misunderstood them. If you were thinking that Boanerges might be a cool name for a band, you might just want to go with Sons of Thunder instead. Linguists might eventually figure out this puzzle and it might totally change the way we understand the word—and the meaning could turn out to be something that wouldn't serve your band's musical aspirations well. Even better, perhaps some reading this will decide to make this nickname a focus of their research and eventually crack it. If you do, please let me know so I can feature your work in future editions of this book!

For Further Reading

Bailey, Kenneth. *Paul through Mediterranean Eyes: Cultural Studies in 1 Corinthians.* Downers Grove, IL: IVP Academic, 2011.

Casey, Maurice. *Aramaic Sources of Mark's Gospel.* New York: Cambridge University Press, 1999.

Culpepper, R. Alan. *John, the Son of Zebedee: The Life of a Legend.* Columbia: University of South Carolina Press, 1994.

Fitzmyer, Joseph A. *According to Paul: Studies in the Theology of the Apostle.* Mahwah, NJ: Paulist Press, 1993.

———. *To Advance the Gospel: New Testament Studies.* Grand Rapids: Eerdmans, 1998.

Garrett, Susan R. *No Ordinary Angel: Celestial Spirits and Christian Claims about Jesus.* New Haven: Yale University Press, 2008.

Gómez, Alfredo Delgado. "The Reception of the Codeswitches of the Syriac Versions in the Gospel of Mark." *Collectanea Christiana Orientalia* 19 (2022): 25–43.

Grabbe, Lester L. *An Introduction to First Century Judaism: Jewish Religion and History in the Second Temple Period.* London: T&T Clark, 1996.

Horbury, William. *Messianism among Jews and Christians: Biblical and Historical Studies.* London: Bloomsbury, 2016.

Law, Timothy Michael. *When God Spoke Greek: The Septuagint and the Making of the Christian Bible.* New York: Oxford University Press, 2013.

Messmer, Andrew. "*Maranatha* (1 Corinthians 16:22): Reconstruction and Translation Based on Western Middle Aramaic." *Journal of Biblical Literature* 139, no. 2 (2020): 361–83.

Newman, Carey C., Gladys S. Lewis, and James R. Davila, eds. *The Jewish Roots of Christological Monotheism: Papers from the St. Andrews Conference on the Historical Origins of the Worship of Jesus.* Leiden: Brill, 1999.

Novenson, Matthew V. *The Grammar of Messianism: An Ancient Jewish Political Idiom and Its Users.* New York: Oxford University Press, 2017.

Zetterholm, Magnus. *The Messiah: In Early Judaism and Christianity.* Minneapolis: Fortress, 2007.

H

Hate Your Enemies

There are a few instances in which Jesus has been accused of misquoting scripture. In Mark 2:26 Jesus mentions the high priest Abiathar when he presumably meant Ahimelek. Matthew and Luke drop the name, presumably because they are aware of the issue. When listing the commandments to the rich man in Mark 10:19, Jesus adds "You shall not defraud," which presumably has Leviticus 19:13 in view but isn't one of the Ten Commandments, whereas the rest of those listed are. This one could simply be a case of Jesus drawing attention to the fact that "the commandments" doesn't just mean the ten. He scarcely needed to do that as a general point, since ancient Jews were less likely than modern Christians tend to be to mistakenly think the Ten Commandments cover everything. It may be that Jesus thought a rich man might need that particular commandment drawn to his attention.

For at least one person I know, neither of these cases I've just mentioned concerns them as much as the fact that Jesus, in the Sermon on the Mount, said that his audience had been told, "You shall love your neighbor and hate your enemy" (Matt 5:43). It isn't the first part that bothers them. Hardly anyone is troubled by the command to love your neighbor. Of course, nowadays some Christians make the mistake of thinking that the command to love one's neighbor in the Bible originated with Jesus. Jesus was quoting Leviticus 19:18. It seems that Jesus had a particular liking for Leviticus 19, doesn't it? Be that as it may, the issue is with the flip side of that commandment as Jesus quotes it. There is no command to hate one's enemy, even if there might be some texts that at least seem to give permission to do so.

Until someone else insisted I take a closer look, I had been quite comfortable in my own assumptions about what the text meant. Jesus, I assumed, was being ironic about the implications some might detect in a command to love one's neighbor. If you must love your neighbor, you are presumably free *not* to love those who do not fall into that category. I assumed that Jesus was being sarcastic, as I might be in similar circumstances. As it turns out, not everyone is as prone to appreciate sarcasm as I am, and they are not as inclined to view Jesus as having utilized it (as helpful a teaching tool as it is, I'm sure you'll agree). While I might still be correct (I sometimes am, I believe), my understanding of the text is an assumption. There are other possibilities, and they deserve consideration. It may be more hyperbole than sarcasm, or Jesus may have had in mind a group like the Essenes, since one of the Dead Sea Scrolls speaks of loving the sons of light but hating the sons of darkness (1QS 1:9–10). Rather than dig into those other options here, let's focus on what is clear: Jesus emphasized the need to love one's enemies rather than hate them. This chapter will explore some of the specific categories of people that Jesus mentioned as illustrations of his point, as well as places where Jesus's words and actions have been accused of being at odds with his stated principle.

Who Is My Neighbor?

In the previous section I mentioned the story about a rich man asking Jesus how to inherit eternal life (Mark 10:17–31;

Matt 19:16–30; Luke 18:18–30). Luke adds another story, which begins with the same question but which follows a different course thereafter. After agreeing that the greatest commandments are to love God and love one's neighbor, a follow-up question is posed: "And who is my neighbor?" (Luke 10:29). It is a natural question to ask. If the commandment meant that you should love everyone, presumably it would have said that. The category of neighbor restricts the demand—but how much? The man who asked the question expected an answer, but instead he was offered a story (Luke 10:30–35). Rather than providing a clear and clarifying definition, the story challenges our human inclination to delineate and categorize. It starts off in a way that makes it sound like the ancient equivalent of the modern jokes about a priest, a rabbi, and a minister. Like some of the best jokes, the ending has a twist. The twist in Jesus's story, however, is not just in the different action taken by the third person but in who that third person turns out to be.

For many people today, there is only one Samaritan they know of: the good one. The expression "good Samaritan" should give us pause as it is reminiscent of a way of speaking you may have encountered in the present day. But before we get to that, we need to introduce the Samaritans. They are not only a group that existed in Jesus's time but also a group that exists in our time. They got this name because the region they historically inhabited came to be named after the capital city Samaria. That region was historically where the tribes of Ephraim and Manasseh dwelt, the

Samaritans: a name given to Israelites living in the region between Judea in the south and Galilee in the north.

heartland of the northern kingdom that was known simply as Israel. Although few in number, the Samaritans are still there to this day, worshiping on Mount Gerizim on holidays and in their synagogues on shabbat. If you visit the Holy Land, be sure to visit Mount Gerizim and the Samaritan Museum. Googling "Samaritans" will likely get you to a crisis helpline, but if you google "Samaritan Passover," you'll see how the Samaritans of today celebrate that holiday.

Nowadays Samaritans and Jews coexist, the latter recognizing the claim of the former to be Israelites and thus to share a common heritage as the descendants of Abraham, Isaac, and Jacob. Relations were not always amicable, however, and the very existence of separate kingdoms of Israel and Judah reflects just how deep the tensions ran. In the centuries before the time of Jesus, rulers in Judea had extended their kingdom to include Samaria as well as Galilee. They also called their kingdom Israel. The dynasty in question, known as the Hasmoneans (introduced elsewhere in this book), destroyed the Samaritan sanctuary on Mount Gerizim. During Jesus's childhood some Samaritans are said to have thrown bones into the Jerusalem temple to desecrate it. You could say they didn't get along. The tribes of Ephraim and Manasseh that historically lived in Samaria were descended from Joseph. You may recall the story of Joseph and his brothers in Genesis 37. Jews and Samaritans traced the ongoing sibling rivalry to the very beginning of the story of the children of Israel.

It is against that backdrop that readers need to understand the parable of the good Samaritan, as well as the story of Jesus's encounter with a Samaritan woman recounted in John 4. As I pointed out, the epithet "good" for the Samaritan should trouble you in ways that are not exactly the same as the way the character in the parable would have troubled Jesus's hearers, although they are certainly related. You may have heard someone with discriminatory views say that a particular individual is "one of the good ones." The disturbing assumption, of course, is that people with the same skin color or religion as the "good one" are as a rule bad. Continuing to call the hero of Jesus's story the "good Samaritan" sounds too much like that way of speaking for my tastes. Jesus's story made its impact precisely because of the assumption held by many of his Jewish contemporaries that Samaritans were generally bad. If we call him the "good Samaritan," it sounds like we are embracing the very assumptions about Samaritans that Jesus told his story to challenge.

Returning to our analogy with modern jokes, Jesus's story initially sounded like it was setting up for a punch line at the expense of the clergy. If a priest and a Levite pass by without helping, then Jesus's Jewish audience may have expected this Jewish storyteller to feature an ordinary Jewish individual as the one who helps where others did not. Substituting a Samaritan was the equivalent of telling a story in a Christian context in which there is a negative view of Islam and the three characters on the road are a pastor, a Sunday school teacher, and a Muslim. If we do not take into account the prejudices people held in Jesus's time, the story will seem like an unnecessarily convoluted way to say that we should be nice to people. When we take the often-sour relations between Judean and Samaritan Israelites into account, we are better poised to understand how the story functioned as a response (if not exactly an answer) to the question Jesus had been asked. The question "Who is my neighbor?" asks for clarification of one's responsibility in relation to a divine commandment in the Torah. The man asked Jesus for help clarifying what the commandment required him to do. In essence Jesus turns the question from "Who is my neighbor?" into "To whom am I a neighbor?" Understood in that manner, the appropriate response to the commandment is to put oneself in another's shoes and empathize with them. If you would want to be helped if you were in a particular situation of need, then you should help someone who is in that situation. The story embodies Jesus's famous saying known as the Golden Rule: do to others what you would want them to do to you.

Gentiles

"Gentile" is an English word that denotes everyone who is not Jewish. When you encounter that word in English translations of the Bible, the underlying Hebrew (*goyim*) or Greek (*ethnē*) literally refers to "peoples" or "nations." The idea was that there was Israel, God's chosen people, and then everyone else, the *other* nations. In most circumstances it was enough to say "the nations" and have it be clear that one meant all other peoples. Indeed, it would be even clearer and more precise if we translated the word as "the peoples," as in "the other peoples of the world," to avoid conveying the sense that in ancient times nations existed of the sort we are familiar with today, sometimes called nation-states. There were peoples, cities, kingdoms, regions, and empires, but not nations in the modern sense. In some English translations the word is rendered not as "gentiles" or as "nations" but as "pagans," which is misleading. The term "pagan" derives from a Latin word for a rural as opposed to urban person, reflecting the persistence of traditional religions that were not monotheistic in the countryside in an era when Christianity was gaining adherents in cities around the Roman Empire. It was an insult akin to calling someone a hick, a country bumpkin, or a redneck. It eventually came to denote people who worshiped a deity (or deities) different from that of one's own group, but apart from that it has little in common with the meaning of peoples/gentiles. The biggest problem with translating the relevant words as "pagans" rather than "gentiles" is that the former reflects the Christian view of those who are not Christians while the latter reflects the Jewish view of those who are not Jewish. They may be comparable, but they are not the same thing. If nothing else, keeping "gentiles" in the text can remind us that the New Testament authors for the most part did not yet think of themselves as

"Christian" (if only because that terminology was still in the process of being invented and catching on). They were Jewish authors who believed Jesus was the anointed one they had been expecting.

The nations or other peoples are viewed as enemies in a number of works in the Jewish scriptures. Psalm 2 speaks of the nations raging against both the Lord and his anointed one (i.e., the king reigning in Jerusalem). That psalm is echoed in the New Testament more than once (Acts 4:25-26; 13:33; Heb 1:5; 5:5; Rev 2:26-27; 12:5; 19:15). In Jesus's time the entire geographic region of Palestine was part of the Roman Empire. Galilee was ruled by the Jewish tetrarch Herod Antipas and was not under direct Roman rule by a Roman governor the way Judea was. People may have viewed foreign rulers as enemies to a greater or lesser extent, resenting the added burden of taxation as a result of being part of an empire if nothing else. If there was a more general sense that the nations were "enemies," it was because they were felt to be hostile not merely to the Jews as a people but to their exclusive commitment to worshiping one God alone without images. Jews had fought hard for special exemptions when civic rituals required everyone to participate in worship of the Roman gods. Jesus's teaching to love one's enemies has implications beyond the level of personal individual animosities. Foreign rulers who were felt to be oppressive or to tax excessively were included, as were those whose religious beliefs and practices were not merely different but were prohibited in the Jewish Torah. For some people at least, someone with an opposing theology or political ideology may be harder to love than someone who "merely" steals from or gossips about them. We see Jesus applying his own teaching when he recognizes the faith of a centurion as

A **tetrarchy** is when a kingdom is divided into four parts, each with a different ruler, as happened after the death of Herod the Great.

not merely equal to but greater than that of members of his own group (Matt 8:10 // Luke 9:7). Yet in at least one (presumably earlier) incident, Jesus's response to someone from another people is troubling to many readers.

Mere Dogs?

Some passages seem difficult because they appear to contain contradictions. Those mainly raise issues for the subset of Christians who subscribe to a doctrine of biblical inerrancy. Other passages present difficulties for *all* Christians because Jesus's behavior doesn't seem very, well, Christlike. If you ask people for the most obvious passage of that sort that springs to mind, they will likely point to Mark 7:24–30 (parallel Matt 15:21–28). In that story, a woman comes to Jesus seeking healing for her daughter, whose condition is said to be caused by an unclean spirit. Rather than immediately providing healing, or at least saying something kind and comforting, Jesus contrasts the woman (described as Syrophoenician in Mark and Canaanite in Matthew) with his own people. Jesus's fellow Jews and Israelites are the children in God's kingdom. What are Canaanites or Syrophoenicians? According to what Jesus says in this story, they are dogs. There have been attempts to soften what Jesus said by claiming that he had cute little puppies in mind. Rather than debate the terminology, I will simply point out that saying one's own people are human beings while others are animals is inherently insulting, even if the animals in question are so cute that you can literally spend hours watching videos of them.

If you've heard this story before, I'm sure you have also encountered some of the standard ways to mitigate the extent to which it makes Jesus look bad. The most common is to say that Jesus was only testing the woman. I honestly don't know why anyone thinks this makes Jesus seem nicer.

If he insults a woman with a sick child just to see what kind of faith she has, why is that better than if his words expressed a bias ingrained in him by his upbringing and culture? No culture in the Mediterranean world in that era was completely without negative stereotypes concerning other peoples. In this specific case, moreover, the negative view could be said to be grounded in scripture. The depiction of Canaanites in biblical stories that Jesus grew up hearing is mostly negative, although occasional figures like Rahab and Melchizedek (both mentioned in the New Testament) leap out as exceptions to that characterization. Phoenicians were not a distinct people; this was just the name given to the Canaanite culture that had cities like Tyre and Sidon, to Israel's north, as their center. Even today one will frequently encounter Christian preachers who insist that the Canaanites were so terrible that genocide against them was justified.

Keep in mind as well that this woman was there not in her own interest but on behalf of her young child. If being insulted as an individual is painful, having one's child included in the insult will hurt all the more. The natural instinctive response is anger. What makes this woman's response so impressive is not merely the cleverness of her retort but the fact that she manages her anger and hurt sufficiently to be able to turn the tables on the one who provoked her. Clever comebacks are harder to come up with when you've just been insulted. Notice how she wins the argument. If her child is a dog as Jesus claimed, she would at least have access to the crumbs that fall from the table. To withhold even such scraps from a dog is to be unjustifiably cruel. I hope you're impressed with this woman's response, because Jesus was. Having not shown willingness to do so initially, he decides to heal the woman's daughter. We get the impression that the woman's clever comeback changed Jesus's mind.

"The Jews"

Having spoken about Jewish assumptions and stereotypes about others, we now turn to the ironic fact that in the Gospel of John the opponents of Jesus are often referred to simply as "the Jews." Scholars try to consistently enclose the phrase in quotation marks when they mention this language from the Fourth Gospel, to emphasize both that it is not their own choice of words and that the phrase is somewhat odd even as part of this particular text. The references to "the Jews" in the Gospel of John have had an influence on Christian antisemitism down the centuries. Christian interpreters cannot ignore this subsequent history of interpretation and influence. No matter one's view of what the author of this gospel may or may not have intended, Christian interpreters must take seriously the fact that the depiction of "the Jews" as "from your father the devil" (John 8:44) had an influence on the individuals and societies responsible for the Holocaust, pogroms, and other horrors. Even today one may encounter conspiracy theories who blame "the Jews" for this or that. The problem has not gone away, and interpreters of the text need to address these issues. On the other hand, deducing what we can about the author and context of this text is crucially important to making sense of it and tackling its difficulties. A helpful place to begin is John 7:13, where the reader is told that "no one would speak openly about him [Jesus] for fear of the Jews." What can it possibly mean for Jewish crowds at a Jewish festival to discuss a Jewish man and yet be afraid of "the Jews"? Clearly the expression does not denote the entire Jewish people in that time, never mind throughout all history. Given that Jesus's own Jewish identity is clear in the Gospels, and particularly clear in stories in which he interacts with non-Jews, how can "the Jews" have ever come to be understood as enemies of Jesus?

There are various ways to understand this expression in the Gospel of John. One possibility is that the label "Jews" is used in its geographical sense. English has different words for "Jews" and "Judeans," whereas in Greek the same word covers both meanings. Judaism and its adherents were not yet separable from Judea either conceptually or linguistically in the way they have since become. Even when Jews lived half a year's journey by road from Jerusalem, they still perceived themselves as being a diaspora, a dispersion of people whose identity was still connected with the place that they or their ancestors were from. A geographical distinction—contrasting Judeans and Galileans, for instance—will work in some instances in the gospel but not all of them. Judeans could indeed be dismissive of Galileans at times. Another possibility is that the reference is to the Jewish authorities. If I were to say that the British refused to allow me to enter the United Kingdom (this never happened, I hasten to add), I would not mean that every British person worked together to prevent my entry, or even had an opinion on the matter. The reference would be to the British government authorities. "The Jews" would make sense as a way of referring to the Jewish leaders. This meaning would fit John 7:13, but as with the previous suggestion, this meaning does not fit all occurrences. The Fourth Gospel does not use the phrase in one consistent way with a single clear meaning. The expression had a range of possible meanings and connotations, so this is not surprising. Nevertheless, it still leaves us with instances in which the phrase remains puzzling and potentially troubling.

I mentioned that scholars place "the Jews" in quotation marks to make clear that they are quoting language from the Gospel of John and not expressing their own views or way of speaking. I use them for another reason in addition to that. Ancient Greek lacked punctuation marks, but if the full range available to us in English had existed in the time in which the Gospel of John was composed, I suspect that the author might have used scare quotes around the expression "the Jews." The Gospel of John explains that the crowds' fear of the Jewish authorities was focused on the possibility of exclusion from the synagogue. In Judaism, there was (and is) no unified hierarchy of leadership that was in charge. Being part of a local community's gatherings was a local matter. In the context in which the Gospel of John was written, it seems that leadership in the community came to be in the hands of some who found belief in Jesus as Messiah unacceptable. To claim that God's anointed king was a man who had been crucified was offensive to many. Some considered it beyond the pale. They defined being Jewish in a way that excluded Christian views of Jesus. In response, those who had been expelled may have referred ironically to "the Jews"—that is, those who defined themselves as the only ones who deserved that label. The story of Jesus found in the Gospel of John would in that case work on two levels, reflecting not only the time of Jesus in which the stories are set but also the circumstances of the community of the author and its readers. All literature about the past mediates between past and present to some extent, but in some cases considering both contexts can be particularly crucial to understanding why a work was written and what it meant for its own time.

The Gospel of John uses "Israelite" positively, reflecting Jesus's vision for all twelve tribes as the people of God. When Jesus talks with a Samaritan woman in John 4, he does so as a Jew and says that he and his fellow Jews worship a God they know, whereas Samaritans are ignorant about important matters. There are two major possibilities here. One is that this text comes from one source while the statements in John 8 (to the effect that "the Jews" are not Abraham's descendants nor children of God) come from a different source or redactor (editor). Another is that these statements are reconcilable because neither is literally saying that an entire people has particular characteristics. If one understands one or both kinds of sweeping generalizations in absolute terms, it contradicts the statements within the gospel that people were divided about Jesus (John 9:16; 10:19).

Some of these same issues come up elsewhere in the New Testament. The book of Revelation might seem the natural place to turn our attention next. Yet although the author of that work identifies himself as John, Revelation and the Gospel of John are not by the same author. The Greek is *very* different. Revelation mentions some who claim to be Jews but are not, calling them a "synagogue of Satan" (Rev 2:9; 3:9). The polemic is every bit as heated as in the Gospel of John, but here it is the Christian author who denies that his Jewish opponents are "really Jews." The feeling may have been mutual. As noted in an earlier chapter, the book of Revelation takes more of a hardline stance on a key matter of Jewish identity than the apostle Paul did. While the latter encouraged the members of the church in Corinth to refrain from eating food sacrificed to idols but ultimately considered it a matter of indifference, the author of Revelation considered it on the same level as sexual immorality (Rev 2:14, 20). Paul did not think of himself as spearheading a new religion but as grafting gentiles into Israel (Rom 11). Paul's opponents, however, thought that he put Jewish identity at risk at a time when the people could least afford to do so.

If, like most Christians today, you read these texts as someone whose ancestry is mostly or entirely non-Jewish, and who lives in a world in which Judaism and Christianity are largely distinct world religions, it can be difficult to read the earliest Christian literature as part of a debate *within* Judaism. Separation between the two might have begun to occur in some places, but the "parting of the ways" was a long process. As we explore in another chapter, in Paul's letters we are at such an early point in the process that Paul doesn't even have a clear label for the communities he brought into existence through his proclamation. They were gatherings of people united by faith in Jesus as Messiah. The Greek word translated as "church" in English did not yet have the connotation of a specifically Christian congregation. The term "Christian" would be coined only later, or at least had not caught on yet. As non-Jewish readers and interpreters of texts that emerged within and as part of first-century Judaism, hopefully you can read them in ways that do not perpetuate stereotypes, generalize, or turn any group whatsoever into enemies. But if you insist on doing that, hopefully you'll then proceed to love them as Jesus taught.

For Further Reading

Anderson, Robert T., and Terry Giles. *The Keepers: An Introduction to the History and Culture of the Samaritans*. Peabody, MA: Hendrickson, 2002.

Bernier, Jonathan. *Aposynagōgos and the Historical Jesus in John*. Leiden: Brill, 2013.

Bourgel, Jonathan. "The Destruction of the Samaritan Temple by John Hyrcanus: A Reconsideration." *Journal of Biblical Literature* 135, no. 3 (2016): 505–23.

———. "The Samaritans during the Hasmonean Period: The Affirmation of a Discrete Identity?" *Religions* 10, no. 11 (2019): 628.

Johnson, Luke T. "The New Testament's Anti-Jewish Slander and the Conventions of Ancient Polemic." *Journal of Biblical Literature* 108, no. 3 (1989): 419–41.

Martyn, J. Louis. *History and Theology in the Fourth Gospel*. Louisville: Westminster John Knox, 2003.

Peppard, Michael. "Torah for the Man Who Has Everything: 'Do Not Defraud' in Mark 10:19." *Journal of Biblical Literature* 134, no. 3 (2015): 595–604.

Pummer, Reinhard. *The Samaritans: A Profile*. Grand Rapids: Eerdmans, 2016.

Rollens, Sarah, Eric Vanden Eykel, and Meredith Warren. "Confronting Judeophobia in the Classroom." *Journal for Interdisciplinary Biblical Studies* 2, no. 1 (2020): 81–106.

Sechrest, Love L. "Enemies, Romans, Pigs, and Dogs: Loving the Other in the Gospel of Matthew." *Ex Auditu* 31 (2015): 71–105.

———. *Race and Rhyme: Rereading the New Testament*. Grand Rapids: Eerdmans, 2022.

Smiga, George M. *Pain and Polemic: Anti-Judaism in the Gospels*. Mahwah, NJ: Paulist Press, 1992.

I

Intent, Interpretation, and Intertextuality

I thought about calling this chapter "Intermission" because you've made it about a third of the way through the book. (Well done! By all means get up and stretch your legs or refill your coffee cup.) As I considered this, I began to think about the way biblical texts would have been experienced by ancient readers. Were gospels meant to be read all the way through by individuals, or read out loud story by story in churches—or both? Did the earliest hearers and readers get an intermission? Paul's letters are rarely read today in one sitting, yet that is definitely how they were experienced by their original intended audiences. When the church in Philippi received Paul's letter, someone didn't read chapter 1 to them and then tell them to come back next Sunday for chapter 2. Indeed, there were no chapter and verse divisions. The New Testament writings are experienced today in small snippets even when the type of literature being read requires that it be heard from beginning to end in order for the point to come across clearly. Hence my decision to focus in this chapter on interpretation.

You may have heard people claim that they don't interpret the Bible, they just read it. Hopefully having read this far you'll know, if you didn't already, that such claims are nonsense. No one today is a native speaker of the Greek language as it was spoken in the first century. But even if they were, all communication involves interpretation. When someone speaks to you directly, you hear their words and understand something from them. Hearing and reading involve interpretation. The field of study that examines what is involved in interpretation is known as hermeneutics. It comes from the Greek word that means interpretation. You will also encounter the word "exegesis," which refers to the act of explaining the

*Hermeneutics means interpretation, more specifically the study of what interpretation entails and the processes involved. **Exegesis** means clarification of the ancient meaning of the words of a text.*

meaning of a text, especially with focus on critical study that seeks to clarify the meaning of the ancient words in their original context. This word also comes from Greek, as do many other technical terms in English. So the good news is that when terms like this are introduced, you aren't just adding to your English vocabulary. You'll also recognize and understand more Greek words if you read the Greek New Testament.

The process of finding meaning in a text as well as making meaning in the act of reading deserves reflection. It is possible to become better interpreters of texts. The question is how. Reading the same text over and over can lead to new insights. But did any New Testament author envisage that their words would be read over and over again, whether in large chunks or in small snippets? Did Paul think that his letter to the Romans would be read often by the Christians in Rome, never mind by Christians in other parts of the world at later times in history? From what Paul wrote in 1 Thessalonians 4:17 we can tell that he understood his generation to be the last in human history before the arrival of the kingdom of God. He says that the dead in Christ will be raised first when the general resurrection of the dead takes place, and then "we who are alive" will be caught up into the air and transformed. The "we" in this context must mean Paul himself and at least some of his readers in Thessalonika. The very act of reading Paul's letters today involves reading them in a way Paul did not intend or foresee.

It is perhaps just as well, then, that the focus on recovering the author's intention has become less central to the study not just of the Bible but of texts in general. To be sure, it can be useful to ask about the author, their cultural context, and other such things. The point is not that seeking to understand what an author intended cannot enhance reading and lead to insight. The issue is that, when we read ancient texts, we have no independent access to an author and what they intended. We can only deduce it from what they wrote. Texts can be understood in more than one way even by those whose aim is to understand them as their authors intended. On the other hand, some will say that everyone has their own interpretation and thus there is no objective meaning. Yet I often point out to my students the irony of the fact that semester after semester, year after year, different students will write and say that everyone has their own opinion and so there is no right or wrong answer. They all seem to agree on this point. You can, I hope, see the irony. The very fact that they share the view that everyone has a different opinion proves that everyone's opinion is *not* different. The words of a text place constraints on how it is possible to interpret them. As a result, diverse readers often agree on what they understand a text to mean. Everything is not completely clear, and everything is not completely ambiguous. Some things fall at one end of the spectrum or the other, and many fall somewhere in between.

No View from Nowhere

There are ways in which people are unique and ways in which we are basically the same. In between is the realm of society and culture in which people share assumptions, values, language, and other things in common. All of this impacts our understanding of texts. Often a particular way of understanding a text, or a particular approach to interpretation, comes to be treated as the default. You may as a result find feminist, womanist, ecological, and other kinds of interpretation treated as niche areas of interest distinct from "plain old biblical interpretation." There is no such thing as the latter. As the saying goes, there is no "view from nowhere," and the Bible itself emphasizes that human beings do not have a God's-eye perspective on things. We must each recognize our positionality, which means that we read from somewhere. Men in Europe and North America have dominated the academic study of the Bible for a long time, which has led to their perspective being treated as though it not only is but ought to be the default. That scholarship has provided much insight. It has also at times missed things that are immediately apparent to women scholars, to those reading from a perspective of poverty rather than relative wealth, and to those who have experienced oppression rather than privilege. Those whose sympathies lie with their own empire do not always pick up on jabs made at the Romans, and when they do, they may not interpret them in the same manner as those whose sympathies are with those who were conquered or enslaved. Just as none of us has a view from nowhere, none of us has a view from everywhere. However, by listening to those who read from a different cultural, socioeconomic, gender, or other standpoint than our own, we can enrich our understanding, just as the perspective offered by two eyes allows depth of vision impossible with only one.

I used that last turn of phrase intentionally. Most people reading this book will not have noticed it. A person with a vision impairment may have had a different reaction. The way the Bible refers to blindness, using it as a metaphor for

incomprehension and sometimes for culpable deliberate ignorance, deserves analysis, but depending on your own life
experience and perspective, it may not even occur to you to
do so. The story of the man born blind in John 9 provides but
one of many possible examples. Even as it perpetuates some
assumptions about disability, the story challenges others, not
only by questioning the assumption that blindness is caused
by sin, but also by making the man the hero of the story. In
addition, the man impressively makes his way to the Pool
of Siloam, which is downhill from the old city of Jerusalem.
Whether a reader has topographical knowledge of a location
mentioned in a text can have an impact on what they notice
and how they interpret it.

The term "intersectionality" denotes the way people
may have multiple identities. It is possible to be privileged
in some ways yet disadvantaged in others. This applies as
much to the act of reading and interpreting texts as anything
else. Having wealth or belonging to the dominant social class
doesn't necessarily mean you will be a better reader of texts,
especially texts written by people whose background is very
different from your own. Your background and assumptions
may result in your missing things that seem obvious to someone else reading the same text.

Allusions

The story in John 9 is echoed in the famous hymn "Amazing
Grace." The interpretation of the Bible through art and the
influence of art on how we understand the Bible are aspects
of the hermeneutical process worthy of study and reflection
in their own right. The way songs may echo a phrase from
scripture in another context also provides a useful illustra-
tion of how echoes and allusions work. In some instances if
the original context of words from the Bible is called to mind

as we listen to a song, even if this happens only at a subconscious level, it can have a profound effect on our experience of the song and our perception of its meaning. In other cases it may seem clear that the songwriter had no interest in the original context of the words. In a great many instances it will be difficult or impossible to tell. Music and scriptural allusions may intersect within the New Testament itself inasmuch as several key christological texts (i.e., texts having to do with the nature and exalted status of Jesus) may be quotations from early Christian hymns. At the very least the passages are poetic, and that fact makes their interpretation more challenging in important ways. Poetry abounds with metaphor, symbol, and wordplay, yet many read passages like Philippians 2:6-11, Colossians 1:15-20, and John 1:1-18 seeking precise and literal answers to their questions about Jesus. Figuring out their significance often depends on scriptural allusions in the text. In the case of Philippians 2 there is the question of whether the passage echoes the story of Adam and contrasts Jesus with him. In Romans 5 Paul offers an explicit contrast between Adam and Jesus in prose. Whether the Philippians passage does the same in poetic form has received a great deal of discussion. In Colossians 1 and John 1 there are echoes not only of Genesis but of Genesis as understood and interpreted in relation to the Word or Wisdom of God in the writings of Philo of Alexandria and Jesus ben Sira as well as in the work known as the Wisdom of Solomon. Each of these New Testament passages is key in discussions about Christology, and a key to interpreting each one is not just what they say but what they echo, and what the significance is of those other texts for the meaning we find in the passage.

This topic is sometimes referred to as "the use of the Old Testament in the New." Yet labeling the Jewish scriptures as the "Old Testament" affects how those writings are understood by Christians. The New Testament authors did not think of those writings the way you do. For them they were simply the writings, the scriptures. The New Testament authors were interpreters of sacred texts, regularly quoting from them and alluding to them. When you read the New Testament, you are thus interpreting interpreters. Texts never stand in complete isolation from other texts; this is called *intertextuality*. We saw in an earlier chapter how Matthew's Gospel echoes the story of Moses and sets up a comparison between him and Jesus. Later we will see examples of how John 6 offers a synagogue sermon by Jesus that reflects the Jewish practice (later adopted by Christians) of reading two scriptural texts and connecting them in a sermon. Whole books have been written on intertextuality, sometimes digging deeply into one example or engaging in a detailed survey of how a particular author or text interprets the scriptures they quote and allude to. Although we can only scratch the surface of this topic here, remembering the main concepts can deepen your future reading of the New Testament. Pay attention to the footnotes in your Bible; they will draw to your attention related passages and scriptural echoes that you might otherwise miss.

Allegory

"Allegory" is another term derived from Greek. As an English word, "allegory" denotes something more than mere figurative language. It indicates that most or all of the major characters and details in a text actually stand for something else. In Galatians 4:24 Paul says that he is offering an allegorical interpretation of the story in Genesis about Hagar and Sarah and their children Isaac and Ishmael. Paul's opponents, whom he is responding to in this passage, made natural descent from Abraham the focus of how they identify God's chosen people. Paul argues that this is not the case. He begins by identifying Hagar with Mount Sinai, which he says is in Arabia. Ishmael was viewed as the ancestor of the people of Arabia, allowing Paul to make a symbolic connection. Paul highlights that Ishmael and his descendants are Abraham's descendants, yet they do not become part of the covenant people. Natural descent from Abraham, a characteristic of both the Ishmaelites and the Israelites, is clearly not enough. Paul harnesses these details to argue that the gentiles who come to Christ and worship the God of Abraham are more like Isaac, the child of Abraham through miraculous means, than those who relate to Isaac through what we today would call a biological connection.

As you reflect on allegory as a way of interpreting scripture, a key point to recognize is that Paul uses it to invert and thereby combat what seemed to his opponents to be a more natural reading of the "plain sense" of Genesis. Paul's opponents in Galatia may have said that the gentile Christians were like Ishmael, people who had some connection to Abraham yet were not heirs to the promise. Paul turns the tables on them, much as he also does in Romans 4 where he discusses Abraham, the covenant, faith, justification, and circumcision. There too he is probably taking a favorite prooftext of his opponents and seeking to invert it, to harness it in support of his own viewpoint and message. Since allegory can be used to insert just about any meaning imaginable into a text, including one that stands directly at odds with its surface-level sense, we ought to use it cautiously if we use it at all. Paul's example suggests nonetheless that there might be a place for taking the favorite passage of those who seek to use the Bible to exclude others and finding ways to interpret it so as to include them instead.

People have allegorized all sorts of passages, but the parables have proven particularly germane for this approach.

Jesus's parable of the sower is given an allegorical interpretation in the New Testament gospels (Mark 4 and parallels; contrast the Gospel of Thomas, which lacks the explanation for this and other parables). Scholars debate whether the interpretation offered in Mark is the "original meaning" intended by Jesus when he told the story. Even if it is, that may not justify treating *every* parable as an allegory. In a famous allegorical interpretation of the parable of the Samaritan (Luke 10:25-37), the man who is robbed is identified with Adam, left spiritually dead when robbed by the devil, and left unassisted by the law and the temple sacrifices, until the Samaritan who represents Jesus comes along, administers the sacraments and brings him to the church. It is hard to imagine that anyone can seriously believe that Jesus meant this and expected his hearers to understand this when he told the story. Indeed, the meaning that this interpretation imports into the story makes it less relevant to the context in which the Gospel of Luke says it was told. Allegorical interpretations can be clever, but should rarely be considered what a text originally meant to its author and earliest readers.

For Further Reading

Blount, Brian K. *Cultural Interpretation: Reorienting New Testament Criticism.* Minneapolis: Fortress, 1995.

Carter, Warren. "'The Blind, Lame and Paralyzed' (John 5:3): John's Gospel, Disability Studies, and Postcolonial Perspectives." Pages 129-50 in *Disability Studies and Biblical Literature.* Edited by Candida R. Moss and Jeremy Schipper. New York: Palgrave Macmillan, 2011.

Hays, Richard B. *Echoes of Scripture in the Letters of Paul.* New Haven: Yale University Press, 1989.

Hooker, Morna D. *Beginnings: Keys That Open the Gospels.* Philadelphia: Trinity Press International, 1997.

McCaulley, Esau. *Reading While Black: African American Biblical Interpretation as an Exercise in Hope.* Downers Grove, IL: InterVarsity, 2020.

Moss, Candida R. *Divine Bodies: Resurrecting Perfection in the New Testament and Early Christianity.* New Haven: Yale University Press, 2019.

Oropeza, B. J., and Steve Moyise, eds. *Exploring Intertextuality: Diverse Strategies for New Testament Interpretation of Texts.* Eugene, OR: Cascade, 2016.

Soon, Isaac T. "Disability and New Testament Studies: Reflections, Trajectories, and Possibilities." *Journal of Disability & Religion* 25, no. 4 (2021): 374–87.

Taylor, Marion Ann, and Heather Weir. *Women in the Story of Jesus: The Gospels through the Eyes of Nineteenth-Century Female Biblical Interpreters.* Grand Rapids: Eerdmans, 2016.

Thiselton, Anthony C. *Hermeneutics: An Introduction.* Grand Rapids: Eerdmans, 2009.

Watson, Francis. *Paul and the Hermeneutics of Faith.* London: Bloomsbury, 2004.

J

Jokes Aside

Joking. Joviality. Jesting. Joshing. Since Jesus gets attention in every chapter, the letter j seemed to be the place to tackle what is in fact a very serious topic. In this chapter we will ask whether Jesus (or anyone in the New Testament) was funny. Obviously, if you believe Jesus was divine, then you'll want to attribute to him all the relevant attributes, which must include not only omniscience and omnipotence but omnihilarity. If that isn't your theological stance, then the historical approach we take to the question here should be more to your liking. Humor is one of the most difficult things to translate between languages. It is also hard for scholars studying texts from not only another language but also a different time period and culture to even know when something is supposed to be funny. This chapter surveys some of the evidence for humor in the New Testament. I apologize in advance if in the process of explaining these jokes I ruin them. There is no better way to spoil a joke than by explaining it, but when it comes to ancient humor, we seem to have no alternative.

Puns

Some people will want to put puns in a category other than humor. Good jokes make people laugh; bad jokes make people groan. Most puns make people groan, even the supposedly good ones. Whatever your view of them, as an avid pun maker myself, I am happy to inform you that Jesus made puns. Earlier in the book we discussed puns Jesus made involving camels. Others are attributed to him in the gospels, some with stronger evidence in favor of their historical authenticity than others. Even if there may be reason to doubt that Jesus made this or that specific play on words, the fact that the gospels independently depict him as doing this kind of thing is strong historical evidence of his penchant for puns.

Some plays on words in the gospels only work in Greek, and even if one considers Jesus to have spoken that language (most scholars do not), when a specific conversation is set in the Aramaic linguistic environment of Jerusalem or the towns and villages of Galilee, the likelihood that Jesus made the pun in question is very small. For instance, the use of a Greek word that can mean both "from above" and "again" in John 3 is difficult to view as historical when a conversation between Jesus and Nicodemus would almost certainly have been conducted in Aramaic. Luke 4:19 and 24 use the same Greek word (often translated as "favor" or "acceptable") in reference to both the time (likely the year of Jubilee) and Jesus himself. Jesus says that the year acceptable to the Lord has arrived, and then that a prophet is not acceptable in his hometown.

Some puns actually do work in multiple languages. For instance, Peter in Greek and Kepha in Aramaic were both nicknames that derived from the words for rock or stone in those languages. We thus find Simon referred to using both (Kepha in John 1:42, 1 Corinthians, and Galatians; Peter in the Gospels of Matthew, Mark, and Luke, in Acts, and also in Galatians as well as throughout the rest of the Gospel of John). Magdalene may also have been a pun, indicating that Mary was from Magdala while simultaneously depicting her as a tower of strength. Jesus seems to have given nicknames to at least some of his disciples that involved plays on words.

John the Baptist may have made at least one pun, although it is not clear from the Greek gospels whether he used words for sons and stones in Aramaic that were similar (Matt 3:9 // Luke 3:8). If he did not, he missed an opportunity to make a pun, which would be very disappointing.

Political Satire

The story of the demon-possessed man and the pigs (Mark 5:1-20 // Matt 8:28-34 // Luke 8:26-39) is set in different places depending on not only which gospel you read but which manuscript. Comparing Mark and Matthew and looking at different copies of these works, you will be told that it took place in the region of the Gerasenes, Gadarenes, or Gergesenes. Sometimes variations creep in because place names are unfamiliar, but this degree of disagreement is unusual and so something else is likely going on. The differences probably reflect an awareness that Gerasa is much too far and Gadara is closer but still not close enough for the grand finale of the story, in which the pigs hurl themselves into the lake, to make much sense. The pigs would have to run nonstop for hours if the story took place in Gerasa. Sometimes these kinds of issues tell us that the story was created or transmitted by people unfamiliar with the geography of the places Jesus visited. In this case, however, it may be a clue that the story ought to be taken not as a straightforward, factual report of an actual event but as something else.

The man who lives among the tombs comes to Jesus and immediately adjures him by God Most High. The word "adjure" (to command someone with an oath) is a technical term in stories of exorcism. An exorcist will adjure a demon by a spiritual power higher than the demon to submit to the exorcist's commands. That means that the demon-possessed man was trying to exorcise Jesus! He invokes God, implying that no lower angelic power would be superior. The irony of a demon trying to call on God to keep Jesus in check is just one of many ironies in the story. When Jesus asks the demon its name, it says, "Legion." This indicates that it has a Roman title: it is not just a large group but a large group of Roman soldiers. They then beg Jesus, the king of the Jews, not to throw them out of the country. Are you picking up on the satirical elements yet? Imagine a story set in Nazi-occupied France involving a man possessed by a demon that identifies itself as "panzer division." You would recognize, on the one hand, that the story is probably political satire and, on the other, that it reflects the fact that people are disturbed mentally as well as in other ways by the experience of occupation.

The Speck and Beam Skit

Some of Jesus's stories and sayings would have been quite comical if anyone acted them out. We don't know whether Jesus enlisted his followers to depict the story visually in this way. It was probably enough if listeners envisaged in their minds what Jesus was describing. Take, for instance, his saying about someone who points out to someone else that they have a speck in their eye, like a bit of dust or an eyelash, but who is oblivious to the fact that they have a plank of wood coming out of their own eye (Matt 7:3-5 // Luke 6:41-42). The Three Stooges would have had a field day with this, with the plank swinging as someone else ducked to avoid it. Another story that seems to have a comedic element, if less of a slapstick one, is the parable of the wedding banquet (Luke 14:16-24). A man tells people that he has prepared a banquet and invites them to attend. Their excuses are ridiculous. To purchase a plot of land before seeing it is like buying a house without seeing it. To purchase oxen and now need to urgently try them out is like saying you have bought a car and now will be too busy taking it for a test drive to accept the invitation. These excuses are so poor as to be insulting, indicating an element of humor in them. But the last one is the most striking and potentially humorous, amusing precisely through what is left unsaid. The third excuse is from someone who says he has just married. If he has literally just married, then what exactly are he and his wife busy doing? Oh . . .

I have heard that some cultures may not even have sarcasm in their repertoire of humor. Perhaps the person who told me that was just being sarcastic. Sometimes it is hard to tell, and never more so than when you're dealing with text that lacks indicators like an eye-roll emoji or a sarcasm hashtag. (The New Testament doesn't have those, just to be clear.) Even with those indicators, we sometimes miss sarcasm, while at other times we perceive it when it is not intended. A couple of places where there seems to be sarcasm in the New Testament are John 9 and Acts 2. In John 9:27 and 30 the man who had been blind responds to those interrogating him in a manner that I cannot help hearing with sarcastic overtones. When the Pharisees question him for the second time about what Jesus did to heal him, he says, "Why do you want to hear it again? Do you want to become his disciples too?" I think he knew they didn't but was goading them. Then, when they deny being disciples and knowing where Jesus comes from, he exclaims, "Now that is remarkable!" (John 9:30 NIV). Maybe it is just that I would be sarcastic in the same circumstances, but that's how I hear his retorts to those questioning him. In Acts 2:13 the crowd remarks that the Christians must be drunk on new wine. Since this happens on the Jewish festival of Shavuot (which Christians typically know by its Greek name Pentecost), the newest batch of wine has had plenty of time to ferment. Thus the crowd isn't saying something about grape juice, just making an accusation of drunkenness. When Peter responds (Acts 2:15) that it is only 9:00 a.m., I think this must be sarcasm. It would be rare to have a crowd drunk at that time. They've scarcely had time to get drunk, and the bars aren't even open yet!

Lost in Translation

As you have presumably seen here, humor can be hard to translate. It is also true that translation can result in unintentional humor. There are things in the New Testament that seem funny to us that may not have seemed that way to the author and earliest readers. There are things that may have been humorous for ancient author and readers that go completely over our heads. There may be instances in which translators of the New Testament have accidentally made things funny. Not necessarily laugh-out-loud funny, but at least smile-inducing funny. In at least a few instances there may be subtle humor that comes across in both English and Greek—but not in the same way. When Jesus called the fishermen to become fishers of men, the wordplay is arguably even better in English than it was in Greek. The Aramaic would have been different again. The Aramaic word that Jesus most likely used covered hunting as well as fishing, including hunting for human fugitives. The image of these specialists in catching fish becoming "evangelistic bounty hunters" is certainly striking. Whether it is funny, I will let the reader decide.

For Further Reading

Bednarz, Terri. *Humor in the Gospels: A Sourcebook for the Study of Humor in the New Testament, 1863–2014.* Lanham, MD: Lexington Books, 2015.

Burge, Gary M., and Gene L. Green. *The New Testament in Antiquity: A Survey of the New Testament within Its Cultural Contexts.* 2nd ed. Grand Rapids: Zondervan Academic, 2020.

Carter, Warren, and Amy-Jill Levine. *The New Testament: Methods and Meanings*. Nashville: Abingdon, 2013.

Jónsson, Jakob. *Humour and Irony in the New Testament, Illuminated by Parallels in Talmud and Midrash*. Leiden: Brill, 1985.

K

Keep On Keeping the Commandments

Tenses are funny things. Languages have such different ways of expressing the timing of actions, when they happened in relation to other events, whether the action was completed or ongoing, and so on. Some languages make these things clear through the form of the verb. Others use the same verb form to express a range of situations that other languages distinguish between. This doesn't mean that some languages have concepts that others do not. It just means that it may take more words to say something in one language than another, and that something may be specified in one language that is left ambiguous in another.

"Are you saved?" became a classic challenge question of born-again Christians in the twentieth century. I wonder how the apostle Paul would have answered if he were confronted with precisely that question. We can at least see what he wrote, and he refers to salvation in an array of tenses. In Romans 5:9–10, for instance, he uses it in the future tense: we will be saved. First Corinthians 1:18 has a present participle giving it a continuous sense: we are being saved. In 1 Corinthians 15:2 both the NRSV and the ESV use four words to translate one Greek verb: "you are being saved." Many other translations use only three English words and render it "you are saved." If Ephesians is an authentic letter by Paul (a subject about which there continues to be debate, but most scholars conclude that it is not), then that would introduce another tense into Paul's repertoire. Ephesians 2:8 has the perfect tense: "you have been saved." Assuming that some other terms like "justified" are roughly equivalent with "saved" for Paul, then we can safely say that he thinks of salvation as past, present, and future. Romans 2:13 talks about justification in the future, while Romans 5:1 and 9 say we have been justified. Paul is not contradicting himself but rather indicating that salvation involves a process and has aspects that are past, present, and future. That in itself suggests that Paul would have thought the question "Are you saved?" to be misguided, precisely because it demands an answer in one tense about a subject that involves a process that no one tense does justice to.

Keep Keeping the Commandments?

Salvation and justification relate directly to our next topic. As we began to explore in an earlier chapter, the early church wrestled with the question of whether non-Jewish Christians need to observe the Jewish law. Some of today's Christians consider it a relatively simple matter. The "moral law" still applies, while the "ritual law" does not. On the one hand, we will see that Paul may have made a distinction among laws that is not entirely different from this. On the other hand, Paul did not feel as though one could pick and choose from part of a covenant that God had made. Either you kept what God commanded or you excluded yourself from the covenant in question. A further difficulty is that some laws seem to fall into both categories. The Sabbath is a prime example. It is precisely the sort of thing that might be set aside as a ritual that no longer applies. Yet its rationale is given in terms of justice (Deut 5:15). Colossians 2:16-17 mentions the observance of the new moon alongside the Sabbath as something that Christians could disagree on, since it was merely "a shadow of the things to come." Yet even if some Christians have shifted the Sabbath to Sunday with no basis in the New Testament for doing so, they are still often adamant that the Sabbath must be observed, in ways that only vaguely correspond to the actual Jewish Sabbath. The Torah requires abstaining from work. The Christian adaptation may require attendance at church and abstinence from things considered frivolous pursuits. Paul was not selective like this. Yet he does seem to have made a distinction among the commandments, and in what follows we will try to clarify his basis and rationale for that distinction.

Paul often uses the phrase "works of the law" when referring to commandments that gentile Christians need not observe. Of the works of the law, the one he mentions most often is circumcision. (It should be mentioned that circumcision is practiced as a matter of course in the United States. Thus the average gentile Christian man in the United States has no need to worry about this commandment since the matter was taken care of soon after he was born.) Genesis is unambiguous that circumcision is required of all males who are born into or become part of the family of Abraham. Genesis 17:9-14 is emphatic and leaves no room for exceptions. Whether born to a member of Abraham's family or purchased by them as a slave, every male must be circumcised or else they are cut off from his people. (I do hope that pun was intended by the author of Genesis.) Paul nonetheless became persuaded that God was welcoming those previously excluded. In Galatians 3-4 and Romans 4 you can see how Paul tries to make the case. In Galatians (the earlier of these two letters) he argues that the inclusion of gentiles as gentiles in Abraham's family, without them converting to

Judaism through circumcision and embracing the other requirements in the Torah, was predicted in the Torah itself.
It is easy for English speakers to miss it. Three times it says
that all nations will be blessed through Abraham (Gen 12:3;
18:18; 22:18). The same word in Hebrew (and also in Greek) is
translated into English both as "nations" and as "gentiles" because the word was and is used by Jews to refer to the nations
other than Israel. Paul takes it that God's blessing of gentiles
through Abraham means they are included in the covenant
with and the promises to Abraham.

Paul's opponents were not convinced. By the time he
wrote Romans, Paul had formulated a different argument:
Abraham is said to have believed God and had it credited to
him as righteousness (Gen 15:6). Paul mentions that verse in
Galatians as well, but in Romans he points out that this happens prior to the covenant and the introduction of circumcision in Genesis 17. Thus Abraham was justified even before he
was circumcised. Paul's opponents would have responded by
saying that this doesn't mean one shouldn't respond to God's
grace and election by doing what God commands. Hence
Paul's need to say that the law of Moses and the covenant
at Sinai have been set aside, replaced by a new law and a
new covenant. Yet he still says the commandments are important, in puzzling phrases like that in 1 Corinthians 7:19
(see also Gal 6:15). There Paul says that being circumcised
or uncircumcised doesn't matter, but only keeping the commandments of God. Paul's opponents would have responded
by saying that circumcision is a commandment.

Paul surely knew that the works of the law that he said
did not apply to gentile Christians were commandments just
as the famous ten are. When he discusses works of the law,
he seems to focus in particular on those works that separated
Jews from gentiles. Romans 2 makes his view clear, in a passage that fits poorly within the traditional Protestant ap-

proach to the letter, which takes "works of the law" to be efforts to earn one's way to heaven. In Romans 2:6–13 Paul says that it is not the hearers but the doers of the law that are justified, and that God will render to each according to their works. How can this be the same Paul who says that justification comes through faith apart from works of the law? One solution that has a long history, yet was sufficiently neglected until recently so as to become known as the "new perspective on Paul" when it was proposed, is that Paul is not focused on works done to earn salvation but works of Torah that were specific to the Jewish people and to the covenant that set them apart as God's chosen people. Paul believed that calling gentiles to worship the one God of Israel was a fulfillment of the plan that led God to make a covenant with the Israelites, even as he said that covenant was being set aside so as to allow gentiles to enter.

*The **new perspective on Paul** proposes that Paul's contrast between faith and works was critiquing not legalistic efforts to earn salvation but overreliance on elect status as symbolized by circumcision and other "works of the law" that served as boundary markers and identity badges of God's people.*

When we interpret Paul's letters in relation to these issues, it allows us to make sense of things Paul wrote that will otherwise baffle us. While he may not have made a facile distinction between moral and ritual laws, if the reason the Sinai covenant was superseded was its exclusion of gentiles, then any law that was not a distinctive boundary marker of the Israelites could still be looked to for guidance within the framework of the new covenant. This will also allow us to understand how Paul can say that salvation is not by works of the law and yet say that those who practice the works of the flesh will not inherit the kingdom of God (Gal 5:19–21). For Paul, what people do matters. He was not opposed to people seeking to value what God values and live accordingly.

On the contrary, he emphasized that, and—returning to Romans 2—he pointed out that one could be circumcised and yet otherwise do evil, or be uncircumcised and yet seek God. Thus, Paul reasoned, other things must matter to God more than circumcision. If God lets someone off the hook for evil simply because they belong to a particular people, and condemns those who are just and pure because they belong to a different people, then God would be unjust. Paul was arguing against an overemphasis on election, a fact that will seem ironic to those who have seen his teaching about justification by faith leveraged to say that, in practice, a Christian can do anything and still be saved, while a non-Christian can be a better person than the Christian and not be saved. What Paul said on this subject has been turned into its opposite. Recovering Paul's emphasis on salvation as a process rather than simple before and after, which we explored earlier in this chapter, fits naturally with this "new perspective" but less well with the traditional Protestant understanding.

It is hard for those who consider Paul's letters scripture to read them as they would have been heard by their original recipients. However you would respond to someone saying, "The Bible plainly teaches X, but God is doing something new in our time as demonstrated by God's Spirit at work in the lives of these believers, and so God accepts them as they are," that is presumably how you would have responded to Paul's letter to the Galatians. In Paul's view, the experience of God's Spirit by the Galatian gentile Christians indicates that God has accepted them as they are, uncircumcised (Gal 3:2-5).

Paul and the Jerusalem Council

I mentioned in an earlier chapter that we would need to come back to the question of how Paul's letters relate to the information in Acts 15 about a council that took place in Jerusalem.

This council, at which Acts says Paul was present, addressed many of the same questions that arose in Paul's churches. Yet the decision of that council is never mentioned in Paul's letters, at least not explicitly. A key aspect of the question is how Paul's visits to Jerusalem mentioned in Galatians relate to the information in Acts. This is a subject on which lengthy studies have been written, and yet disagreement remains. Some view Paul's meeting with the Jerusalem leadership described in Galatians 2 as corresponding to Acts 15, while others view it as corresponding to the meeting in Acts 11:27-30. In the latter case, Galatians 1:18-20 would constitute Paul's first visit after his radical reversal of attitude toward the Christian movement, corresponding with Acts 9:26-30. Questions about the historicity of Acts intersect with this subject. All ancient historical sources, like modern biopics, compress, conflate, and adjust historical information in the interest of telling a compelling story. We cannot press too far either the correspondences or the discrepancies, which is why the question continues to be debated.

Setting aside the subject of whether Galatians and Acts match up and if so how, there is still the question of what the decision of the Jerusalem Council was and why Paul does not explicitly mention it. It has to be said that by calling it the Jerusalem Council we are viewing it through the lens of later councils like the famous ones at Nicaea and Chalcedon. Being so much earlier, this meeting must have been a much smaller one. This is important if for no other reason than to make clear why scholars think it might correspond to one of the meetings that Paul writes about in Galatians 2, both of which sound like small-scale affairs. It is also possible that Galatians was written precisely in the heat of the debates that led to the council. Paul had encountered people who claimed to represent the leaders in Jerusalem, and who opposed what Paul was doing. He had reason to doubt whether he and the Jerusalem apostles were still on the same page. He thus emphasizes that his own authority does not depend on them or anyone else but on Christ who called him. Later, writing to the Corinthians, he would emphasize the extent of agreement between him and other apostles (1 Cor 15:1-11). For now, however, Paul feels betrayed and angry, and it shows— for instance, when he says in Galatians 5:12 that he wishes his opponents would go further than merely removing the foreskin and cut off the whole of what it is attached to.

The letter from the church in Jerusalem asks gentile Christians to observe a small number of restrictions in order to facilitate fellowship and church unity. Why precisely those things? There are different ways of interpreting them, reflecting actual differences among the New Testament manuscripts at this point. It seems that ancient scribes differed in their understanding of the rationale for the list and how to interpret it. One possibility is that the rules are based on the Noachian laws, the commandments given to Noah. The view developed within Judaism that gentiles were not obligated to obey all the laws given to Israel in order to be righteous. The commandments given to Noah, however, applied to all his descendants and thus all human beings. These were also thought to be the basis for the laws in the Torah that explicitly applied to resident aliens living among the Israelites. While there was disagreement about precisely what had been revealed to and imposed on Noah, Genesis explicitly mentions capital punishment for murder and not eating meat with blood still in it (Gen 5:4-6). Some manuscripts of Acts and some interpreters see the focus as moral rather than ritual, with blood referring to the shedding of human blood rather than the consumption of blood that has not been drained from meat, omitting the reference to things strangled. When there is this level of uncertainty about the original form of the text, it makes it that much harder to

decide what the author of the work meant. The meaning of
the different variants nonetheless point in two directions:
either these were a few basic moral requirements, or they
were a small number of matters related to purity and eating
that would help gentile Christians to not do things that would
be offensive to Jewish sensibilities.

There is also no way to definitively answer the question
of why Paul never mentions the decree. I sometimes suspect
that even though a decision may have been reached and a
letter sent, Paul might not have been informed about it at
the time, but only later, as depicted in Acts 21:25. Another
possibility is that the gist of the decision is woven through
Paul's letters, but he saw no reason to make reference to the
Jerusalem leaders as though their authority overruled his
own. This was clearly a major concern of Paul's, especially
in Galatians, where his opening introduction emphasizing
his own authority must be read as a response to challenges to
his authority (Gal 1:1). Some feel that Luke-Acts, in the interest of promoting church unity, played down the seriousness
of the tensions and disagreements between Aramaic- and
Greek-speaking Christians, and between Paul and James the
Lord's brother.

James versus Paul?

Martin Luther was not fond of the Letter of James. Having
felt burdened by his own inability to live up to God's standards, he found relief in Paul's letters with their emphasis
on salvation by grace through faith apart from works (which
he interpreted as any human effort). James, however, emphasizes that faith without works is dead (Jas 2:14–26). It
isn't surprising that Luther reacted as he did, given how
much Paul influenced him. The "new perspective on Paul"
that we've discussed in this chapter has challenged the way

Luther understood Paul, which has in turn influenced how many modern scholars have understood him. We should therefore revisit the question of how much James and Paul disagreed. That they put things differently is beyond dispute. Salvation by faith without works and salvation by faith that is inseparable from works are not the same. Paul and James use the same Greek words in their discussion of faith and works. Yet if we look closely at how they use these words in their letters, we find that these two authors may not have been using them in precisely the same way. The words are the same, but the connotations and emphasis differ. In Paul, what is to the fore is *faith in* (trust) and *faithfulness*. In James, the faith that demons have is not trust in God but mere belief *that* there is only one God. In Paul, the "works of the law" focus on circumcision and things like that, while James mentions things we might call "good deeds." It takes close attention to how authors use words to understand what they meant.

This is why you should never, ever write in an assignment that "Webster's dictionary defines X as . . ." If a professor asks you about the Pharisees, or about faith in Paul's writings, they aren't asking you for the information you'd find in a dictionary. That isn't just because the New Testament wasn't written in English. Looking up Greek words will often be necessary, but the list of possible meanings in a reference work like Liddell and Scott's lexicon (or the definition that comes from who-knows-where when you click a word in an online hyperlinked interlinear) ultimately poses the same problems as occurs in English. A question about what Paul meant by faith is asking which of the range of possible meanings (i.e., semantic range) of the Greek word is to the fore, what nuances it has in his writings, and how he used it in distinctive ways. This also applies to things you may have heard about the Greek word *agapē* (pronounced "ah-gah-

pay" and not like the English word that is spelled the same
but describes the way some readers' mouths will hang open
when they read what I write here). *Agapē* does not *mean* God's
selfless love. That may be what God's love is like, but just as
in English, so too in Greek, a word like "love" can be used in
a variety of ways. It is not that the word in Greek or English
always inherently means divine love with all the characteristics thereof. When Christians talk specifically about *God's*
love, they are defining that love as having particular attributes and connotations, ones that go beyond the meaning of
the generic word for love.

While some Christians in the modern era have used slo-
gans such as "Christianity isn't a religion, it's a relationship,"
the Letter of James advocates explicitly for "true religion,"
which it defines as caring for widows and orphans and avoiding pollution from the world (Jas 1:27). The word translated as
"religion" is also sometimes rendered as "worship" or "service
to God." The Greek word has a range of meaning, much like
the English word "religion," making that quite a good translation. While we're on the subject, I'll let you in on a little secret
in the field of religious studies. Scholars find themselves unable to come up with a good working definition of "religion."
For every proposed definition, there always seems to be something that we naturally consider a religion that doesn't quite
fit. Hopefully you'll believe me when I say that this doesn't
show there's something wrong with the academic study of
religion, or that religious studies scholars are just a bunch of
incompetent fools. The word is challenging to define because
words are like that. They point to concepts; they lump things
together that could be separated and split apart things that
could potentially be categorized together. It is appropriate,
then, to end this chapter by highlighting the vagueness and
flexibility of the English word "religion." Words don't just
have definitions; they have nuances and overtones and conno-

tations. Words in one language overlap with words in another but rarely if ever do so perfectly. That is why different words in Greek are rendered into English as "religion," and none of them is *always* translated into English that way.

Looking up words in a dictionary when you don't know them is still important, however. Not everyone in this field will stop to tell you what a "semantic range" is, to make sure you don't mistake it for some sort of oven. The English word "range" is a good one to end with, since its range of meanings illustrates nicely the point I've been making here.

For Further Reading

Bockmuehl, Markus. "The Noachide Commandments and New Testament Ethics: With Special Reference to Acts 15 and Pauline Halakhah." *Revue Biblique* 102, no. 1 (1995): 72–101.

Dunn, James D. G. *The New Perspective on Paul.* Grand Rapids: Eerdmans, 2008.

Hartog, Pieter B. "Noah and Moses in Acts 15: Group Models and the Novelty of the Way." *New Testament Studies* 67, no. 4 (2021): 496–513.

Hooker, Morna D. *Paul: A Beginner's Guide.* Oxford: Oneworld, 2008.

Pifer, Jeanette Hagen. *Faith as Participation: An Exegetical Study of Some Key Pauline Texts.* Tübingen: Mohr Siebeck, 2019.

L

Language, Please

You may have heard that Jesus talked about hell more than any other topic. Or you may have heard that hell doesn't actually appear in the Bible. You may in fact have heard both statements if you have a broad and diverse circle of friends. Both cannot possibly be true—or can they?

Modern English Bibles vary widely on the number of times the word "hell" appears. By my estimation the Contemporary English Version has roughly a third more occurrences than the New Jerusalem Bible. That may or may not say something about the traditions that produced them. The Message has a lot more than other versions (and not only because it includes the word "hello" where others do not, and "hello" shows up in searches for "hell"). It has hell-raisers, one-way tickets to hell, rotting in hell, and all hell breaking loose. (The Common English Bible is another translation that might seem to have more references to "hell" until you filter out the many occurrences of "hello.") What should readers of the Bible make of this? Why have some translators decided to give 'em hell to an extent that others have not? We should back up a bit before New Testament times if we want to get a clear sense of what is going on here.

Sheol and Hades

Belief in rewards and punishments in an afterlife was a relatively new thing in Judaism in Jesus's time. Except for late works like the book of Daniel, the viewpoint most expressed in the Jewish scriptures is that all people go to a place called Sheol, the realm of the dead. Often it is hard to know whether the word simply denotes the grave, or refers to an underworld where the dead persist as some shadowy remnant of themselves. (My favorite answer to the question "What is Sheol?" was offered by a student who noticed that in Jonah 2:2 the prophet says he cried out to the Lord "from the belly of Sheol." Thus clearly Sheol is the name of the big fish that swallowed Jonah.)

The prophets regularly warn the people of Israel that judgment is coming, but they never say, "Repent or you'll go to hell." They threaten the nation with plague, famine, exile, and other calamities in *this* world rather than with punishment in an afterlife. This changed, however, during the era in which the Syrian ruler Antiochus IV (sometimes called Antiochus Epiphanes) persecuted those who observed the Jewish law. It is one thing to try to make sense of why bad things seem to happen to good and bad people alike. It is another matter entirely to try to make sense of why the most faithful are at the same time the most persecuted, liable to be killed precisely because of their obedience to God, while those who abandon God's laws are spared and even rewarded for doing so. To preserve their conviction that God is just, some Jews developed the idea that even death would not prevent God from rewarding God's faithful servants. Had such developments in Jewish thought not occurred, it would have been pretty much impossible for Jesus's followers to retain faith in him after the crucifixion. The development of a doctrine of afterlife in Judaism is truly crucial and central to the phenomenon of Christianity.

It appears that by the time of Jesus belief in an afterlife had caught on, with most people embracing the teaching of the Pharisees that God would raise the dead at the end of time and judge all human beings in bodily form. The Sadducees were more conservative and stuck with the view that there is no meaningful afterlife to speak of. The Essenes (according to Josephus and confirmed by the Dead Sea Scrolls) believed that God held people accountable whether in this life or hereafter but without positing (or at least without emphasizing) bodily resurrection as the means to accomplishing this. Summarizing these major streams of thought in this way doesn't answer a crucial question: *Where* would God ensure that justice was done and that God's faithful were rewarded? If it was in a corporeal afterlife, would they inhabit the earth? If it was in an incorporeal afterlife, would that be in heaven?

One of the words in the Greek New Testament that is sometimes translated as "hell" is *hadēs*. Hades (as it's rendered in English) was the Greek god of the underworld, and his name eventually became synonymous with the underworld itself. Like the Hebrew Sheol, the Greek Hades was a place where *all* the dead went, and not a place where only the wicked went. The King James Version rendered the word as "hell," but the term "Hades" did not normally mean the same thing that modern English speakers think of when they read or hear the word "hell." In some Christian traditions Hades is thought of as the place where all souls go until the time comes for God's judgment. Needless to say, that isn't what most modern English speakers mean by "hell." Because of a lack of clarity on the nature of punishment and its duration, people often envisage Hades or something like it as an intermediate state, with bodily resurrection to follow. Sometimes the resulting system becomes convoluted, with people being punished in a spiritual afterlife as they await bodily resurrection, at which point they are judged and punished bodily. That seems rather redundant, and not surprisingly some simply envisage an afterlife featuring heaven and hell as places one goes directly when one dies, to remain there for eternity.

Gehenna

Another term that occurs in the New Testament is transliterated from Hebrew: Gehenna. It occurs in a number of places, with the preponderance of them in the Gospel of Matthew (see Matt 5:22, 29–30; 10:28; 18:9; 23:15, 33; 25:41; Mark 9:43–47; Luke 12:5; Jas 3:6). You may have come across online memes and blog posts discussing whether Gehenna meant something like the English word "hell." The word *Gehenna* comes from the Hebrew name Ge Hinnom, Valley of Hinnom. If you visit the Old City of Jerusalem, you will undoubtedly see this valley. I won't recommend that you go there, however, just to make sure no one accuses me of having told them to "go to hell." The relation between the geographical location and references in Jewish and Christian literature to Gehenna requires discussion. Many preachers commit the etymological fallacy. Etymology looks at words diachronically—that is, studying their origin and history over time. The meaning of a word in any given time may be quite different from what the word meant originally or at any previous point in history. The etymological fallacy makes the mistake of thinking that the origin of a word tells you its meaning, what we might call its lexical (or dictionary) definition.

Grammatical forms change. An example related to the Bible is the second-person singular pronoun "thou" and associated verb forms, which became obsolete. Words can become archaic or fall out of use entirely. Verily, if thou hastenest anon to the King James Version, thou wilt haply find words such as "concupiscence" and "chambering" therein. Returning to Gehenna, the fact that the word comes from the name of a valley does not necessarily tell us what the word meant in Jesus's time. However, because the valley was still there in Jerusalem, and the scriptures mentioning it were still read and familiar (see Jer 7:31; 32:35), the meaning of Gehenna is unlikely to be completely unrelated to the actual place. Some have claimed that the place was used for burning trash in Jesus's time, but there is no clear evidence for this. We are probably dealing with another case of a hypothetical suggestion subsequently spreading and being repeated so widely that eventually it came to be treated as though it were something demonstrated and known to be true. That happens quite often with the Bible, and unless you jumped straight to this chapter, you have already encountered other examples elsewhere in this book.

Gehenna appears in Jewish texts from closer to Jesus's time, such as 1 Enoch 27, where it is still the "accursed valley." In rabbinic literature it is contrasted with the Garden of Eden (e.g., b. Berakhot 28b; Hagigah 15a) and is mentioned alongside it in lists of things that were created before the world (b. Pesahim 54a; Nedarim 39b). By this point Gehenna clearly denotes a place of judgment in the afterlife. In the Babylonian Talmud (b. Sukkah 32b) a distinction is made between Gehenna and the Valley of the Son of Hinnom, the latter being the location of the gate that leads to the former. When the Valley of Hinnom is mentioned in the Jewish scriptures, it is sometimes a place where child sacrifice was practiced, described as making children pass through the fire. Gehenna remains a place of fire and burning even as the meaning of the term develops. Yet the fires of the Valley of Hinnom were made by people, and so Gehenna could perhaps be understood in terms of God allowing the consequences of human actions to befall them, rather than God kindling a fire and then taking pleasure in roasting the wicked. Whether this interpretation could fit the various references to Gehenna as a place of punishment in an afterlife is unclear. The main point here is that different words are used to refer to places a person might find themselves after death. However one interprets these terms, and whether they are understood to denote the same or different things, behind the word "hell" in some English translations is an array of terms, the precise meaning and connotations of which cannot be determined simply by tracing the origin of the word in question. There's a helluva lotta room for misunderstanding if one doesn't know that.

Before departing from Gehenna, I should mention that there are other texts (for instance, Matt 13:42, 50; 25:41) that refer to punishment in the form of burning but do not mention Gehenna, at least explicitly. An important question is whether this language conveys destruction, which is usually the effect that burning has, or a sensation of burning that lasts forever without end. In Judaism punishment in the afterlife was not usually envisaged as lasting forever, although given that there were differences of opinion on whether there would be an afterlife and if so what form it would take, we should assume that there were likely differences of opinion on this topic as well. In some places it is said explicitly that Gehenna is temporary and that there are only a few exceptions to the general rule that everyone eventually ascends from there (b. Rosh Hashanah 16b–17a; Bava Metzi'a 58b). The fire and the smoke are said in places to never end, but those are symbols of its consuming power and do not necessarily indicate that the one thrown into the fire is never consumed by it. Another place of punishment mentioned in the New Testament is Tartarus. The name appears only in 2 Peter 2:4 as a reference to a place to which angels who sinned were sentenced (see also the parallel in Jude 1:6). Bringing us full circle, the book of Revelation has a lake of fire, and into it are cast not only evil angels and human beings but also death and Hades, suggesting that death itself is destroyed (Rev. 20:10-15). A whole book would be necessary to tackle the questions that come up when we seek to interpret the varied references in the book of Revelation. At the end of the book, the New Jerusalem has descended from heaven to earth and God's home is among human beings. Even then, although the gates of the city never shut, wrongdoers apparently still exist, although they are only to be found outside the city (Rev. 21:27; 22:14-15).

Feasting by the Pearly Gates

In Luke 16:19-31 Jesus tells a story about a poor beggar named Lazarus and a rich man outside whose gate he sits, contrasting the situation of the two in life and then in the hereafter. In that story the reversal that is expected with the kingdom of God appears to occur immediately after death. When Jesus talked about the kingdom, he emphasized that the last will be first, that those who are currently hungry will be filled while those currently well fed will be hungry. He often spoke about the kingdom through the image of a feast, sometimes called by commentators the "Messianic Banquet." The image of feasting in Isaiah 25:6-9 influenced Jewish and thereby Christian depictions of the time when God would restore his people and defeat his enemies and theirs. Those who have sought to construct a coherent view of the afterlife from all the things the New Testament has to say on the topic have struggled with this story. It seems to depict judgment as occurring to each individual when they die, instantaneously, rather than awaiting a final resurrection and judgment of all. This seems to be confirmed by the fact that while the rich man finds himself in torment, his brothers are still alive on earth and can be warned about the place that they too will presumably end up if they don't change their ways. Yet this seems unlike a purely spiritual afterlife given that there is a request for water. Lazarus's position "in the bosom of Abraham" is an expression that simply means "alongside Abraham." It presumably reflects the position of individuals when they reclined at meals, as was the custom in the Greco-Roman world. The same idiom is found in the Gospel of John in 1:18 and 13:23. In the prologue of the gospel, Jesus sits alongside the Father. In the latter instance, people have sometimes misunderstood the idiom and the dining custom and, as a result, envisaged the disciple whom Jesus loved literally lying on Jesus's chest. The meaning is rather that the disciple in question sits alongside Jesus. In the parable in Luke, the poor beggar has been elevated to an honored position and is seated alongside the illustrious patriarch, perhaps at the Messianic Banquet.

One simple solution to the issue of how to understand the scenario and whether it agrees with other depictions of afterlife in the New Testament is to treat it as a "pearly gates story." You know the kind of amusing story or joke that this label refers to, the sort that starts something like this: "A Baptist arrives at the pearly gates and St. Peter says to him . . ." As a member of a Baptist church, I can tell you that most Baptists do not really expect a scenario like this to unfold in the afterlife. But most Baptists can get the jokes and may even tell them. (I would have said "all Baptists," but one thing I know for sure as a Baptist is that all Baptists never agree about anything.) The image of the "pearly gates" comes from Revelation 21:21, where it is a feature not in heaven but in the new Jerusalem that descends from heaven to earth to become the dwelling place of humans and God together. A "pearly gates story," on the other hand, often features clouds and perhaps even St. Peter standing watch to decide who enters. Most Christians today speak of their hope in terms that sound more like the parable in Luke: their immediate destination will be their final destination. Most of the New Testament, however, depicts the hope not in terms of people "going to heaven when they die" but in terms of a new creation in which there is a new heaven and a new earth, with God deigning to dwell with the resurrected righteous in the latter. (See chapter 4 for more on that topic.)

Interpreters have often been so focused on figuring out how to make sense of the scenario depicted and how it might fit into a systematic theology about afterlife that the interesting details of the story as story get neglected. The scenario depicts a literal reversal of the situation of rich and poor, with no questions asked about whether either of them had any sort of faith, much less the kind of faith that Protestants tend to insist is the only thing that matters when it comes to salvation. This story is not the only place that the message seems to be not "believe" but "woe to you who are rich" (Luke 6:24–25). Those of us who live in relative luxury (as compared to what is typical globally and not as compared to the top 1 percent who have things even better than we do) tend to prefer Matthew's version of the beatitude that says it is the poor *in spirit* who are the ones who have something to celebrate, with no addition of woes aimed at the prosperous (Matt 5:3). The parable is supposed to be disconcerting if we are in that category. Perhaps the most striking detail in the story about Lazarus and the rich man is that a great chasm has been situated between them. The implication is that otherwise both the rich and the righteous would continue to do what they had been inclined to on earth. The rich would take the water from those who now have it in order to quench their own thirst. And even though the reversal is just, the righteous have to be physically prevented from showing mercy and helping those who are suffering even though they deserve to. It is, like so many of Jesus's parables, a powerful story that reveals new facets of meaning as we ponder it and let it sit with us—provided, of course, that we don't miss the point and become fixated on squeezing it into a systematic theology about life beyond death. By depicting an afterlife in which things are reversed, so that those who withhold crumbs now long for a drop of water but do not get any, the story aims to get us to notice those in need around us.

The Sign of Jonah

Jonah has more to offer in this chapter than just the amusing anecdote I shared earlier. The Gospels of Matthew and Luke depict Jesus talking about the "sign of Jonah." In Luke 11:29 and Matthew 16:4, the saying seems to have the same meaning as what Jesus says in Mark 8:12: "no sign will be given to this generation." After all, what sign or miracle did Jonah perform? None. (Smelling like fish doesn't count as a miraculous sign.) The "sign of Jonah" can naturally be understood to mean that just as Jonah delivered his warning and the inhabitants of Nineveh either accepted it or didn't on its own merits, so too in the case of Jesus with respect to his detractors. Matthew 12:38-41, however, takes the "sign of Jonah" in a different direction, adding, "For just as Jonah was three days and three nights in the belly of the sea monster, so for three days and three nights the Son of Man will be in the heart of the earth." Friday until Sunday morning (the time during which Jesus was in the tomb) is not, of course, "three days and three nights," but presumably the point is less the precise timing than the relevance of the resurrection as a sign from the perspective of the author of Matthew's Gospel and its readers. Since Jonah cried out "from the belly of Sheol," there was a basis for connecting Jonah's experience to that of Jesus. Even if Jonah 2:2 doesn't give us the name of the fish, it may have provided the basis for the deeper significance Matthew saw in Jesus's reference to Jonah.

For Further Reading

Bailey, Kenneth E. *Jesus through Middle Eastern Eyes: Cultural Studies in the Gospels.* Downers Grove, IL: InterVarsity, 2009.

Elledge, C. D. *Resurrection of the Dead in Early Judaism, 200 BCE–CE 200.* Oxford: Oxford University Press, 2016.

Long, Phillip J. *Jesus the Bridegroom: The Origin of the Eschatological Feast as a Wedding Banquet in the Synoptic Gospels.* Eugene, OR: Pickwick, 2013.

Nickelsburg, George W. E. *Resurrection, Immortality, and Eternal Life in Intertestamental Judaism and Early Christianity.* Cambridge, MA: Harvard University Press, 2006.

M

Mud in Your Eye

This chapter could perhaps have been about Jesus's reputation as "a glutton and a drunkard" (Matt 11:19 // Luke 7:34, an allusion to the law about rebellious sons in Deut 21:18–21). The phrase "Here's mud in your eye," after all, is most frequently encountered as a toast when drinking. (Not that anyone has said it to me, but I've seen it in movies.) Here I mean it literally, however, which I gather is not the sense intended when the phrase is used as a toast. The theme of the chapter also connects with another toast, "To your health." In the interest of healing people with visual impairments, Jesus is said to have literally put mud in their eyes. John 9:6–15 contains the famous story about Jesus healing a man born blind. In it he spits on the ground and makes mud, places it on the man's eyes, and sends him to wash in the Pool of Siloam. In Mark 8:23 Jesus uses only spit without mixing it with dirt. Mark 7:33 also mentions Jesus spitting in the process of healing, although it is less clear there how the spitting relates to the touching of the man's tongue.

Some readers of the Bible, used to thinking of Jesus as unlike any other figure in history, may find it troubling to realize that Jesus used methods of healing that were also used by his contemporaries. This included application of saliva, a mud paste, or a touch, as well as prayer and sometimes exorcisms. Illnesses were generally blamed on malevolent spirits. This was not only the case when the symptoms were strange behaviors of the sorts depicted in horror movies about "demonic possession." The "bent woman" in Luke 13:10–17 is said to have been afflicted by a demon, and yet her condition had to do with posture and mobility rather than her mind. Jesus's actions as exorcist parallel what we know about other ancient exorcists. This should not surprise us, since Jesus relates his own exorcistic practice to that of others among his contemporaries. He asks those who accuse him of casting out demons by harnessing a demonic authority, "If I cast out demons by Beelzebul, by whom do your own exorcists cast them out?" (Matt 12:27 // Luke 11:19). Luke emphasizes that Jesus healed through the power of God's Spirit or power at work in and through him (e.g., Luke 5:17), just as would presumably have been said about anyone else who performed healings.

Miracles and the Historians

Beginning students and the wider public often have the impression that historians are skeptical, maybe too skeptical, when it comes to the Bible. The stereotype is not entirely inaccurate, but it reflects a problematic assumption, namely that skepticism is a bad thing. Yet there is a long history of skepticism grounded in and allied with religion. The Catholic Church, to prevent people being frivolously elevated to the ranks of sainthood, appoints a "devil's advocate" to investigate the claims that someone had performed miracles. René Descartes famously doubted everything he could, but some are unaware that his motive for doing so was religious. He wanted to ground his own beliefs on a solid foundation. He also wanted to find an unquestionable foundation on which to build an argument that would effectively persuade skeptics to believe in the Christian God.

Most religious people doubt the claims of other religions, and they critically examine the arguments that are brought by those who disagree with them. The historian cultivates and hones precisely these tools, the key difference being that they seek to apply them fairly across the board. This too is at the very least compatible with Christian values, if not indeed an expression of them. Jesus taught us to do to others what we would want done to us. We should treat the arguments and claims of others the way we want our own to be treated. Conversely, if we treat the claims of others with what we consider appropriate skepticism, we should be willing to subject our own assumptions and views to the same sort of skeptical analysis. Far from being something antithetical to faith, this rigorous analysis can be considered an expression of faith. If we take God seriously, then avoiding deception and error ought to be a high priority. If we are unwilling to allow our assumptions and views to be challenged, how will we ever discover if we are wrong about something? Historical tools are skeptical, and for that very reason Christians should embrace them, however difficult and painful the result may be.

The rigorous evaluation of evidence that characterizes historical investigation may usefully be compared to a court of law. Evidence is gathered, cases are made, and a group of fallible but hopefully well-informed and well-meaning human beings decide what to conclude on the basis of the cases and evidence presented. When it comes to ancient history, the modern juridical standard for criminal cases—proof "beyond reasonable doubt"—sets the bar unrealistically high. When it comes to ancient history, our evidence is always piecemeal. As a result, few things are genuinely beyond doubt, and whether a doubt is reasonable can be hard to determine. Civil cases set the standard of evidence as "more probable than not," and that seems more appropriate for the investigation of ancient history.

Miracles are by definition events that are out of the ordinary. (I think this is probably true no matter what precise definition of miracle one may have in mind.) They are inherently improbable. History, on the other hand, is about probability. The tools of the historian cannot ever be legitimately expected to declare the inherently improbable to be probable. If a modern-day miracle claim would require significant evidence in its favor to persuade those not predisposed to believe, how much more in the case of an ancient one for which the only evidence is in the form of stories? On the one hand, those who wish to believe in ancient miracles may take comfort from the fact that historians cannot disprove that miracles occurred. On the other hand, those who wish to believe in ancient miracles not with blind faith but on the basis of evidence will have to wrestle with the fact that historical study cannot declare a miracle likely, much less a certainty. While a few New Testament scholars have tried to make a case for an approach to history that makes room for the miraculous, the field of history as a whole has not embraced their views. To return to the analogy of criminal investigations, if a dead body is found in a locked room with no evidence who did it, the appropriate thing for the police to do is leave the case open, labeling it unsolved, rather than pronouncing it a miracle since an explanation in everyday human terms is lacking.

You may be surprised to learn that, despite what I have just written, historians most certainly can talk about Jesus as a healer and exorcist. The fact that Jesus did what other healers and exorcists in his time also did makes things easier for historians, since having a basis for comparison is crucial to estimating probability. Jesus had the reputation not merely of being a healer and exorcist but of being a particularly good one. Even a historian who does not believe in miracles as part of their worldview can study the evidence and conclude that some people must have experienced healing as a result of contact with Jesus, just as people do today who seek healing from faith healers. The Gospels tell us that some people were not healed and connect it with a lack of faith. Explanations in psychosomatic terms will help some and offend others, but the end result is the same, leaving us with a historical conclusion that believers and nonreligious people should be able to agree on: Jesus was a healer.

Spitting Image

Spittle was used in healing in ancient times. People may have observed dogs licking their wounds and deduced that saliva had healing properties. The association is so ancient that we cannot recover when precisely it originated, much less what the reasoning behind it was. Although we are dealing with texts from a prescientific era, that doesn't mean that observation of the natural world and deductive inference were not part of how people sought to understand it. The main thing that distinguishes the modern approach to medicine and wellness from that of all previous eras is the effort of researchers to exclude the placebo effect through double-blind studies. In less technical terms, some people have been documented to experience improvement even when they are given a pill that contains no medicine, because their belief can have an impact. Modern medical studies give some participants the medicine being tested while others receive sugar pills, and they keep those involved ignorant of which they are receiving. If the actual substance of the drug being tested has a significant effect, that will become clear in the data. Not only before modern medicine, but alongside it even today, people rely on anecdotal evidence. When one person says an alternative medicine helped them, others will assume that they should experience the same result. Some likely will, but it may not have much if anything to do with the thing they ingested.

In Mark 8:22–26 we find a story about Jesus trying to heal a blind man and having partial success on the first attempt. It is not surprising that Matthew and Luke omit the story. On the one hand, because Jesus is not depicted as an infallible source of divine power, a historian may judge the tradition as having a basis in history. On the other hand, a skeptical reader will wonder how it would occur to a man who had never seen trees before that the blurry shapes he saw moving around resembled trees. The story of a man who had been born blind in John 9 may be inspired by this story in Mark. That man moves from an initial estimation of Jesus as a good man to worshiping him as the Son of Man. John's Gospel may take Mark's story of gradual healing of physical blindness and adapt it into a story about increasing spiritual insight. At the end of John's story (John 9:39–41), what has been largely implicit and symbolic is brought to the fore. The man with the visual impairment had spiritual insight even before his physical eyes were healed, while those who expelled him persist in their failure to perceive even though their physical eyes are healthy. The story about a step-by-step process of gaining literal sight in Mark may have inspired a story of a step-by-step process of gaining spiritual insight about Jesus in John. Today in most churches, including ones in which people are encouraged to believe in and expect miracles, it is common for sermons on miracle stories to treat them as symbolic of spiritual realities. The story of Peter walking on water and then beginning to sink (Matt 14:22–33) is typically used to encourage people to "step out in faith" in more mundane circumstances, and to keep their eyes on Jesus and not lose focus when the metaphorical "winds and waves of life" are stirred up about them. It is rare for anyone to use this text nowadays as guidance on how to get across a literal body of water.

Unwellness and Unclean Spirits

Later in the book we will have a whole chapter about things that are not mentioned in the New Testament. Here we will get ahead of ourselves slightly by mentioning a few such things. There is no mention of viruses, nor of bacteria, anywhere in the Bible. People were unaware of what caused most illnesses. Ancient people blamed the evil eye, black magic, and malevolent spirits. There were also theories about the origin of unclean spirits (which is the phrase used in the New Testament, rather than "evil spirits"). One view was that they were the spirits of the Nephilim, a race of giants whose bodies perished in the flood in Noah's time but whose spirits could not be destroyed so easily since they were the offspring of angelic fathers. Those homeless spirits wandered the earth looking for bodies they could inhabit, and of course the only ones available still had their original occupants in them, leading to much unpleasantness, to say the least. The New Testament does not mention things people then did not know about illness. Nor does it explicitly mention things that were widely assumed about spirits, exorcisms, and healing in that time. The interpreter of the New Testament must for that reason think about and investigate what isn't said. It isn't enough to just look at what is said. All communication leaves some things implicit. One of the big challenges when reading ancient texts is figuring out what was left unsaid that is crucial to understanding what the text does say.

Signs and Symbolism

In the story of the healing of the man born blind in John 9, Jesus sends him to wash in the Pool of Siloam. After the man does so, he is able to see. We are not told how he made it to the pool, and the story is not explicitly set in close proximity. The author of the gospel points out that Siloam means "sent," conveying the impression that the man had to make his way there. Yet he had to make his way there while still unable to see. The journey would have been fraught with literal and metaphorical pitfalls. Did people help him make his way? We aren't told, and if the man simply found his way there on his own, that in itself might be part of the miracle, or an indication of the man's determination as well as his trust in Jesus. Even though for the most part the miracles of Jesus are presented as literal occurrences, they have served from the outset as "signs," and deeper symbolism has been found in them. The sending motif in the healing in John 9 presumably relates to the theme of Jesus as the one whom the Father sent, which runs through the entire gospel.

So too when Jesus multiplies loaves and fish in the wilderness, readers would not have missed that he took bread, gave thanks, broke it, and gave—words familiar from the celebration of the Lord's Supper (Matt 14:19-21; 26:26; Luke 9:16; 22:19; John 6:11). There is also an allusion to the manna in the wilderness. John 6 builds on that symbolism, presenting Jesus as the bread from heaven. The Gospel of John includes the feeding of the multitude and walking on the sea as one of its few points of major overlap with the other gospels. Yet it lacks the words that connect Jesus's final meal with his disciples to the celebration of the Lord's Supper. Through his exploration of Jesus as the bread from heaven, the manna that God provided—which is connected in this synagogue sermon (John 6:59) with the word of God—the author may make up for what he omits in his account of Jesus's final meal with his closest followers. The connection between manna and the word of God had been made as far back as Deuteronomy 8:3, which says that the manna was provided to humble the Israelites and teach them that humans do not live only through bread but through the word of God. Jesus's sermon in John 6 also alludes to Isaiah 54–55 (John 6:45 quotes Isa 54:13). In close proximity, the book of Isaiah depicts God's word coming down from heaven to accomplish God's purposes (Isa 55:10–11). This background informs the depiction of Jesus in this chapter. Those who hear him take offense at his words. Who wouldn't if someone started saying people should eat his flesh and drink his blood? If you're sure that you wouldn't, you aren't really imagining yourself into the story. Even the disciples who remain with Jesus have not understood him or found his words easy to digest but remain with him nonetheless because they are convinced that Jesus is God's holy one even though they do not always understand him (John 6:68–69). Jesus himself emphasizes that the words were not offered as literal instruction to eat his flesh, saying that "the flesh counts for nothing" and that it is the Spirit that gives life (John 6:63 NIV). Don't expect that to settle the long-standing debates about this passage, though. If you've found the things Jesus says in John 6 hard to swallow, you may have to chew over some of the things discussed in this book and then give them another look, at some point when you don't have too much else on your plate.

For Further Reading

Borgen, Peder. *Bread from Heaven: An Exegetical Study of the Concept of Manna in the Gospel of John and the Writings of Philo.* Leiden: Brill, 1965.

Carroll, John T. "Sickness and Healing in the New Testament Gospels." *Interpretation* 49, no. 2 (1995): 130–42.

Porterfield, Amanda. *Healing in the History of Christianity.* New York: Oxford University Press, 2005.

Reed, Annette Yoshiko. *Demons, Angels, and Writing in Ancient Judaism.* New York: Cambridge University Press, 2020.

Stuckenbruck, Loren T. *The Myth of Rebellious Angels: Studies in Second Temple Judaism and New Testament Texts*. Tübingen: Mohr Siebeck, 2014.

Twelftree, Graham H. *Jesus the Exorcist: A Contribution to the Study of the Historical Jesus*. Tübingen: Mohr Siebeck, 1993.

Wright, Archie T. *The Origin of Evil Spirits: The Reception of Genesis 6:1–4 in Early Jewish Literature*. Tübingen: Mohr Siebeck, 2013.

N

Naked Truth

This chapter was inspired by a phrase uttered by someone in my Sunday school class: "Jesus didn't wear pants." I consider it particularly fitting to begin a chapter on an array of New Testament references to clothing with something that an ordained woman said, since readers who have strong feelings about male and female clothing distinctions may also have similar feelings about female ministers. Yet ancient clothing was not like anything that most people reading this book have ever worn. Take a look at ancient depictions of Jesus in art and mosaic. Look at depictions of people in general from his time. They all agree. *Jesus didn't wear pants.* The modern male who feels the need to be the one who "wears the pants in this family" is thus not following the example of Jesus, at least not literally. Don't miss the important implication: you can be doing the same exact thing as in New Testament times, yet it may mean something different or even the opposite today. Conversely, you can do something very different, yet the significance may be more similar than if you merely mimicked ancient people's precise actions.

Distinctions between men's and women's clothing have blurred in certain respects over the past century. Yet while it is now perfectly acceptable in most places for a woman to wear pants, a man wearing a dress remains unusual. Whether that should be the case or not is not a topic we can discuss here. The fact that it is so is nonetheless worth noting since it shows how identities and apparel remain related even today. What men and women wear has changed. That men and women do not always wear the same kinds of clothes is something that has persisted through most ages and in most cultures. It is thus something that we and the characters in the New Testament share in common, even though their clothing is mentioned infrequently.

Gird Up Your Loins

In 1 Peter 1:13, if you read the King James Version, you are told to "gird up the loins of your mind." If you read a more recent translation, it says to "ready your mind for action" or something similar. The King James is more literal in this instance, but far less helpful. Even if you know what loins are (whether thanks to your broad knowledge of English, a *Friends* episode, or the cuts of meat you are in the habit of purchasing), you are quite certain your mind doesn't have them. Girding the loins is also mentioned in Luke 12:35 and Ephesians 6:14. The expression also occurs in the Hebrew scriptures. Modern translations correctly convey the meaning, but it is worth explaining *why* the expression means what it does. Ancient men wore tunics that hung down far enough that they were prone to interfere with strenuous physical activities. To avoid this, one prepared by tying the tunic up around one's waist. Doing this turned this ancient male dress into something more akin to a pair of shorts. If my description is insufficient for you to envisage how the process might unfold (or, rather, how the tunic might fold),

Tunic: a shirt worn by women or men that might be as simple as a single piece of fabric stitched or pinned to make a cylinder with openings left for arms and head.

you should be able to find a visual tutorial online that explains how to gird up one's loins in the biblical sense.

A tunic is one of many items of clothing that has become less standard in our time. It is sometimes translated as "shirt," and it was that, but often extended downward further than modern shirts tend to, sometimes all the way to one's feet. It is mentioned quite often in the New Testament, which is unsurprising since it was one of the most common items of clothing, worn by both men and women. Jesus instructed his disciples not to wear an extra tunic (Mark 6:8-9; see also Luke 10:3 and Matt 10:10, which appear to disagree with Mark on whether sandals were allowed). The various prohibitions on bringing or wearing certain things reflect an overall emphasis that those Jesus sent out needed to rely on the hospitality they received from others. These instructions may also reflect the teaching of Jesus's mentor John the Baptist that if a person has two tunics, they should give one away (Luke 3:11). Of course, Jesus said that his followers must give up *all* their possessions (Luke 14:33), and so the instructions to not bring certain possessions may provide particularly clear evidence that this teaching was couched in hyperbole (exaggeration for effect).

You may have already realized that we have a close equivalent in English to "gird up your loins." It is not similar to the ancient expression with respect to what is done to the clothing or where on the body the action occurs. It is similar in that we recommend that someone rearrange their clothing as preparation for physical exertion. So roll up the sleeves of your mind and read on . . .

The Shirt off Your Back

Those who read Jesus's teaching in Matthew 5:40 and Luke 6:29 may prefer particular translations because they think they get them off the hook. If you don't own a tunic or cloak, surely this teaching doesn't apply to you. The only people who wear cloaks nowadays tend to be renaissance fair attendees or Jedi cosplayers. (For them, faced with Jesus's teaching about giving someone your articles of clothing, a translation that allows them to part with an ordinary coat rather than an expensive part of a custom-made costume may be more ap-

Cloak: in ancient times a rectangular piece of fabric that adorned the upper body. Worn by both men and women as an outer garment above the tunic.

pealing.) The two versions agree on the items of clothing referred to but disagree about the order. Luke's makes more logical sense: If someone takes your outer garment, give them even the shirt off your back. If someone takes your next-to-last piece of clothing, give them the last one as well.

Matthew introduces a detail that may potentially change the meaning. He does something similar in the preceding and following sayings as well, suggesting deliberate editing and adaptation to make a particular point. Matthew sets the scene as taking place in the context of being sued. That suggests the man whose item of clothing is being taken had borrowed money and not paid it back. Today we might say that his shirt is not so much being stolen as being repossessed. If they are taking his shirt or his cloak, he must not have anything else left to offer in lieu of repayment of the money he owes, or perhaps they have already taken everything else and his debt is still not paid in full. Exodus 22:26 and Deuteronomy 24:12–13 both prohibit the taking of someone's cloak as a guarantee against a loan and then keeping it overnight, since it leaves the person from whom it is taken cold. This man had not pawned his clothing for money, but he had borrowed money, and the lender, not having been repaid, is taking the man's possessions to recover his losses. This sort of occurrence was depressingly common in Jesus's time. In the realities of ancient agrarian societies, if your crop failed to produce enough one year, then you had no choice but to borrow money, plant again, and hope for a better outcome the following year. Without modern farming technology, the risk from drought, blight, or locusts was constant. If the crop failed again, you could lose your land to your moneylender and end up a tenant on your own land. Fail to pay rent thereafter and you might be sold into slavery. This was the rationale for the Jubilee Year legislated in Leviticus 25, in which, once a generation, land was returned to the families that originally owned it, debts were canceled, and slaves were set free. The Jubilee Year reset things so as to avoid persistent inequity from which those who sank into poverty could never escape. Commentators have detected echoes of the Jubilee Year in things that Jesus said.

Returning to the man whose shirt or cloak is being taken, some commentators see in the context of legal proceedings an implied inequality of socioeconomic status between the one doing the taking and the one from whom it is being taken. If the taker has more wealth than the takee (to coin a word), what is unfolding would have been considered unjust and unfair even if the latter was in the wrong from the perspective of the law. There is debate among anthropologists about whether ancient Mediterranean cultural values included the idea of limited good—that is, that there was only so much of any good thing to go around, whether arable land, wealth, or honor. In this understanding, if someone has more, it means others have less as a direct consequence. If there is one pie and you take a bigger slice, everyone else's slices will be smaller. Where a modern capitalist would see business success, some ancient people perceived unrighteous gain. Whatever one's view of this cultural model, the Jewish scriptures emphasize throughout that the accumulation of wealth at the expense of others is not merely immoral but sinful, an affront to God. If the scenario Jesus depicted involved a person with nothing but two articles of clothing having one of them taken away by someone with sufficient wealth to be a lender of money, most who heard Jesus would have sided with the man left with just the shirt on his back.

The practical question in this circumstance is this: What can the poor and oppressed do in the face of injustice? If someone takes your next-to-last piece of clothing and you offer your last one as well, that leaves you literally naked. If you offer someone who is leaving you almost naked the "opportunity" to leave you completely destitute in the nude, their sense of shame might kick in and make them reconsider. It doesn't really matter whether they are a thief taking what is yours or a lender taking what might be considered theirs because you defaulted on your payments. Your action might serve as an effective form of nonviolent protest, a third option in between taking up arms or merely accepting your fate. Matthew next turns to a scenario in which someone is struck on the cheek. Matthew's addition of the detail that it is the right cheek that is being slapped (Matt 5:39) has also been viewed as having similar significance to the case of the tunic and cloak. If you gently reenact this with a friend, ideally just pretending to hit them, it may help you grasp the point. Put the book down and see what you have to do to hit someone on the right cheek. Make sure it is someone that will still be your friend even after doing this. Once you're back, hopefully unbruised, we can continue.

Did you instinctively strike their left cheek? Matthew specifies the right cheek, and some commentators consider the detail significant. To hit the right cheek you would either need to give a backhanded slap or use your left hand. Both actions would have been disrespectful in the first-century Mediterranean world. Even today a backhanded slap is something we can imagine being administered by a superior (or someone who considers themselves superior) but would never see as a boxing move. After being struck in that manner, turning the other (i.e., the left) cheek is not merely saying "hit me some more" but asking to be hit in the way one hits an equal, with a punch or smack with the right hand. Luke also includes this saying but without specifying which cheek. His version thus sounds more like passive acceptance of violence rather than nonviolent resistance.

Continuing the comparison with Luke, Matthew alone adds a third instruction to the sequence, that pertaining to going the extra mile. Like turning the extra cheek, this saying has contributed an expression to the English language that remains in regular use, including by people who don't know that it comes from the Sermon on the Mount (Matt 5–7). Both expressions ("turn the other cheek" and "go the extra mile") were literal rather than metaphorical in their original context. A Roman soldier could compel a noncitizen to carry their equipment one Roman mile. Up until that point you were a conscripted nobody, akin to a slave. What happened if at the end of the period of forced labor you continued to offer this service, emphasizing that you were providing assistance not out of obligation but because the soldier needed help? In that moment you would go from being the soldier's victim to being their benefactor. This too could represent a form of nonviolent protest. Matthew seems to have taken some general teaching from Jesus about nonviolence and turned it into something more specific and focused.

We're not quite done with what the Sermon on the Mount says about clothing. In Matthew 6:25–34 Jesus says his followers should not worry about the following day's food or clothing. God feeds birds and clothes flowers, after all.

A Fringe View

The Gospels refer to people being healed merely by touching the hem of Jesus's garment (Matt 9:20; 14:36; Mark 6:56; Luke

8:44). Matthew 23:5 also mentions the edges of a garment and specifically the lengthening of tassels for show. Those tassels or fringes are precisely the part of Jesus's clothing that people are said to touch, or to long to touch, in the hope of experiencing healing. Although the same Greek word may refer to both the edge of any garment and more specifically to the tassels that characterized Jewish clothing, Jesus's clothing would have been like that of his contemporaries. Note that in Matthew's Gospel Jesus does not criticize the wearing of tassels but the lengthening of them, just as he criticizes not the use of phylacteries but their size and showiness. Both the tassels and the phylacteries may be unfamiliar to those who have never witnessed Jewish prayer. While only some people observe the instructions in Numbers 15:37-41 and Deuteronomy 22:12 about having tassels on clothing in general, prayer shawls consistently have them. A phylactery is the small box you can still see attached by those at prayer to their foreheads and arms, following the commandment in Deuteronomy 6:8 and 11:18 that the Israelites must tie God's commandments onto their foreheads and arms.

Phylacteries (Hebrew tefillin*) may denote amulets of any sort, but in Judaism are specifically the small containers holding a portion of scripture that are worn during prayer.*

The desire to merely touch the edge or a tassel on Jesus's cloak expresses the belief that Jesus's healing power had such potency it would permeate through every fiber of his clothing. That is what the woman suffering from hemorrhaging is said to have touched in the Gospels of Matthew and Luke, whereas Mark 5:25-34 just says she touched his clothing. Note that the story is not saying something negative about Jewish purity laws. Jesus at times criticizes some specific way of observing commandments, but that was a debate about *how* to do what the law required and not *whether* to obey the law. (For a comparison, think of Christians who agree that people should be baptized but disagree about the timing and method.) It was generally accepted that impurity was transmitted from the impure person to the pure through contact, rendering the latter impure as well. When the woman touches Jesus's clothing, however, healing power flows out of him into her. That is what would have struck an ancient reader of the story: Jesus's purity and power are strong enough not only to resist impurity but also to flow out from him and make the impure pure and the unwell well.

Matthew places the story about a woman touching Jesus's clothing alongside a saying about patching clothing. If you put unshrunk cloth onto an older piece of clothing as a patch, when the new cloth shrinks, it will damage the garment further. Jesus's statement about this and his teaching about putting new wine in old wineskins (Matt 9:16-7; Mark 2:21-22; Luke 5:36-39), building houses on sand, and lighting lamps and then placing a basket over them all depict actions that are foolish or wasteful. Luke's version makes the point most emphatically, depicting the ridiculous action of tearing new, undamaged clothing in order to make a patch for something old. He also emphasizes the superiority of old wine to new. The point is not what many in the history of Christianity have assumed, that Jesus was depicting how his superior new religion comes along and breaks free from the restricting confines of the older worn-out religion of Judaism. Jesus was not even talking about that, much less saying it would be a good thing if it happened. These are proverbs. When I teach on this topic, I point out that much of Jesus's teaching is in the same genre as the memorable sayings in the book of Proverbs. Many of my students are unfamiliar with classic proverbs in the English language such as "a stitch in time saves nine." This is because clothing nowadays is designed to be disposable. Few of my students have stitched anything. I suspect that soon the proverb "there's no use crying over spilled milk" will go the way of the dodo. (Oh, sorry, you had to look that one up too?) For most people in the English-speaking world, a tear in clothing or loss of foodstuff is merely an inconvenience. It was much more than that for Jesus's audience. In today's culture of innovation, bursting out from the seams of convention might be viewed positively, but in Jesus's time the image of damage and repair to clothing or other property would have had different connotations. The parable explicitly emphasizes that the aim is to ensure that neither the wineskin nor the wine is destroyed by putting old and new together. Perhaps the key to understanding the imagery is to connect it with Jesus's call to the nation and to individuals to become new, like little children, reborn of the Spirit, since that is the only way that the kingdom of God can come into our midst and be a source of joy rather than destruction.

While we're on the subject, don't forget Jesus's saying about the damage moths do to clothing (Matt 6:19–20; Luke 12:33).

Running Around Naked

Since ruined clothing can leave you naked, that is the natural (or should that be naturist?) topic to turn to next. There are a couple of characters within the New Testament gospels that are found in various states of undress. Perhaps the most famous is the man wearing only a linen sheet who was following Jesus, and who managed to elude capture by leaving his sheet behind (Mark 14:51–52). The word used here for the linen sheet is the same one that occurs in the passion narratives in reference to the linen sheet used as a burial shroud. While the gospel authors may have seen symbolism in this, we should not make too much of it. Wearing this sort of thing was not uncommon in summer. Indeed, the term *sindōn* is ambiguous, simply meaning linen and not how it was worn nor what it was used for. The big question is why the story of the man who ends up fleeing naked is included. Some have suggested it is an autobiographical anecdote from the author. While not impossible, that is at best a guess. On the literary level it serves as a counterpart to the story of the women fleeing in fear from the tomb in Mark 16. If their initial response to the empty tomb is fear, at least they stick by Jesus during the crucifixion. The male disciples, in contrast, flee in fear even earlier and don't even make it to the cross and the tomb. One of them was in such haste to save his own life and abandon Jesus to his fate that he left his wrap behind.

Next we turn to someone who was surprisingly naked and then gets even more surprisingly clothed. In John 21 Peter is fishing and is said to be "naked" (21:7). It seems unlikely that he was *completely* naked (pics or it didn't happen), but at the very least he had taken off most of his clothing. If you've visited the Sea of Galilee, you'll know that it can get quite warm there. If you were wearing multiple layers, you too may have removed some article of clothing. What you've probably never done, however, is spot someone you recognize on the shore and, before jumping in the water and swimming toward them, put your shirt or jacket back on first. Why does Peter do this?

My favorite answer (shared with me in my Sunday school class but apparently originating in an online discussion forum) is that Peter was an "exuberant goober." While I can think of additional symbolic significance to clothing in the story that might make for an interesting sermon, the main point is perhaps simply that Peter was so eager to get to Jesus that he wasn't thinking straight. Peter throws his clothes on and throws himself in the water. Whatever the opposite of skinny dipping is, that's what Peter does. If it seems undignified, unbecoming of the one who is arguably preeminent among Jesus's twelve apostles, that seems to be the point. Peter doesn't even take time to think properly before jumping (literally!) into action. Similarly, in the transfiguration story we are told that Peter didn't know what he was saying (Mark 9:6). While seeing someone that you know is dead ought to instill at least as much fear as the transfiguration, Peter is clear on what he should do—make a beeline (or a fish line?) for Jesus. Even if he wasn't sure how to dress for the occasion.

Notice as well that in John 21:18 Jesus says to Peter that in the future he will no longer clothe himself. This is taken as an indication of how Peter will die. Peter decided to clothe himself in order to rush to be with Jesus. It was a strange decision, but if Peter is truly committed to following Jesus, a future fate awaits him in which his clothing and movements will no longer be under his control.

Camel Cloth

Let's end the chapter by returning briefly to John the Baptist's clothing. He is often depicted in movies as though he dressed like a stereotypical caveman. Camel hair has gone out of fashion and so is unfamiliar to many people, but you can still get a camel hair suit even today if you shop around. It won't look like caveman attire—and unless you buy it from a costume shop, it won't have humps and four legs. Camel hair produces material that is less flexible and rougher than most other fabrics. John wore clothing made from this material, not (as some cinematic portrayals of him might lead you to believe) the skin of a camel that he ripped from it with his bare hands and casually threw over himself.

The reason we are told what John wore is the similarity to the clothing of Elijah mentioned in 2 Kings 1:8. If you read the King James Version and versions dependent on it, you'll read instead that Elijah was a "hairy man." Other versions say he wore a garment of hair. The Hebrew has been understood both ways. The phrasing of Mark 1:6's description of John the Baptist's clothes is very close to the Septuagint's rendering of 2 Kings 1:8, especially what it says about his leather girdle. It is thus clear, despite the ambiguity in the description of Elijah, that Mark thought John had styled himself after that famous prophet. We also find people discussing whether John is Elijah at various points in the New Testament. It is hard to say whether John thought he in some sense embodied the spirit of Elijah, much as Elisha had done, or simply thought of himself playing a comparable role to Elijah's. He definitely mirrored Elijah in his speaking out against the ruler.

They say that clothes make the man. The New Testament emphasizes that this should not be the case for those who follow Jesus. In Matthew 11:8 Jesus explicitly contrasts John with people who have fine clothes. James 2:3-4 emphasizes that favoritism should not be shown to those in expensive apparel. Yet it is important to get John's clothing right in our minds despite the influence of misleading on-screen depictions. If we envisage John as a wild man eating bugs and shouting in the desert where few people would hear him, we will find it impossible to explain why political and religious leaders paid so much attention to him, and how he could have disciples as far afield as Ephesus (Acts 19:3). Clothing definitely makes an impression on people, even those whose values challenge them to look beyond externals to the heart. The visual depictions we encounter of people mentioned in the New Testament also make an impression on us and may influence our understanding of them and their stories.

For Further Reading

Asikainen, Susanna. *Jesus and Other Men: Ideal Masculinities in the Synoptic Gospels.* Leiden: Brill, 2018.
Jeal, Roy R. "Clothes Make the (Wo)Man." Page 393-414 in *Foun-*

dations for Sociorhetorical Exploration: A Rhetoric of Re-
ligious Antiquity Reader*. Edited by Vernon K. Robbins,
Robert H. von Thaden Jr., and Bart B. Bruehler. Atlanta:
SBL Press, 2016.

Kennedy, John G. "'Peasant Society and the Image of Limited
Good': A Critique." *American Anthropologist* 68, no. 5 (1966):
1212–25.

Malina, Bruce J. *The New Testament World: Insights from Cultural
Anthropology*. Louisville: Westminster John Knox, 2001.

Moss, Candida R. "The Man with the Flow of Power: Porous Bodies in Mark 5:25–34." *Journal of Biblical Literature* 129, no. 3
(2010): 507–19.

Oakman, Douglas E. "The Biblical World of Limited Good in Cultural, Social, and Technological Perspective: In Memory
of Bruce J. Malina—Pioneer, Patron, and Friend." *Biblical
Theology Bulletin* 48, no. 2 (2018): 97–105.

Reid, Barbara E. "Violent Endings in Matthew's Parables and
Christian Nonviolence." *The Catholic Biblical Quarterly* 66,
no. 2 (2004): 237–55.

Taylor, Joan. *The Immerser: John the Baptist within Second Temple
Judaism*. Grand Rapids: Eerdmans, 1997.

Thiessen, Matthew. *Jesus and the Forces of Death: The Gospels'
Portrayal of Ritual Impurity within First-Century Judaism*.
Grand Rapids: Baker Academic, 2020.

Wink, Walter. *Jesus and Nonviolence: A Third Way*. Minneapolis:
Fortress, 2003.

O

Only One God

Jesus is probably the only person in history about whom one could say that he was the greatest human being to ever live, inspired like none other before or since, esteemed by God and exalted to become God's literal and metaphorical right-hand man, second only to God himself, and yet still be accused of having sold him short, of engaging in blasphemous heresy. How can such superlatives be considered not only inadequate but insulting? The short answer is that the Christian view of Jesus as God incarnate that developed over the centuries has led many Christians to have little or no room for his humanity. Where traditional categories like rabbi, prophet, and anointed one were felt by Jesus's early followers to together do justice to what he meant to them and all they perceived him to be, many Christians today would not utter any title or descriptor without an explicit or implicit "more than a" in front of it. The earliest Christian sources, on the other hand, are not at all ambiguous about Jesus as a full-fledged human being. Was there more to be said than that? Certainly. But what that something more was, and how to best articulate it, was not something that the New Testament authors all agreed on, and most New Testament scholars will say that there is significant development detectable across the New Testament writings as well as in subsequent centuries.

The Early High Christology Club

Do scholars have clubs? We're more likely to belong to things called professional organizations. But in recent years a group or movement emerged that came to be nicknamed the "early high Christology club." Whether or not "club" is an appropriate label, all the other words in that moniker need to be explained and unpacked. First, Christology. Let's start by noting that the word is pronounced with a short i sound, reflecting the sound of the Greek word *Christos*, from which we derive our English word "Christ" with its long *I* sound. Nothing gives away a newcomer to the field like pronouncing it as the English word "Christ" with "-ology" stuck on the end. Enough about pronunciation—what does the word mean? There are enough academic fields with "-ology" at the end that you likely already know it denotes "the study of" whatever goes before it. That makes figuring out the meaning of "Christology" seem straightforward. But what exactly does it mean to be engaged in "the study of Christ"? The field of Christology is focused on how people view and understand who Jesus is, his nature and role. In systematic theology the aim is to articulate what the theologian believes, and what they consider to constitute appropriate belief and the right language to express it. New Testament Christology is focused on understanding how the various New Testament authors viewed Jesus. This has often focused on their choice of titles and placement of them on the lips of characters. "Son of God" in the Gospel of Mark is a good example. Human characters debate who Jesus is throughout the Gospel of Mark, but no human being offers the identification that God offers at Jesus's baptism and transfiguration—no one, that is, until the centurion at the cross utters the famous line "Surely this man was the Son of God!" (Mark 15:39 NIV).

But what does it mean to call someone the Son of God? There were no capital letters in ancient Greek or Aramaic, and so the English distinction between "son of God" and "Son of God" (or "son of man" and "Son of Man") simply did not exist. There was no indefinite article in Greek or Aramaic, and so "son of God" and "son of a god" were expressed using the same words. This left quite a bit of room for ambiguity, although knowing something about who was using the phrase narrowed the range of possible meanings. Among those who could be referred to as "son/sons of God" were righteous humans in general (see Wisdom of Solomon 2:12–18, a passage echoed in Matt 27:43), the king (implicit in John 1:49, 11:27, and 20:31, where it is at least related to and perhaps identical to being the anointed one), the nation of Israel as a whole (Hos 11:1–2, quoted in Matt 2:15), angels (perhaps the meaning in Ps 82:6, which is quoted in John 10:34), and, within the wider Greco-Roman world, literal offspring of the gods through intercourse. Titles and descriptors are important, but they do not help us understand a text unless we can determine what the label or phrase meant in that time and place. Having determined that, we can explore whether a particular author used the phrase in the same way as their contemporaries. As a rule, if a word or phrase consistently had a meaning in a given language during a given time, that is what it ought to be understood to mean when we encounter it *unless* an author indicates otherwise. Could you imagine if you used an everyday word but gave it your own meaning and never told anyone you were doing so? Even if readers are uncertain what precise connotations "son of God" had in certain contexts in the Gospels, they can be quite certain that Jewish characters who utter the phrase did not mean "offspring of Zeus and Hera" and that likewise none of them meant "God the Son" in the sense that title would come to have in later doctrine. Even in the Gospel of John, which (unlike the other New Testament gospels) views Jesus as the Word-become-flesh and the Son of Man who came down from heaven, the Father is still "the only true God" while Jesus is the one whom the one God has sent (John 17:3). The earliest Christians, being Jewish, were monotheists in the sense that the rest of their Jewish contemporaries were. They proclaimed that Jesus was the Messiah, the anointed one descended from David. They didn't proclaim a radical redefinition of the nature of God. On the contrary, Jesus is depicted as reciting the Shema (Deut 6:4), Israel's statement of faith in one God alone, in Mark 12:29. Paul too emphasizes that there is one God (Rom 3:30; 1 Cor 8:6; Gal 3:20; 1 Thess 1:9; see also Eph 4:6; 1 Tim 2:5).

Paul is rather unambiguous in saying two things. One is that Jesus has been exalted by God to the highest place, second only to the one God. The one God places all things under Jesus's feet, and ultimately once all is subject to Jesus, he in turn hands all things over to God so that God may be all in all (see Phil 2:6-11; 1 Cor 15:20-28). Students will regularly encounter scholars who refer to this as "low Christology," which seems very strange indeed. It may not be the Christology of the later Nicene Creed, but it is scarcely "low" when Paul says that God *hyper*-exalted or *super*-exalted Jesus and gave him the name above every name, which presumably means the divine name. You will sometimes encounter terms like "adoptionism" (the idea that Jesus was a human being whom God "adopted" as his Son) and "divine identity" (Jesus shares in God's identity). Neither of these terms in itself brings clarity to who Jesus was and how he was understood. One may bear a name as a result of adoption into a family or by being born into it and always having been a member.

The divine name Yahweh (rarely if ever pronounced in Jesus's time out of reverence) was central to the unique identity of Israel's God, and yet that didn't mean the name could not be shared. The angel Yahoel, who features in the text known as Apocalypse of Abraham, likely dating from the first century AD, is said to bear the divine name. In Samaritan literature Moses is said to be clothed with the divine name. In both instances these figures are not confused with the one God but instead are authorized to function as God's agents. Today if someone has an agent, we assume they are an actor, musician, or author. When New Testament scholars discuss agents and agency, it has nothing to do with these particular lines of work, even if it is not entirely unrelated. An agency or an agent is someone that represents the other person, serving as a go-between. If today many authors and celebrities utilize agents, they were more widely used in the ancient world when there were no fax machines, no email, not even a postal service in the modern sense. The only way to get one's will done in a far-off place was to authorize some-one else to act on your behalf. The one sent as emissary or ambassador had authority to represent the one who sent them, and any disrespect shown to them was considered an insult addressed to their sender. Jesus did what God alone normally did as God's authorized agent and representative. Texts like Matthew 10:40 and John 13:20 emphasize this: Jesus sent the apostles to represent him, just as God the Father sent Jesus to represent him. So, just to be clear, when scholars talk about God's agents, they don't mean people employed to make bookings for God to perform at clubs on weekends. They mean angels, prophets, and anyone else appointed to represent God in the human sphere.

We thus have something that deserves to be considered a "high Christology" from the very beginning, our earliest New Testament writings, if what we mean is affirmation not of later creedal statements regarding the divine nature but of Jesus as the supreme emissary of God who has authority to speak and act on God's behalf. And as exalted as the status of Jesus is in our earliest Christian writings, there clearly was development over the course of the New Testament period, and the development continued thereafter as well. At no point within the New Testament are all the elements of later Christian orthodoxy laid out in every detail. In the letter of Paul to the Philippians (in a passage that might even be Paul quoting an earlier hymn or poem), Jesus has the divine name bestowed on him when, after being obedient even to death on a cross, God exalts him to have authority over all things other than God himself (Phil 2:6-11). By the time we reach the Gospel of John, written after Paul's letters, it sounds as though the name had been given even before creation to the one whom God would later send into the world (John 17:6, 12, 24). In both, the name is given by God to one who is authorized to serve as God's supreme agent and bear unique authority as God's viceroy, God's "second in command."

Scholars sometimes work in contexts that require adherence to a statement of faith or simply have lots of people with strong feelings about matters of doctrine. As a result, they may couch their statements in wording that doesn't deny their historical conclusions yet avoids unnecessarily upsetting the faithful. (I don't particularly want to upset the faithful, being one of the faithful myself.) You will thus encounter language that seeks to avoid suggesting that the New Testament is in any way different from, much less in tension with, what later Christians came to believe. But there are differences between the New Testament and the later creeds, and it isn't clear why this is controversial in some circles. Human thinking about God has always developed as languages and cultures have changed. The impact of Jesus may have been viewed even more clearly with the benefit of hindsight than it was in the moment. The question of what Christians today ought to believe cannot (for Protestants in particular) be separated from what the New Testament authors wrote, but it isn't exactly the same thing either. The question for theologians is what to do with the material in the New Testament to articulate a Christology for us, to express the faith of people today. The aim of a New Testament scholar is to reconstruct as accurately as possible what the earliest Christians thought. The inevitable tension between those two tasks has led to controversies, but it doesn't necessarily have to, as long as we understand that the theologian's task is to apply and rearticulate for today, and the historian and biblical scholar's task is to contextualize the scriptural material in its original ancient context. Although how we bridge the gap between the two remains a topic of some debate, understanding the difference between the two endeavors should hopefully lessen the likelihood of unnecessary controversy.

So when you encounter language that articulates what an early Christian author believed, read what is being said carefully. The scholar who is writing is undoubtedly trying to describe what they understand these texts to mean as precisely as possible. The assumptions that you bring to the topic may lead you to think they are saying something other than they are. When they say that Jesus speaks and acts with the authority of the one God, they are likely neither affirming nor denying anything about what we might call the "nature" of Jesus. When some say that Paul "redefined monotheism" or "split the Shema" (the Jewish statement of allegiance to one God alone found in Deut 6:4), in most cases they don't mean that Paul had already formulated the doctrine of the Trinity in the form that the later church would produce after much debate. They are more likely to be saying that, for Paul and other early Christians, the very identity of the one God and of the people of God revolved in a central way not only around God but around God and Christ, so that the two came to be inseparably associated for them. "For us," Paul says in 1 Corinthians 8:6, "there is one God, the Father, from whom are all things . . . , and one Lord Jesus Christ, through whom are all things." That is the language of agency, and how it related to what was going on in the fabric of Jesus's being is not spelled out. The few statements that Paul makes simply cannot provide a basis for saying precisely how "in Christ God was reconciling the world to himself" (2 Cor 5:19). He affirms that God was working in and through Jesus. The whole reason that the debates about the nature of God and of Christ unfolded as they did over many decades and centuries is that the earliest Christian authors did not explicitly answer the questions that arose for their readers in later times and different contexts. When New Testament scholars describe what early Christians believed, it may seem like we are sidestepping questions about divine nature and Jesus's personhood. If we are, it isn't just to avoid getting entangled in controversy (as good as it may be to do that whenever possible). We're trying to be precise, to not claim that we can know that Paul, or Mark, or John assumed or meant something they didn't in fact say.

If you are looking for answers to questions about how best to think about God and Jesus in your own context, you'll want to consult not only New Testament scholarship but also the work of theologians.

For Further Reading

Bauckham, Richard. *Jesus and the God of Israel: God Crucified and Other Studies on the New Testament's Christology of Divine Identity.* Grand Rapids: Eerdmans, 2008.

Brown, Raymond Edward. *An Introduction to New Testament Christology.* Mahwah, NJ: Paulist Press, 1994.

Dunn, James D. G. *Christology in the Making: A New Testament Inquiry into the Origins of the Doctrine of the Incarnation.* Grand Rapids: Eerdmans, 1996.

Ehrman, Bart D. *How Jesus Became God.* New York: HarperOne, 2015.

Hurtado, Larry W. *Lord Jesus Christ: Devotion to Jesus in Earliest Christianity.* Grand Rapids: Eerdmans, 2005.

———. *One God, One Lord: Early Christian Devotion and Ancient Jewish Monotheism*. London: Bloomsbury, 2015.

Kirk, J. R. Daniel. *A Man Attested by God: The Human Jesus of the Synoptic Gospels*. Grand Rapids: Eerdmans, 2016.

McGrath, James F. *The Only True God: New Testament Monotheism in Its Jewish Context*. Urbana: University of Illinois Press, 2009.

Schüssler Fiorenza, Elisabeth. *Jesus and the Politics of Interpretation*. London: Bloomsbury Academic, 2001.

P

Plagiarism in the Gospels?

I mentioned earlier in this book that Matthew might have received a failing grade if his gospel had been submitted as an assignment for a class at a modern university or seminary. There are no footnotes in the original Greek manuscripts. (There probably are footnotes in your modern printed or online Bible, and you should read them, but be aware that they are not present in our ancient Greek manuscripts. Indeed, they are often added by translators to tell you about things that *are* in different Greek manuscripts.) Would Matthew be judged to have plagiarized from Mark by today's standards? If he were accused today, perhaps he would shift the blame: "I didn't copy from him—he copied from me!" How do we determine who copied from whom? Those same skills that lead educators to deduce the answer to that question also apply to the Gospels. Those of us who teach and research on the Gospels are often more adept at catching plagiarizers than others. (You've been warned.)

Extensive verbatim agreement is one clue that a written source is being used. Now, you may think that memory or being eyewitnesses to the same events may be an adequate explanation. However, studies of the psychology of memory show that without a written text from which to read the same words repeatedly, there is no way to fix exact wording in the mind. Indeed, without a written text the whole notion of "the exact words" disappears or at least changes its meaning. Even when scribes worked with a source, they didn't always have it open in front of them, so memory may have played a role even in a case of direct literary dependence. This is one reason why the "Synoptic problem" remains a problem with no solution that is universally agreed on. The evidence is not clear-cut, and that is unsurprising, since authors who use sources do not always use them in a consistent manner. They will often draw on information in their own minds. They may read a source and then write without having it open in front of them one day, while copying parts of it directly the next. In seeking an overall solution to the Synoptic problem, we seek answers to general questions like "Which gospel came first?" and "Which gospel author used which other gospel(s) when writing their own?" Yet in the case of each specific pericope, the answer may be different from the answer that is generally the case. We will explore here some of the evidence about the direction of borrowing and influence that indicates the overall relationship and order between the Gospels of Matthew, Mark, and Luke.

The **Synoptic problem** is the puzzle of how the Gospels of Matthew, Mark, and Luke relate to one another, including which of their authors knew one or more of the other gospels and used it when composing their own.

A **pericope** is a small excerpt from a larger text. Your professor will be impressed if you use this word, provided you catch it when your spellchecker changes it to "periscope."

It can sometimes be difficult to know whether the direction of borrowing is from the shorter version to the longer or vice versa. Sometimes people use a source and leave things out in the process. At other times someone may use a source and expand on it. We cannot always tell, but often there are important clues that make one seem much more likely than the other. For instance, compare Mark 13:14 with Matthew 24:15–16:

> But when you see the desolating sacrilege set up where it ought not to be (let the reader understand), then those in Judea must flee to the mountains. (Mark 13:14)

> So when you see the desolating sacrilege, spoken of by the prophet Daniel, standing in the holy place (let the reader understand), then those in Judea must flee to the mountains. (Matt 24:15–16)

The English of the New Revised Standard Version Updated Edition accurately conveys that the words of the parenthetical remark and what immediately follows it are identical in Mark and Matthew. There were no parentheses in ancient Greek, and anyway one cannot hear a parenthesis when someone is speaking. The translators nevertheless are surely right that parentheses are needed here. The phrase "let the reader understand" is the gospel author addressing the reader of his text, rather than Jesus addressing his hearers. When Jesus wanted to say something similar verbally, he said, "Whoever has ears, let them hear"—or, in more colloquial English, "If ya got ears, use 'em." The ones addressed are not the hearers of Jesus but the readers of the gospels. Yet readers of *both* gospels are addressed here in precisely the same way, using the very same words. There is a natural explanation, and only one explanation fits the evidence: one of these authors borrowed material from the other. But who borrowed from whom? The fact that the parenthetical remark asks the reader to understand is an important clue. Mark merely says the desolating sacrilege is standing where it should not be. Matthew says that it is standing in the holy place and is mentioned in the book of Daniel. Is it more likely that Mark kept "let the reader understand" but removed things that help the reader understand, or that Matthew added additional information to help the reader understand?

This one instance might seem inconclusive on its own, but it is not on its own. As another example, compare Mark 8:27–30 with Matthew 16:13-20. Is it likely that Mark used Matthew and decided to omit the words praising Peter for recognizing Jesus as the anointed one? It isn't impossible, but it certainly seems more likely that a Christian author would add words praising the confession of Jesus as Christ than that a Christian author would deliberately leave out something like this that was in his source. This book cannot discuss all the relevant evidence, but if you take time to read the Gospels and books about them, you will find that Matthew has a penchant for adding explanatory material. He spoils the riddle "If salt has lost its saltiness, how can you season it?" (Mark 9:50 and Matt 5:13). In the famous prayer that Jesus taught his disciples, he explains that God's kingdom coming means God's will being done on earth as in heaven, and that not being led into temptation means being delivered from evil (Luke 11:1-4 and Matt 6:9-13). The list of similar examples could go on.

Another of the things that gives away the use of sources in many student assignments is an abrupt change of style or point of view. We sometimes see this in the Gospels and other biblical literature. In both Mark's and Matthew's accounts of Herod's beheading of John the Baptist, Herod is saddened by the request for the head of John the Baptist on a platter. Yet in Mark Herod sought to protect John, while in Matthew he was looking for an excuse to kill him. Why, then, would he be sad in Matthew's telling of the story? He shouldn't be, and the logical explanation is that Matthew used Mark's

Gospel as a source, and although he made changes to it, he didn't always consistently remember to make changes. This is sometimes called "editorial fatigue." The editor relies lazily on their source to the point of including a detail from it that contradicts or at least sits awkwardly with the story they are telling. Here too it is not just one example like this one but the preponderance of evidence that convinces scholars that Matthew used Mark rather than vice versa. This is an important conclusion for historians, since it indicates which of the gospels is closer to the events that it describes.

This does not mean, however, that Mark's Gospel *always* includes the earliest form of a saying of Jesus or a story about him. We can readily imagine Mark doing something creative with the stories he knew, and later Matthew reads Mark's account and thinks, "That's not the way I've always heard the story," and decides to rely on his own information and memory there. Matthew's Gospel might in such instances reflect or preserve an earlier version of the saying or story than Mark does. Consider the case of Matthew 15:17–18 and Mark 7:18–19. It would be easy to assume, in light of our discussion above, that Matthew wrote first and Mark added the parenthetical statement that Jesus, in saying what he did about defilement, "declared all foods clean." Matthew, however, may have recognized and disagreed with Mark's parenthetical statement and dropped it.

When it comes to Luke, we find the same kind of agreements with Mark that we find in Matthew. Usually when either Matthew or Luke departs from Mark's order, the other does not follow. This leads many scholars to conclude that Matthew and Luke each relied on Mark independently of the other. In a handful of places, however, Matthew and Luke both change Mark in the same way or make the same addition to Mark, which might indicate that Luke used both Mark and Matthew or Matthew used both Mark and Luke.

You can see why this is called the Synoptic *problem*. Just when the clues seem to clearly be pointing in one direction, an exception appears. That is why we said earlier that scholars are trying to puzzle out the overall pattern and relationship among the gospels, and yet in each instance it is possible that the situation might be different. If Matthew used Mark, it doesn't mean that he had no other source that overlapped with yet differed from Mark. Nor does it mean that Matthew knew a particular story or saying of Jesus *only* from Mark.

There are also agreements of Luke with Matthew on material that is not in Mark. Sometimes they are quite extensive. Luke 6:20-49 includes a lot of material that is in Matthew 5-7 in the same order. Luke also includes some other material that is in Matthew 5-7 elsewhere in his gospel. These two passages are sometimes called the "Sermon on the Plain" and the "Sermon on the Mount." Mark doesn't include this material. Is it more likely that Luke took Matthew's neatly organized blocks of discourse and scattered parts of them throughout his gospel, or that Matthew gathered the material into blocks of discourse? The latter seems more likely, but there is a third option: both may have used a common source rather than either Luke or Matthew

*The letter **Q** is used as an abbreviation for a hypothetical source that many scholars think Matthew and Luke used. It is thought to have been a collection of Jesus's sayings with little or no narrative.*

having borrowed from the other directly. This is referred to as the "Q hypothesis" because of a tradition of referring to this hypothetical source Matthew and Luke shared in common as "Q." One reason that many (but by no means all) scholars posit the existence of such a source is that the earliest version of a saying or story sometimes seems more likely to be that in Luke while at other times it seems more likely to be that in Matthew. If we look at the Beatitudes in Matthew 5 and Luke 6, did Matthew change it from second to third person (from "Blessed are you who . . ." to "Blessed are those who . . .") and add phrases like "in spirit" and "for righteousness," yet drop the woes entirely? And what are we to make of the infancy stories and the genealogies in the opening chapters of Matthew and Luke? Neither seems like an obvious direct reworking of the other.

There are always scholars who propose something different from what the majority in a field conclude. That is the essence of what academics do when not teaching: we engage in research, and one form of research is to try to find new interpretations and new explanations of the things we find in the New Testament. In the case of the Synoptic problem, however, there is significant disagreement. The two main views are the following:

- Two-source hypothesis: Independently of each other, Matthew and Luke both used Mark and Q.
- Farrar hypothesis: Mark wrote first, Matthew used Mark, Luke used Mark and Matthew.

There are other views too, including that Mark created a briefer gospel based on Matthew and Luke, or that Matthew used Mark and Luke, not to mention proposals that include still other hypothetical sources or propose that some of the known gospels circulated in significantly different editions.

Knowing which authors used which sources is important for both literary and historical approaches to the Gospels. From a literary perspective, it makes a difference to our perception of the meaning of a text if we think it is omitting things from a story, or if we think a different text is adding things to the story. From a historical perspective, knowing which source takes us closest to the events allows us to trace the ripples of Jesus and his first followers back toward their source. But there is another reason I consider this topic important. I mention plagiarism and the use of sources more than once in this book. It is because I expect some readers to be students who might be tempted to make the poor choice not to cite sources they use. Following ancient norms of writing and citation in the present day simply won't cut it, so the procedures followed by the gospel authors is not one that you should follow. Remember, ancient Greek writers composed their works with no spaces between words and no punctuation. Modern English is different from ancient Greek in the very manner in which it is written. Writing and research are different now too. So when you write, whomever you may be writing for, give credit where credit is due. No one should be disappointed that an author had to read and look things up. That's what we're expected to do when researching a book. Citing sources doesn't demonstrate ignorance or a lack of originality. It shows diligence and seriousness in research. If you read academic books not aimed at a general audience, they will be full of footnotes. The only way to see further than others who came before us is by standing on their shoulders.

By the way, if you think popular and introductory books should have more footnotes since it helps make this point, you should write to publishers and tell them that. This one doesn't—but it easily could have if I believed my intended readers would want them.

For Further Reading

Dunn, James D. G. *The Oral Gospel Tradition*. Grand Rapids: Eerdmans, 2013.

Goodacre, Mark. *The Synoptic Problem: A Way Through the Maze*. London: Continuum, 2001. Available for free online: https://markgoodacre.org/maze/

North, Wendy E. S. *What John Knew and What John Wrote: A Study in John and the Synoptics*. Lanham, MD: Lexington Books/ Fortress Academic, 2020.

Richards, E. Randolph. "Was Matthew a Plagiarist? Plagiarism in Greco-Roman Antiquity." Pages 108–33 in *Christian Origins and the Establishment of the Early Jesus Movement*. Edited by Stanley E. Porter and Andrew W. Pitts. Leiden: Brill, 2018.

Rollens, Sarah E. "Did the Authors of the Canonical Gospels Know Each Other?" Bible Odyssey, https://www.bibleo dyssey.org/en/tools/bible-basics/did-the-authors-of-the -canonical-gospels-know-each-other.

Stein, Robert H. *Studying the Synoptic Gospels: Origin and Interpretation*. Grand Rapids: Baker, 2001.

Q

Quotation Marks Required

Our earliest Greek manuscripts lack punctuation marks. There were no periods, commas, or apostrophes. People had yet to invent things like quotation marks and parentheses. Indeed, capitalization of names and the beginnings of sentences was also a development that lay in the future. Even putting spaces or other separators between words was not the universal practice. People had previously begun to use dots to separate words, but in the era of the New Testament the general scribal practice was to write continuously without spaces. When writing materials were expensive, this would certainly have cut costs. If you have ever added extra spaces to an assignment to reach the minimum number of pages a professor has specified, you already know how much the amount of space between words can impact the length of a document. (What, you thought we didn't know about that trick?)

Understanding these details about New Testament texts is of practical relevance for a number of reasons, not least of which is that just because the early Christians wrote a certain way doesn't mean you should do the same. Use a space (and only one) where our modern practice requires it. Use periods, commas, and even semicolons and learn to use them appropriately. And of particular importance, use quotation marks. Putting an apostrophe where it does not belong (e.g., when making a noun plural) may cost you points or merely make a bad impression. Failing to use quotation marks, on the other hand, may lead to failure or even a lawsuit. Professors are writers, among other things. We work hard on this aspect of our professional activity. We are thus particularly sensitive to the stealing of words and ideas. We expect students we teach and others who quote us to give credit to the sources they use. Even when paraphrasing (which doesn't mean merely changing a few words) there still needs to be a footnote or other reference indicating where the information comes from. And today when we quote someone's exact words, we are expected to put them in quotation marks.

Systems for citing sources did not exist yet in the era in which the New Testament texts were written. That is why scholars cannot offer an answer with absolute certainty about which of the New Testament gospels was used by the authors of the others. As we saw in a previous chapter, Mark, Matthew, and Luke overlap substantially, and none of them has footnotes indicating their sources. That's another thing that hadn't been invented yet. This is why students of the New Testament learn about the academic tools labeled "source criticism" and "redaction criticism." Source criticism focuses on identifying and, when possible, reconstructing sources behind a text. Redaction criticism is related but focuses on how the author of a work has edited their sources: changing wording, rearranging order, omitting or adding material, and so on. In some cases it seems clear that a source was used and that we know what that source is. The clearest example is Matthew and Luke both appearing to have used Mark, reproducing

Redaction means editing. Redaction criticism is thus the careful study of how New Testament authors made edits to the sources they used.

much of its content in the same order. There is much more debate about whether John knew any of the other gospels in written form. When it comes to the overlaps of Matthew and Luke in material not in Mark, as we explored previously, some scholars believe that Luke used Matthew, a much smaller number believe Matthew used Luke, and many conclude that Luke and Matthew each independently used a source we no longer have, nicknamed Q. Many scholars have detected behind the Gospel of John a source referred to as the "Signs Source" or "Signs Gospel" because of its use of the term "sign" for Jesus's miracles and its numbering of them. Obviously the existence of such a source, and what the author of John did with it, is much more hypothetical than what Matthew did with Mark, a case where we have both texts and can compare them to one another.

Asking these kinds of questions about the gospels is important for many reasons, both historical and literary. With respect to history, knowing which of our gospels was earliest tells us which brings us closest in time to the events that these texts purport to describe. If Matthew and Luke used Q and that hypothetical source was written several decades earlier than either of the gospels that drew on it, the material in Q was written down that much sooner after Jesus said and did the things attributed to him. The closer we get to the time of events, the more confidence historians can in principle have in the accuracy of what was recorded. Even though human memory and storytelling are equally capable of preserving information and distorting it from the very beginning, all other things being equal, it is more likely that someone will remember what they experienced or were told soon afterward than they will much later. As for the literary importance of these approaches, you will often find redaction-critical approaches contrasted with literary ones. Redaction criticism and historical criticism seek to get behind a text to understand processes that led to its production. Literary criticism as a rule focuses on the finished product and treats it as literature, setting aside questions about what events if any lie behind the narrative and how accurately they are recorded. Yet, at the intersection of the two, redaction criticism can help us recognize the emphases of a work as literature. We understand Matthew's perspective better when we know that the author chose to omit the parenthetical remark in Mark that Jesus declared all foods clean (Mark 7:19; Matt 15:17) than we would have if we did not have Mark's Gospel and were unaware of Matthew's editorial activity.

Red Letter Edition

The absence of quotation marks from the Greek texts that make up the New Testament means we have no straightforward way of telling the difference between these two sentences:

- Jesus said X
- Jesus said "X"

For us, the former may be a paraphrase of what Jesus said, while in the latter case we are given to understand that he literally said "X." This is a challenge for historians but perhaps even more so for those who create red letter editions of the New Testament, which print the words of Jesus in red. When are we dealing with something like an exact quote (even if in translation), when are we dealing with a paraphrase, and where do the words of Jesus end and those of the narrator or gospel author begin? This problem is particularly acute in John 3. You would think that one of the most famous verses in the New Testament (John 3:16) ought to be a clear-cut case. Yet if you watch movie versions based on the Gospel of John, you will find that when they reach chapter 3, some switch from Jesus speaking to the narrator at around the same point that many modern translations end the quotation marks, whereas others have Jesus continue speaking all the way through 3:21. If you read the footnotes of a translation like the New International Version, you will see that it mentions more than one option for where to end the quotation. If it were up to you, which words would you put in quotation marks—or, if you prefer, which words should be printed in red?

I really would like readers to try this activity. Imagine you are working on a Bible translation and have been given the task of evaluating a proposal for where to place quotation marks in John 3. How would you evaluate the choice made by the translators of the Bible version you usually use, being aware that other English translations make different choices? As you think about it, keep in mind that there is a uniformity of style between how the narrator, Jesus, and John the Baptist speak in this chapter. The question about where to put quotation marks applies to the whole chapter, including toward the end. It gets complicated because the same kind of language about Father and Son, above and below, belief, and eternal life is found throughout no matter who is speaking: Jesus, John the Baptist, or the narrator. Further complicating matters, similar style and vocabulary is found in the Johannine Epistles as well. The natural conclusion to draw is that everything is couched in the author's own distinctive style. If he had written today, he would not only have had the option of beginning and ending quotation marks to make clear who is speaking. He would have had the option of not using them, thereby indicating that we are hearing his paraphrase. Since they did not exist in his time, the author's not using them offers us no clues. If you think of *all* the dialogue in the Gospel of John as paraphrase, it may help you make sense of the way that Jesus, John, and the narrator all speak in the same distinctive style. The fact that English Bibles need to place some words in quotation marks creates something of an impossible challenge for translators. When your own language makes distinctions that ancient Greek did not, what is the appropriate thing to do?

We should not move on from this topic and our discussion of red letter editions without mentioning the Jesus Seminar. That organization famously brought together a group of scholars to vote on the authenticity of the sayings attributed to Jesus in the Gospels. They voted using colored beads, with red indicating they thought the words were those of Jesus, pink indicating they were close to what Jesus said, gray indicating a greater degree of distance from what Jesus said, and black indicating that the words and ideas expressed the viewpoint of the later church rather than Jesus. They calculated the results of the votes and published them in a form that aimed at getting the attention of the press and of the wider public. The Jesus Seminar thus produced not a red letter edition but a four-color edition of the Five Gospels (including the Gospel of Thomas), color-coded to reflect the outcome of

*An **eclectic critical edition** of the Greek New Testament offers a printed Greek text that is not precisely what is found in any manuscript, but reflects the judgment of experts on what the original likely said based on the differing manuscripts we possess.*

their voting. The words attributed to Jesus in the New Testament may thus be in red, pink, gray, or black. Not many are in red, but the fact that any are is noteworthy given the innate skepticism of many of the likeminded voters the Jesus Seminar assembled. The voting process and this way of presenting the results were both considered controversial. Yet voting when a committee disagrees is nothing new, and committees working on the Bible are no exception. The *Textual Commentary on the Greek New Testament* explains how the committee that worked on the United Bible Societies' editions of the Greek New Testament decided what to include in the text of their eclectic edition and what to relegate to a footnote.

To help students understand the process involved, and also to get an anonymous sense of what students think, I have often staged a reenactment of the work of the Jesus Seminar in my classes on the historical Jesus. We discuss a particular saying and then vote on it. Since I don't have a collection of colored beads, I got students to bring M&Ms and use them to vote. Eventually I decided to take things a step further and get custom-colored M&Ms in red, pink, gray, and black for use in this activity. (Yes, you really can do that, and if you're reenacting the Jesus Seminar, it is worth the added expense since otherwise you have to decide what green and orange stand for, whether peanut M&Ms count extra, and so on.) In keeping with the group we were emulating and the way we tweaked the method of voting, I decided that we should call ourselves . . . the Jesus SeM&Minar! Once you have finished groaning, I will point out that this activity has an added benefit in the context of American universities. Most schools in the United States use a four-point scale to calculate students' grade point average (GPA). Most students have never learned to do the math necessary to figure out how they are doing in an individual class or overall. In order to calculate the average of our four-color scale of authenticity, we have to assign numerical values to the beads or M&Ms—one for black, two for gray, three for pink, four for red. If everyone votes red, it will then be 4.0. In the process of doing the math to see what color a saying should be in our class's edition, students also get to see how one poor grade in a class does not mean you won't get an A. Likewise, despite the fact that you didn't get a B or a C in any course, or that no one voted gray or pink, that might be the overall outcome nevertheless. Averages are funny like that. In the same way, if the participants in the

Jesus Seminar were evenly divided on a saying, some certain it was authentic and some certain it was not, the pink result would not make this clear, since the same color could indicate that everyone involved thought it sounded rather like Jesus but not his exact words. The four-color edition is interesting in many ways, but knowing the actual results of each vote would tell us something much more significant.

Quoting the Corinthians

The Gospels are not the only place where translators need to make decisions about quotation marks. In 1 Corinthians Paul explicitly says that he is writing to them about matters concerning which they had previously written to him. In view of that, and the fact that Paul repeatedly introduces a phrase only to immediately qualify it, we have good reason to think that Paul in places was quoting from the Corinthians' letter to him. To make things more complicated, it is possible that they quoted him in expressing their own views, which may have necessitated that Paul quote his own earlier statement, and the Corinthians' statement about his statement, before stating what he wants to now emphasize to them in light of their correspondence. Confused? I didn't try to smooth over the wording of that sentence because its muddiness conveys precisely the challenge that faces anyone who wants to say that someone said that we said that they said what they said. It gets complicated. We have single and double quotes to allow us to place a quotation within a quotation, but anything beyond that and the system pretty much breaks down. Is it any surprise there is ambiguity in a letter written in an era that didn't have quotation marks at all?

So where does Paul appear to be quoting the Corinthians? Phrases like "it is good for a man not to touch a woman" (1 Cor 7:1) and "all things are permitted for me" (1 Cor 6:12) are strong candidates. It is possible that the Corinthians heard Paul say that all things are lawful to him, which they then applied in a manner that shocked and horrified him. In the process of correcting the Corinthians he may thus be clarifying or tempering things that he himself said. If you've ever said something and had it quoted back at you, and been forced to insist that even though the person has your words right they are mistaking your meaning, then you'll understand how Paul likely felt. First Corinthians 11 is a place where the possibility that Paul is quoting the Corinthians opens up several avenues for making sense of this otherwise puzzling passage. Toward the beginning of the section about women's hair or head coverings (the very terminology is ambiguous), we might get the impression that Paul is emphasizing that women must do something particular with their hair or scarves, because in the Genesis story the woman was taken from man. Yet by the end Paul has insisted that just as woman came from man, every man comes from a woman, and so a woman should have authority over her head. Yes, believe it or not, that's what Paul's words in 11:10 mean. Some translators have been so certain Paul couldn't have meant that—despite that being the only possible sense of what the Greek text says—that they substituted what they thought Paul must have meant in place of what Paul actually wrote. Thus the King James Version turns the woman's authority over her head into a sign of authority on her head. Later translators have gone even further in altering the meaning, changing it into a sign of her submission. If we understand Paul to have been quoting the Corinthians (and perhaps quoting the Corinthians quoting him) in the first part of the passage, then we can understand how Paul could have begun where he did and yet ended up with the woman's authority over her head. This also fits well with his emphasis that the churches of God do not have the practice of being contentious about such matters (1 Cor 11:16).

Sometimes when we look at the decisions certain translators have made, we can identify biases and assumptions that were at work. Not that any translator or translation is unbiased. People sometimes ask what the best translation is. The best course of action (apart from becoming very proficient in ancient Greek) is to read multiple translations that reflect different backgrounds, assumptions, and approaches to translation. No translation can ever be perfect. Yet that has not stopped people from occasionally making really dubious arguments based on their understanding of the wording of one particular translation, wording that conveyed to them something other than what the Greek New Testament meant. Again, other than learning the relevant ancient languages, reading many different versions in English is the best and perhaps the only way to avoid that pitfall.

The Use of the Old Testament in the New

While we are on the subject of quotations, whole books have been written on the quotations from the Jewish scriptures or Old Testament that are found in each of the New Testament books. Studying how a text alludes to other works beyond itself provides us with important clues about what Paul (for example) knew and assumed that the recipients of his letters would understand as well. Paul is known as the apostle to the gentiles, one who proclaimed the message to non-Jews and founded churches that at least welcomed them and often consisted primarily or entirely of people from such backgrounds. Yet he quotes the Jewish scriptures as an authority and alludes to them in ways that might well be imperceptible to someone not steeped in those texts the way Paul was. We've already begun to wrestle with how Paul cites and alludes to the Torah. He says that gentile Christians are not under the law, yet he also cites Deuteronomy 25:4 in 1 Corinthians 9:9 ("you shall not muzzle an ox while it is treading out the grain") in order to make the case for missionaries like himself receiving support. How can Paul say Christians are "not under law" and yet cite the law in support of his arguments? He also says things such as that "circumcision is nothing, and uncircumcision is nothing, but obeying the commandments of God is everything" (1 Cor 7:19; compare Gal 5:6; 6:15), and that it is not the hearers but the doers of the law who are justified before God (Rom 2:13). These statements and many more are liable to puzzle those who have heard that Paul considered the law of the "Old Testament" to have been abolished. The issue is with the modern interpreter and not Paul, who says adamantly in Romans 3:31, "Do we then overthrow the law through this faith? By no means!"

As we discussed earlier in the book, a significant amount of scholarship in recent years has highlighted how interpreters since Martin Luther have read the issues of the Protestant Reformation back into Paul. Paul's own concerns were different from the legalism that Luther and other Reformers made the focus of their attention. The "works of the law" that Paul was arguing against were not love of God, love of neighbor, the Ten Commandments, or refraining from muzzling oxen. Instead, his concern was with circumcision, kosher food laws, and other things that separated Jews from gentiles. He was arguing against those who were born into the people of Israel thinking this automatically gave them a favored status with God even if they ignored what God commanded, while gentiles were by definition outsiders to God's people however righteous they might be. The irony, of course, is that any Protestants today who emphasize that it is Christians alone or their group alone that is saved sound much more like Paul's opponents than like Paul if we understand him in this way.

Quotation from the Jewish scriptures is also crucial to understanding how Paul thought about Jesus. Some interpreters have suggested that in 1 Corinthians 8:6 Paul "split the Shema" (the traditional affirmation of Jewish belief in one God alone found in Deut 6:4), adding Jesus as Lord within the definition of the one God. When we read 1 Corinthians all the way to the end, we will realize if we hadn't earlier that the one Lord remained for Paul subordinate to the one God (1 Cor 15:28). One could allude to the Shema by writing about "one God" and be understood as affirming Jewish monotheism, but it would have taken more than allusion to redefine or depart from monotheism. The same applies to the language taken over from Isaiah 45:23-24 in Philippians 2:6-11. The exalted status of Jesus includes accolades couched in language emphatically about the one and only supreme God in the context of Isaiah 45. Such worship was acceptable not because Paul redefined monotheism but because he affirmed it and understood Jesus's exalted status to be rule on behalf of the one God which was "to the glory of God the Father." Paul's quotation from the same passage in Isaiah in Romans 14:10-12 makes this clear. Whole books have been written on *how* Paul's statements about Jesus's exalted status relate to Jewish monotheism, and those who are interested can spend a lifetime if they wish (as I have!) pondering such things. The point here is that Paul is not redefining Jewish monotheism but affirming it, and he clearly understands his view of Jesus to be compatible with his emphasis on God as one. We tackled some aspects of that in another chapter. Here you can see how noticing and understanding the references to Jewish scripture in the New Testament makes an enormous difference to how one understands what the New Testament has to say about Christology.

Let's end this section with one more interesting case, one that I suspect many readers of Paul's letters are liable to miss. In 1 Corinthians 3:19 Paul quotes from Job 5:13: "He catches the wise in their craftiness." In context, the words quoted are those of one of Job's friends, Eliphaz, who is condemned at the end of the book for not having spoken rightly about God the way Job had. So is it appropriate to quote Eliphaz positively, or is Paul taking a text out of context? Both are possible. It would be ironic if Paul wrote about God catching the crafty in their craftiness while his clever use of scripture was self-defeating (because he cited Eliphaz, whom the book of Job itself says is not entirely trustworthy). Then again, it may be that Paul was aware of the fact that Job's friends were citing genuinely valid principles a lot of the time, and the issue was how they were applying them to the case of Job. While we should not bend over backward to avoid the conclusion that Paul took this text out of context, as many who have quoted scripture before and after him also did, it is also possible that Paul made his point through this text in full awareness of the context and speaker. Eliphaz could serve as a perfect example of a wise person caught in his own craftiness, someone who knew the classic wisdom well enough to quote it against Job but not well enough to apply these very words to himself.

"As Your Own Poets Have Said"

In Titus 1:12 we encounter the paradox that a Cretan author says that Cretans are all liars. The author of the letter (claiming to be Paul) says that this is a true saying. Yet if a Cretan says all Cretans are liars, then that statement must be false, mustn't it? There's a paradox here, and it isn't clear whether the author of Titus was aware of it. Like the previous example of a quotation from the book of Job, this use of an authoritative source may be either intentionally ironic or self-defeating. Acts 17 also depicts Paul as appealing to authorities other than scripture when addressing an audience for which the Jewish scriptures carried no weight. In the narrative Paul mentions unnamed "poets" who say certain things. The words he attributes to them can be found in Aretus, Epimenides, and Cleanthes, among others. The sentiments are ones that were widely shared, and so it would have made all the more sense to appeal to them. What readers who do not recognize and do not seek the sources of the allusions may fail to realize is that these are all texts that talk about Zeus.

Already in the Letter of Aristeas the God of the Jews is identified with Zeus, even though the behavior of and specific stories about the two deities are significantly different. The Hellenistic age was characterized by a penchant for making such identifications, which led to the Roman and Greek gods being blurred and blended. While both Acts

*The **Letter of Aristeas** is a work in Greek from in or around the second century BC. It narrates a story about how the Greek translation of the Torah/Pentateuch supposedly came to be made.*

and the letters of Paul are adamant that gentiles are welcome in the people of God, stories such as that about Paul visiting Athens in Acts 17 explore the lengths to which Paul was willing to go to communicate that point.

As we reach the end of a chapter about quotations, we should note the willingness of the early Christians to translate what Jesus said so that the meaning was conveyed even if the exact wording was lost. Paul incorporates extensive paraphrases of and allusions to teaching of Jesus, with no sense that it was important or even possible to preserve the exact wording. Only rarely does he indicate that he is repeating something that was told to him. One clear example of this is his repetition of the tradition about the Lord's Supper that he had passed on to the Corinthian Christians previously (1 Cor 11:23). Paul says he received this from the Lord, which indicates its ultimate source and not that no other people were involved in the process. Paul indicates in Romans 16 that he had relatives who were part of the Christian movement while he still opposed it. Even at that stage he must have heard some things, enough to make him dislike what his relatives were involved in. He emphasizes that his gospel message did not depend on the authority of other apostles, which some mistake for a claim to never have learned anything about Jesus from anyone else. Paul has been informed about the teaching of Jesus about divorce, for instance, and appeals to it when he tells the Corinthians that what he taught them about that topic comes from "not I but the Lord" (1 Cor 7:10), which he contrasts with his own judgment about an aspect of the subject not explicitly addressed in the teaching of Jesus (1 Cor 7:12). The gospels had not been written yet, but Paul's reference shows that the material that eventually ended up in Mark 10:2–12 was already known in his time.

In an era in which there were no quotation marks and no recording devices, and in which most communication was in oral rather than written form, expecting verbatim quotations is inappropriate. I still kinda wish the New Testament authors had cited their sources, though. If they had, it would have answered a lot of questions. You can quote me on that.

For Further Reading

Beale, G. K. *Handbook on the New Testament Use of the Old Testament: Exegesis and Interpretation.* Grand Rapids: Baker Academic, 2012.

Dunn, James D. G. *The Evidence for Jesus.* Louisville: Westminster John Knox, 1985.

Eurell, John-Christian. "Paul and the Jesus Tradition: Reconsidering the Relationship between Paul and the Synoptics." *Journal of Early Christian History* 12, no. 2 (2022): 1–16.

Funk, Robert W., and Roy W. Hoover. *The Five Gospels: What Did Jesus Really Say? The Search for the Authentic Words of Jesus.* New York: HarperCollins, 1997.

Hays, Richard B. *Echoes of Scripture in the Letters of Paul.* New Haven: Yale University Press, 1989.

Metzger, Bruce Manning. *A Textual Commentary on the Greek New Testament: A Companion Volume to the United Bible Societies' Greek New Testament.* 4th rev. ed. Stuttgart: United Bible Societies, 1994.

Saenger, Paul. *Space between Words: The Origins of Silent Reading.* Stanford, CA: Stanford University Press, 1997.

Williams, H. H. Drake. "Light Giving Sources: Examining the Extent of Scriptural Citation and Allusion Influence in 1 Corinthians." Pages 7–37 in *Paul: Jew, Greek, and Roman.* Edited by Stanley E. Porter. Leiden: Brill, 2009.

R

Revelations Is *Not* in the Bible

A good quick test of biblical literacy is whether someone at least gets the names of the books correct. I regularly point to Dan Brown's reference to the "Book of Judgments" in *Angels and Demons* as an example of this. The character was actually referring to the book of Judges 13:20. It might seem unfair to pick on Brown when many people make mistakes of this sort. However, since Brown's novel *The Da Vinci Code* has helped promote misinformation about the formation of the canon of the New Testament, while Brown claimed that details about history in that novel were accurate, it is not only appropriate but necessary to evaluate his claims and his knowledge. Christians tend to know the New Testament better than the Old (although they may have just as much trouble locating the letter of Jude as the book of Zephaniah). Yet even among Christians you will occasionally see mention made of the book of Revelations. There is no such book in the Bible. The title is Revelation (with no s on the end). This is short for the Revelation of John. Sometimes you'll hear it called the Apocalypse of John. *Apocalypse* is a transliteration of a Greek word that means "a revelation," as in an unveiling or disclosure of something previously hidden. As a result of the book being called that, and being thought of as having to do with the end of the world, the English word "apocalypse" has come to denote a catastrophe of a sort that might end human existence. The Greek word does not have those connotations. The title Revelation comes from the very first words of the book, which describe it as the revelation (singular) of Jesus Christ.

It is the tendency to preface all the books in the Bible with "the book of" that probably accounts for people getting the title wrong so often. If you call it "the book of Revelation," it does sound odd, ungrammatical. But rather than add an s where there isn't supposed to be one, why not just call it by its actual name, Revelation, or the Revelation of John? While you're at it, get in the habit of talking about Paul's *letter* to the Romans. Calling it "the book of Romans" makes it sound like it is a book

Canon: *an authorized list of the contents of a collection, especially of sacred scripture.*

rather than a letter and that the Romans in general are the focus of that book. This applies to other letters equally. There are letters addressed to Timothy, while talking about "the first (or second) book of Timothy" sounds like it is something else. Getting titles right isn't just nitpicking. The way we refer to things often conveys whether we understand what it is at a deeper level. Just as a Harry Potter fan will know that someone who refers to the first novel as *Harry Potter and the Sorcerer's Apprentice* isn't a genuine fan, if you get the names of texts in the Bible wrong, people who know the Bible will know you are at best vaguely familiar with these texts. That is fine if you have never taken a course on the Bible or read a book like this one before, but should change as a result of your doing so! (Since this often comes up, let me also emphasize that a novel is a work of fiction, and so you should not call a textbook or other nonfiction book, including the one you are currently reading, a "novel.")

Revelation did not get included in the Bible without significant controversy. Both because of that and because people get the title wrong, it is a good place to begin a chapter that explores the debates and processes that led to the formation of the New Testament as we now have it.

What Is "All Scripture"?

Second Timothy 3:16–17 refers to "all scripture," literally "every writing," as being God-breathed. "Scriptures" is an English word that is consistently used for the *sacred* writings of a particular religious tradition. The Greek word that appears in 2 Timothy 3:16 is not that specific, although in context it was probably clear enough what was meant. It is extremely unlikely that the author thought that *anything* that might be written, every writing of every sort, was God-breathed. In Judaism "the Writings" denotes just one subset of the collection of sacred texts (the other two being the Torah and the Prophets). Noticing the ambiguity of the language used here helpfully draws our attention to things that people often assume without discussion: that there is a single, clear thing known as "the Bible," that its contents were divinely inspired, and that this inspiration took a particular form that safeguards the reliability of the contents thereof. It would be a long time before anyone had all the works in the New Testament, and only those works, bound into a single codex. We have remnants of ancient codices that contained a subset of what we today know as the New Testament, as well as ones that included works that are not in Bibles today alongside works that are. It took time for the church to agree on its canon.

*In Judaism the scriptures are called the **Tanak**, an acronym made from the first letters of each of its three sections: Torah (Pentateuch), Nevi'im (Prophets), and Ketuvim (Writings).*

***Codex** (plural **codices**) denotes the ancient equivalent of the modern book form, using separate pages bound together on one side in place of the earlier roll or scroll.*

Before They Were Famous

If there is something scholars take for granted that other readers of the New Testament tend to forget, it is that there was a time when the texts that are now found in Christian Bibles were not yet part of such a collection. Grasping this and its implications is a key part of engaging in historical study of the New Testament. While some scholars use the methods of canonical criticism, seeking to understand works within the context of the New Testament as a whole or even of the entire Bible, historical criticism focuses on understanding Paul's letters as genuine occasional correspondence with specific communities he knew. It attempts to read the Gospel of Mark on its own terms, rather than as a gospel that seems to be missing things because one cannot help comparing it to Matthew and Luke.

When a New Testament text uses a phrase like "the scriptures" to denote an established corpus of authoritative sacred writings, by definition the work in which that phrase appears is not yet part of such a collection. No New Testament text became scripture as soon as it was written. This is crucial information to keep in mind when seeking to interpret the New Testament writings contextually, as they would have been perceived by their earliest readers and hearers. When Paul argued against his opponents, those who received Paul's letter didn't respond by saying, "Well, Paul must be right because his words are in the Bible." They weren't yet. Some readers accepted Paul's authority, but we can tell from the way he defends his authority that not everyone did. Whether he persuaded a reader/hearer depended entirely on the arguments he made. He appealed to works that were already regarded as sacred scriptures in his time, the Jewish scriptures that became the Christian Old Testament. Those works were written on separate scrolls, and there was as yet no official canon, no agreed-upon list of what was or was not scripture, much less a printed table of contents that was placed in front of them in a single bound volume. (Even today the default format for the Jewish scriptures in the original languages is separate scrolls rather than a single book.) This does not mean that things were radically ambiguous, however. For one thing, the Torah or Pentateuch was clearly defined. The collection of the Prophets had also taken shape, although slightly later, with the result that not all Israelite groups accepted them. It is also important to know that the prophetic writings as they came to be categorized in Jewish Bibles included works that are considered "historical books" in Christian Bibles: Joshua, Judges, 1-2 Samuel, and 1-2 Kings. Daniel, on the other hand, is considered part of the Prophets in Christian Bibles but not in Jewish Bibles. This is likely due to the late date of its composition. The third grouping, the Writings, is a catchall for everything else. Jesus is depicted as referring to these three categories in Luke 24:44 when he refers to the law of Moses, the Prophets, and the Psalms. The Psalms is the largest of the works in the Writings.

There is another place where Jesus appears to refer to this threefold collection and even to know its contents in the order that would eventually be made official. When Jesus referred to the blood of all the righteous from Abel to Zechariah (Matt 23:35 // Luke 11:51), he wasn't saying "all the martyrs from A to Z." "Abel" does begin with the first letter of the alphabet in Greek and Hebrew, but Z was not the last letter in either. That is why the phrase "the Alpha and the Omega" is used in Revelation (1:8; 21:6; 22:13): alpha is the first letter of the Greek alphabet, and omega the last. The reason for mentioning Abel and Zechariah is more likely the fact that Abel was the first righteous martyr murdered in the Bible, and toward the end of 2 Chronicles we are told of the murder of Zechariah within the temple precincts (2 Chr 24:20-22). As the Jewish Bible took shape, 2 Chronicles became the last work in its table of contents. Matthew got his Zechariahs mixed up, since the Zechariah killed in the temple was the son of Jehoiada. Zechariah son of Berakiah was a different individual (see Zech 1:1). Matthew wasn't the only one to get confused by fathers of Zechariahs. Ezra 5:1 and 6:14 refer to the prophet as "son of Iddo." The New International Version tries to cover this up by rendering "son of Iddo" as "a descendant of Iddo." Luke decides to avoid getting tangled up in this by simply dropping the name of Zechariah's father in Luke 11:51. After all, Jesus hadn't mentioned that Abel was son of Adam. The confusion about which Zechariah was meant eventually led Christians to take Jesus as referring to Zechariah the father of John the Baptist, and stories developed about his martyrdom. The earliest of these is found in the second-century work known as the Protevangelium (or Infancy Gospel) of James, although it may be an addition made to that work after its original composition. Anyway, confusions and later traditions about Zechariahs aside, the "Abel to Zechariah" reference got the point across. This generation would have to give an answer for the mistreatment of the righteous throughout the ages, and not just those living in that time. They had the stories about how the righteous were mistreated historically and so should know better. It is a recurring theme in the scriptures that those who have scriptures are not off the hook when it comes to what God expects of them, but held to a higher standard precisely because of what they ought to know from reading those texts. If someone has been given much, much will be expected of them (Luke 12:48).

The fact that there was no "Bible" in this period can seem disconcerting. In fact, the same is true today. While Christians eventually agreed on the contents of the New Testament, it took a very long time. Revelation took so long to be accepted among the Eastern Orthodox that its contents are still not used liturgically. At the time of the Protestant Reformation, Martin Luther voiced his qualms about that same work as well as the Letters to the Hebrews, James, and Jude. They are found among the contents of his New Testament, but at the very end as a kind of begrudging appendix. When it comes to the Old Testament, there is even greater divergence. References to Protestants not having the "Apocrypha" obscure the fact that the rest of Christianity has at least somewhat different collections in this category. The prize for the largest Old Testament would go without question to the Ethiopian Orthodox (Tewahedo) Church. It includes works like Jubilees and 1 Enoch, which clearly had an influence on early Christianity. The Letter of Jude quotes from 1 Enoch (Jude 1:14–15; 1 Enoch 1:9).

Apocrypha is often used to denote those works that Protestants removed from their Old Testament at the time of the Reformation, seeking to align their Old Testament canon with that of Judaism (often called the Hebrew Bible even though a few parts of it are in Aramaic). Deuterocanonical is a preferable way of referring to the texts in question, the precise contents of which differ among churches and their canons.

Greatest Hits

The passage with which we began this chapter, 2 Timothy 3:16, refers to "all scripture" or "every writing." I mentioned earlier someone telling me they viewed the entire Bible as equally inspired but not equally inspiring, with the genealogies particularly in mind. As you've seen in this book, if you skip the genealogies, you will miss things that are really important. But as important as certain details in Matthew's genealogy may be, few would say they find that list of names "inspiring" as a whole. It is not surprising that you won't find even a small part of it plastered on T-shirts or bumper stickers. Few die-hard fans of a band like *every* song they ever made, and if they do, they do not like them all equally. The average person will likely only know a band's greatest hits. When Christians learn memory verses, they are approaching the Bible in the same way. It seems fair to say, then, that most people, and perhaps even most Christians, know the "greatest hits" of the New Testament. Everyone knows John 3:16, but far fewer could identify the major distinctive themes in the Gospel of John as a whole. More importantly, they may not be aware of how the rest of what this gospel says about the world, believing, and other things might be relevant to how we interpret that famous verse. Let me repeat the famous saying a third time (just as the Bible repeats things that are important): a text taken out of context becomes a pretext. That is the risk of knowing just the most popular verses. Unless they are situated within their literary context, and those writings are situated in their historical, cultural, and linguistic context, the words of those verses will seem to us to mean what they would if a contemporary English speaker wrote them.

When students learn about the canon, they also learn that different groups and denominations have a "canon within the canon." Baptists preach few sermons on passages in Acts or 1 Corinthians that mention speaking in tongues. Pentecostals, on the other hand, gravitate to those passages. Lutherans and other Protestants may frequently quote Galatians, Romans, and Ephesians on faith, works, and grace. Roman Catholics, on the other hand, are more likely to direct their attention to what the Letter of James says about faith and works. To continue our musical analogy, even those who do not just know a band's greatest hits may have favorite albums. An important corollary is that those who claim to be "Bible-believing Christians" cannot help but be selective. They may or may not speak in tongues. They may or may not affirm the legitimacy of women in ministry. All those who call themselves "Bible-believing" are using a slogan that assumes that what their church teaches or what they personally believe corresponds to "what the Bible says." As a result, someone might offer a detailed case for a particular viewpoint that pays close attention to scripture and still have others reject it because of their assumption that it is not "what the Bible teaches." When someone says the Bible is their ultimate authority, it sounds to me like a form of idolatry. Nevertheless, if someone does claim that, then the meaning of the Bible ought to be so important to them that they take the time to read books, consult commentaries, and, most importantly, familiarize themselves intimately with the entirety of the texts themselves. Smaller fragments of scripture, on the other hand, are easier to weaponize, to hurl at one's opponents in an argument. This seems like a good point at which to emphasize that *canon* and *cannon* are different words, spelled differently. If you use the canon as though it were a cannon, launching prooftexts at your enemies like cannonballs, you are using it wrong. If these authors had wanted churches to have only pithy sayings to use as weapons, they would have provided that. Instead, what we have are books, letters, and other types of literature that need to be read the way you would read a biography or a letter from a friend if you want to understand those: from beginning to end. SparkNotes won't cut it. To truly understand the texts contained in the New Testament, you need to know them as wholes and not just the "greatest hits" from each.

God-Breathed

Christians debate many things when it comes to scripture, but most would agree in calling whichever texts are part of their canon "inspired." That term is often associated with

2 Timothy 3:16. Yet ancient Greek had terminology to express the idea of being inspired, and what is found in this passage is something different. That is why some English Bibles say "God-breathed" or something similar, rather than "inspired." When the New Testament was translated into Latin, the word *inspirata* was used in this verse, and that has undoubtedly influenced English translations. What does the actual language used mean? Does "God-breathed" mean something significantly different from "inspired"? Surely, you might be thinking, either way of putting it envisages God exhaling and scripture being breathed into? Yes, indeed, but when people talk of the Bible being inspired, they often picture God doing something not to the writings but to the people who wrote them. In some cases they imagine the authors hearing exact words they are to write, or being taken over by God's Spirit so that God is the actual author. Saying that the sacred writings are God-breathed, on the other hand, directly echoes the story of God creating a human being in Genesis 2. The human being is made from the ground, the stuff of earth, and comes to life when God breathes the breath of life into the nostrils of the human being. Against this background, the breath of God in 2 Timothy can be understood to animate not the authors (who are not mentioned in the passage) but the texts. The texts would be mere ink and papyrus or parchment, and the words would be mere human words, were it not for the Spirit of God giving life to them. The result, once again according to the passage in 2 Timothy, is not that they are inerrant or infallible. It doesn't say they aren't, but it doesn't say they are. What the texts become is *useful* for purposes related to God's will and plan. That's the focus here. God brings these texts to life.

It should go without saying that a verse in the Bible cannot be used to prove the status of the entire Bible as God-breathed, inspired, authoritative, inerrant, or anything else.

Even if the Bible had been composed all at once as a cohesive whole, a passage that said "this book is authoritative" or "believe what is written here" would not constitute evidence that it in fact deserves your credence. The text might indeed be trustworthy, but any text in any religion can assert its own authority. A circular argument doesn't work. Circular arguments are ones that assume what they need to prove. Put another way, such arguments beg the question. (By the way, don't say, "It begs the question that . . ." and add something else afterward. In such instances what you mean is that it *raises* a particular question. "Begging the question" refers specifically to making an assertion that assumes the very thing it needs to prove.)

Apocrypha and Pseudepigrapha

The terms "apocrypha" and "pseudepigrapha" are not used consistently. When someone refers to "the Apocrypha," they likely mean what Catholics prefer to call "deuterocanonical texts." In neither case does the etymology clarify the way these terms are used today. "Apocrypha" comes from a Greek word meaning "hidden," while "deuterocanonical" means they belong to a "second canon." Yet no one is hiding the texts that are in the Apocrypha, or if they are, they haven't done a very good job of it. So too the deuterocanonical texts are either canonical for a group or not canonical, with only some slight exceptions. In the Anglican Church, for instance, the Apocrypha really does have a status that is almost but not quite like those works that are generally accepted by all Protestants as canonical. Reading of the Apocrypha is encouraged, but one is not to rely on these texts to establish a doctrine or practice. (This is according to the Thirty-Nine Articles, which are themselves authoritative for those in the Church of England but also not canonical.)

The term "apocrypha" also appears in phrases such as "Christian apocrypha" or "apocryphal gospels," which usually denote early Christian works that are in the same genre as works included in the New Testament but are not included in it. These include works like the Epistle of Barnabas, the Gospel of Philip, and the Acts of Thomas. The terms "pseudepigrapha" and "pseudepigraphal" are also ones you will encounter. They derive from Greek words that together mean "falsely written." If a work is pseudepigraphal, it claims to be by someone other than the person who actually wrote it. We have already seen that there may be works in the New Testament that are not by the person they claim. Jewish works in this category are important to understanding the New Testament, providing important information about the cultural and religious context in which Jesus and his earliest followers participated. Works like the Testament of the Twelve Patriarchs, the Apocalypse of Moses, and the Books of Enoch are usually labeled Jewish (or Old Testament) Pseudepigrapha.

An irony in this whole discussion is that most scholars conclude that 2 Timothy, the very letter that says that all scripture is God-breathed, is not an authentic letter composed by Paul. Some religious believers are troubled by the idea that a biblical text would be considered a forgery if judged by our standards. The key point I would make here is that it seems inappropriate to insist that a text must have been written by its purported author since it is in the Bible. If you think that pseudepigraphal works should not be in your canon, then the way to proceed is to honestly evaluate the question of authorship for each work and if necessary remove things. The ancient church considered these very questions, and sometimes they got things wrong. One of the main arguments ancient Christians made in favor of including the Letter to the Hebrews was that it was by Paul, even though it is anonymous. Those who read it in Greek will quickly recognize it is not by Paul. It isn't just a matter of different vocabulary or style. The Greek is much more polished and elegant than what we find in Paul's letters. The theological ideas are also distinctive. So if the church included Hebrews on the basis of a view of authorship that is today evaluated as incorrect, should Hebrews be removed? Not necessarily. Authorship is just one of the things the church considered when discussing the contents of their canon. The long-standing precedent for these works being part of the canon throughout so much of history should also count for something when we discuss the matter in the context of our time.

The formation of the New Testament canon was a long and complex historical process, so much so that, rather than offer students a history lesson crammed into the second day of my class on the Bible, I decided to invent a card game (called Canon) to make it possible to learn about the process inductively. When students play the game, they consistently work out the main facets of the process as it actually played out in the first few centuries of the church's history. Before I invented the game, I used a small group discussion activity to accomplish the same thing. Students were asked what should happen if we were to discover a previously unknown letter of Paul's. Should it be added to the Bible? In response, they inevitably asked how sure we could be who wrote the letter, how early it was, how universally applicable it was, and whether it agreed with the other works included in the New Testament. The early church asked about precisely the same things—although you might miss this fact when you read scholarly works that use technical terms like "apostolicity" (deriving from the apostles or those who learned from them via an unbroken chain of transmission), "catholicity" (meaning universality of relevance and applicability), and "orthodoxy" (teaching correct doctrine).

It is important to get away from two inaccurate ideas about the way the canon formed. One bit of misinformation

that was popularized in Dan Brown's *The Da Vinci Code* is that
the emperor Constantine gathered bishops at the Council of
Nicaea and told them they had too many gospels and should
settle on four. In actual fact, the canon was not even a focus
at the Council of Nicaea. The second inaccurate idea is that
some people think the table of contents for the New Testament simply dropped down from heaven. But the table of
contents in a Bible is not itself part of the canon. In reality,
the process of canon formation was at once much simpler
and much messier than these two popular scenarios envisage. The core of the New Testament emerged as a result of
the sharing of literature among churches connected in a network that naturally developed as the gospel spread and communities formed. The works that were most widely accepted
became canonical. Ones that were not as widely known either caught on or were eventually excluded. Debates about
what constitutes scripture occurred throughout, but there
was also a core collection of gospels and letters of Paul that
took shape organically.

It is important to always remember that the Bible is not
a single book but a compilation. The very word "Bible" itself
comes from the Greek plural for books, *biblia*. Protestants
may find it deceptively easy to talk about scripture as the
foundation of their faith. Martin Luther, however, clearly
recognized that in challenging the authority of the church
he could not then simply take the church's definition of a
scriptural canon for granted, on authority. He had to wrestle
with what constituted scripture. Those texts were to be given
primacy of place not because the church said so but because
they connected Christians with the very beginnings of Christianity. In light of this it is not only appropriate but necessary to ask what should be in a Bible and why, and whether
texts the church has historically held in high esteem are by
the authors they claim. Yet the consensus of my students

(who, for the record, do not constitute a church council, and their decision is not binding on anyone, not even themselves) is that historical precedent and tradition are a major consideration. It matters that something has been part of the New Testament for as long as there has been one. It is acceptable (in academia if not in all churches) both to ask difficult questions about authorship and authenticity and to work with a body of literature that has become an established canon.

Discussions of canon are not limited to the Bible. They occur in relation to English literature, music, and franchises like Star Trek and Star Wars. There is a place for working with an established canon and a place for acknowledging that it is something historically contingent. Even for those who regard the historic canon of the New Testament as sacred scripture, it is important to recognize that these works were not composed in a vacuum. The Gospel of John and the Gospel of Thomas may have been in dialogue with each other. The Acts of Paul and Thecla and the Pastoral Epistles (1 Timothy, 2 Timothy, and Titus) may give us two sides of a debate about the status of women in early churches. The Gospel of Peter may provide clues about how the Gospel of Mark originally ended. Or they may not. For those engaged in the academic study of the New Testament, the point is that the questions must be asked so that we understand our object of study as well as possible. Unless we recognize that Jude 14–15 quotes 1 Enoch and that 2 Timothy 3:8 uses the names given to Pharaoh's magicians not in the Bible but in later tradition (see

Pastoral Epistles *is a term referring to 1 Timothy, 2 Timothy, and Titus. These letters share a lot of characteristics with one another that also differentiate them from other letters attributed to Paul.*

Apocryphon: *singular of "apocrypha," sometimes used in the title of an individual work in this category.* **Targum**: *Aramaic paraphrase of Jewish scriptures.*

the Apocryphon of Jannes and Jambres the Magicians as well as Targum Pseudo-Jonathan to Exod 1:15; 7:11; 13:22), we will not understand the New Testament as well as we can. As we conclude, it is worth mentioning something interesting that happened when Revelation became part of the New Testament and was placed at its end. The warning in Revelation 22:18–19 not to add anything or take anything away can appear no longer to refer just to the words of that one text, which was the sense when the book was first composed. Instead, it can seem like a final statement about the Bible as a whole. Perhaps that too is a reason why some find it difficult to grapple with the process of canon formation and the fact that there were genuine debates about what should and should not be included. If we understand the history, though, we will be poised to understand that in the first Christian centuries people did not encounter the words of Revelation as the finale of a larger compilation and did not experience the New Testament as a compilation that ended with this warning.

I hope that learning about the New Testament canon has been an apocalypse in the sense of the Greek word, a disclosure of information, and has not seemed like the end of the world.

For Further Reading

Bruce, F. F. *The Canon of Scripture.* Downers Grove, IL: InterVarsity, 1988.

Gaventa, Beverly Roberts. *When in Romans: An Invitation to Linger with the Gospel According to Paul.* Grand Rapids: Baker Academic, 2016.

Kalimi, Isaac. "The Story about the Murder of the Prophet Zechariah in the Gospels and Its Relation to Chronicles." *Revue Biblique* 116, no. 2 (2009): 246–61.

McNamara, Martin. *Targum and Testament Revisited: Aramaic Paraphrases of the Hebrew Bible; A Light on the New Testament.* 2nd ed. Grand Rapids: Eerdmans, 2010.

Pietersma, Albert. *The Apocryphon of Jannes and Jambres the Magicians: P. Chester Beatty XVI.* Leiden: Brill, 1993.

S

Scribes and Secretaries

There is a "joke" or "riddle" that asks, "Who was the father of the sons of Zebedee?" The scare quotes in that description are clearly necessary. If that is a joke, it obviously isn't funny, and it isn't genuinely a riddle—more a prank, an attempt to see if someone might be tripped up by a question that provides the answer within the question itself. The question of who wrote the "letters of Paul," on the other hand, isn't a lame attempt at humor or a practical joke disguised as a riddle. It is a legitimate question, and this chapter will explain why. In the case of one of the letters that Paul sent, we have an explicit answer to the question right within the letter itself, and you may be surprised to learn that the answer is not "Paul."

Let's start at the beginning—the beginning of a letter, that is. Authors of letters in the Greco-Roman world placed their names as senders at the beginnings of their letters. That is why Paul's letter to the Christians in Rome doesn't begin "Dear Romans" but "Paul." (If anyone wants to try to revive this custom, I'd be supportive. I don't know about you, but when I receive a letter, the first thing I do is flip it over to see who sent it.) Yet when we get close to the end of this famous letter of Paul's, we read the following in Romans 16:22: "I Tertius, the writer of this letter, greet you in the Lord." If you never noticed that, don't feel bad. Chapter 16 of Romans does not at first glance appear to be a particularly interesting part of the letter. It is mostly filled with Paul's greetings to individuals in the community to which the letter was written. However, when we skip it, we miss important details—not just about Tertius's having written the letter but also about Phoebe the deacon, who is Paul's emissary and delivers the letter, Junia the apostle, and much more. It is not just Paul saying hi to some people you don't know (and some of whose names you may struggle to pronounce).

Returning to Tertius, if you're just finding out about this for the first time, you may understandably be wondering why Paul's name is at the beginning of this letter as author and yet Tertius's name is near the end as the one who wrote it. The answer is a simple one, yet important, as it highlights a major difference between Paul's time and our own. Today, reading and writing are linked, and both are standard parts of education. In the first century, most people received no formal education in reading or anything else. But those who learned to read did not automatically learn to write as well. Sure, they could form for themselves the shapes of the letters that they recognized on an inscription or in a scroll. But serious writing was a task for professionals, trained in how to produce legible text using the necessary tools. There were neither pens nor paper in anything like the modern sense. Writing on papyrus was not like anything most people reading this book have ever experienced.

When writing his letters, Paul did what most people would do in his place: he made use of a trained professional. The technical term for Tertius's role is "amanuensis." Other than for the purpose of dropping impressively long words into conversations to impress your friends, you'll probably prefer to call him a scribe or secretary. Neither of those terms is quite precise enough, however. The word "amanuensis" is still in use today and isn't just a facet of an ancient way of doing things. It refers specifically to an author's assistant who writes (or nowadays more likely types) what the author dictates. That overlaps with the meaning of words like "scribe" or "secretary" but is more specific. That was what Tertius did when Paul wrote to the Romans. Why might Tertius have sent

*An **amanuensis** is someone employed to write down what is dictated by another.*

greetings to the church in Rome, something done by no other amanuensis Paul employed to write any of his other letters? Tertius was presumably a believer who either was known to some in the church in Rome or expected to travel there himself in the near future. Whether Paul compensated Tertius for his work, or whether Tertius offered his services at no cost to support the apostle's work, we do not know.

Paul took over the task of writing and did a small part of it himself on occasion. Galatians 6:11 has Paul refer to the large letters he wrote with his own hand, differentiating his own handwriting from that of a trained scribe. First Corinthians 16:21, Philemon 19, Colossians 4:18, and 2 Thessalonians 3:17 also depict Paul as author briefly taking over writing at those points. The implication is that the rest was written by someone else—an amanuensis. Why might Paul have chosen to do this? Did it convey something about his direct involvement in the process? Did it vouchsafe the authenticity of the letter (at least until they started circulating in copies, at which point the original handwriting was gone and so one could forge a letter and include a section claiming to be written by Paul's own hand)? It may have been any or all of these reasons, and perhaps others as well.

Not everything is different between Paul's time and ours. Today if you get a letter signed by the president or the CEO of a company, you may rightly suspect that the letter was composed by a secretary. They would be given instructions about what it should say, and the end result will likely have been checked to ensure it conveyed the sender's intent, but the actual composition was carried out by someone other than the person whose signature appears on it. Today just as in ancient times, authorship does not always mean that every word is from the mind of the author. It can mean that, but it can also mean many other things besides that. What it means in every instance is that the person named as author authorized the message. Whether they composed the precise wording varied, and readers would rarely be told. In most instances it could be assumed that the author was not the one who did the actual writing. Sometimes letters and other documents are authored by a committee. Sometimes you can tell. The New Testament letters of Paul sometimes mention other senders besides him. Authorship was and is more complicated than we often assume. (What you are reading now was written and typed by the author, in case you were wondering. But that doesn't mean the same is true of another book you read, which may perhaps have been ghostwritten. In most cases you'll never know. Books like this one do get input from editors at the publishing house. It may be that this sentence you are reading was adjusted and improved by input from an editor, or even suggested as something to add by them. Despite their important role in improving what you read, they don't get credited as author, nor do they even get the opportunity to send you greetings toward the end. Pretty unfair, if you ask me.)

Complicating things even further is the possibility of forgery, mistaken attribution, use of a pen name, and other scenarios in which the name associated with a work is not in fact who composed it, nor did they even authorize it. This happened in ancient times and continues to happen today. It is a blurry area, since, as we have already noted, there are scenarios in which an author employs someone either to write exactly what they dictate or to take their notes or general

ideas and elaborate them in fuller form in writing. We would
not consider those to be forgeries. The main difference is the
involvement of the purported author in
the process, if only to start the process
and approve the end result. There are
lots of different categories into which
we might place works that were neither
composed nor approved by their purported author. The technical term that
is often used to cover this range of possibilities is "pseudepigraphy," and it has already come up in
this book. That English word comes from the Greek words for
"false/lying" and "writing." Vocabulary from the Greek New
Testament that is now becoming familiar to you.

Pseudepigraphy is writing in
someone else's name or claiming that the author is someone other than the person who
actually composed the text
in question.

As has already been explained, scholars of the New Testament cannot simply dismiss the possibility of forgery on the
basis of the fact that texts are included in a canon of scripture. The ancient church debated the authenticity of these
works, and modern scholars follow in their footsteps. It is
not only appropriate but necessary that this kind of work
be done. You may feel obligated to trust the judgment of the
ancient church, but unless you view their judgment as infallible, then this is a subject that deserves close scholarly
attention, and serious consideration from you. Shying away
from things that make us uncomfortable is an expression
of fear rather than faith. Whether something that is forged
or misattributed belongs in the canon is another question,
one that you'll find there's disagreement about, just as there
is about the authorship of certain New Testament texts.
The key thing to remember is that what ancient Christians
did, and what scholars today do, in discussing questions of
authorship can be an expression of, rather than an attack
on, Christian faith. Modern scholars who investigate these
topics, far from "attacking the Bible," are respecting it by

paying close attention to what it says and asking how to best explain what they find there. Understanding why a text has the characteristics it does is important. Sometimes the best explanation for why two texts that bear the same author's name are very different from each other is that they were not in fact authored by the same person.

Concern about forgery is already expressed in the New Testament itself. In 2 Thessalonians there is a warning that the recipients should not be unsettled by any word or letter as though it came from Paul and his associates. Clearly people writing in someone else's name was a concern back then and is not just a needless worry invented by modern scholars. When you then find out that some scholars think 2 Thessalonians is a forgery, with this warning about forged letters intended to throw the suspicious off the scent, it may be enough to make your head spin! The main reason many scholars have doubts about 2 Thessalonians is that so much of it seems like it could be a deliberate imitation of 1 Thessalonians, yet its view of the end of time and what should be expected to unfold seems different from (and perhaps even contradictory to) what we find in 1 Thessalonians. Similarity to other authentic works can be a sign of authenticity. Too much similarity, too much difference, or a combination of the two can raise questions and suspicions.

There is a lot more that you may wish to find out about specific letters in the New Testament and what scholars conclude about whether they were authored by the person named at their beginning. One case can be very different from another. When it comes to the letters to Timothy and Titus (known collectively as the Pastoral Epistles), more scholars think they are falsely attributed than think they are genuine. It is not so much any one consideration that leads to this conclusion as the combination of them, including but not limited to

- differences in vocabulary from other letters,
- the same phrases that appear in authentic letters being used in different ways,
- greater similarities with second-century church writings than with Paul's letters, and
- a more elaborate church leadership structure being in view.

In the case of Colossians, you will find comparable numbers of scholars arguing both ways. Ephesians faces greater doubts than Colossians, seeming to share much in common with Colossians that is distinctive of those two letters, yet standing apart from it in other ways.

The fact that Paul didn't *write* the letters he *authored* makes determining a letter's genuineness much harder. Some letters have noticeably different styles, vocabularies, and even theologies. Scholars disagree about when that is most likely due to the input of an amanuensis or coauthors or both and when it is more likely due to forgery and false attribution. This chapter provides you with the basics and key points, each of which you may want to investigate further. If you do decide to look into this topic, you'll be better prepared because you read this book. You now know significantly more about what was involved in writing letters in ancient times than you did a few pages ago.

You may have seen an older Bible that attributed the Letter to the Hebrews to Paul. That letter is in fact anonymous. No author is named, nor are any recipients for that matter. Indeed, it doesn't seem much like a letter until you get to the conclusion. It ends with greetings in the manner a letter would be expected to, but it doesn't begin like a letter. Not only are neither the author nor the recipients specified, there isn't any thanksgiving or other introductory element. Such things were a standard part of a letter in ancient times. As for the question of authorship, not only is the theology very different from what we find in Paul's other letters, but the Greek is much more polished. This isn't a case of pseudepigraphy, however, since the author does not claim to be Paul. Hebrews is simply an anonymous letter by someone other than Paul.

While the majority of the New Testament letters are attributed to Paul, and the one just mentioned is anonymous, other letters are attributed to James, Peter, and Jude, while three traditionally ascribed to an author named John do not explicitly name their author, who calls himself "the Elder" (2 John 1; 3 John 1). The authenticity of each of these, along with the identity of the author even if they bore the name ascribed to them, has to be treated on its own terms. We won't tackle all of these letters here, since you now have the skills and information you need to investigate them further. My only additional advice on this topic is to be appropriately skeptical without being dismissive of an attribution of authorship just because it is traditional. For instance, while many scholars doubt the authenticity of the Letter of James, it is hard to imagine who would have forged it and why. Its focus is on Jewish ethical teaching, emphasizing the points and priorities that Jesus had made central to his own teaching.

I have been referring all this time to the *letters* in the New Testament. Some readers may be wondering why I don't call them "epistles." There is a good reason: the word "epistle" is simply a transliteration of the Greek word for a letter. Ancient letters from Roman times differ from modern ones in English, but there is still enough in common that it is just fine to refer to Paul's letters, using the English word, and many people do just that. As a reminder, a transliteration is when you spell a word from another language using the English alphabet (or more strictly speaking the Latin alphabet, since English borrowed its alphabet from Latin). The Greek word for "epistle" looks like this: ἐπιστολή. Its pronunciation is rather like "epistolay."

Letters are typically part of a conversation, a back-and-forth exchange of messages between individuals or groups in different locations. In 1 Corinthians Paul mentions things that the church in Corinth had written to him about. We are essentially listening in on one half of a phone conversation. I'm sure you've had that experience. (I'm not accusing you of putting a glass up to a door, just saying we've all been in the same room with someone when they've been on the phone.) We don't even have Paul's side of the conversation in its entirety. First

> **Epistle** *means "letter" and derives from the Greek word for a letter.*

Corinthians is the first of Paul's letters to that church that we have in the New Testament. However, as we discussed in an earlier chapter, this was clearly not his first letter to that church. In 1 Corinthians 5:9 Paul makes reference to something he had written to them previously.

Just as the writing of letters differed significantly in ancient times, the sending of letters was also a very different process. When you want to send a letter nowadays, you place it in an envelope with an appropriate stamp on it and drop it in a mailbox. Paul lived in a world without mailboxes, with no postal system. (In case it doesn't go without saying, there were therefore no stamp collectors either.) It may seem hard to fathom that if people wanted a letter delivered somewhere, they had to get someone to travel with the letter and take it to its destination. It may seem that they were really sending a person, and there's some truth in that, at least in many instances. Often a letter's primary function was to introduce the person carrying it to the recipients and authorize that individual to represent the sender in the place to which they brought the letter. In an era before modern modes of communication, this was the only way one could have one's voice heard, one's will expressed, in another part of the world.

We started the chapter with a failed attempt at humor. It therefore seems fitting to end with humor. We have been talking about Hebrews, and it contains what I consider to be the funniest verse in the New Testament. I am referring to Hebrews 13:22. There—after twelve chapters of some of the densest and most elaborate theological exposition in the whole of the New Testament, filled with detailed discussion of the Levitical laws concerning priesthood, sacrifice, and atonement—the author writes, "Brothers and sisters, I urge you to bear with my word of exhortation, for in fact I have written to you quite briefly" (NIV).

Now *that's* funny.

For Further Reading

Adams, Sean A., and Stanley E. Porter, eds. *Paul and the Ancient Letter Form*. Leiden: Brill, 2010.

Doering, Lutz. *Ancient Jewish Letters and the Beginnings of Christian Epistolography*. Tübingen: Mohr Siebeck, 2012.

Ehrman, Bart D. *Forgery and Counterforgery: The Use of Literary Deceit in Early Christian Polemics*. New York: Oxford University Press, 2013.

Klauck, Hans-Josef, and Daniel P. Bailey. *Ancient Letters and the New Testament: A Guide to Context and Exegesis*. Waco: Baylor University Press, 2006.

Richards, E. Randolph. *Paul and First-Century Letter Writing: Secretaries, Composition and Collection*. Downers Grove, IL: InterVarsity Press, 2004.

Sarri, Antonia. *Material Aspects of Letter Writing in the Graeco-Roman World: C. 500 BC–C. AD 300*. Berlin: de Gruyter, 2017.

Stowers, Stanley K. *Letter Writing in Greco-Roman Antiquity*. Philadelphia: Westminster, 1989.

T

Telephone Game?

Seeing, hearing, believing, understanding, speaking, and much more are involved in the process of communication that lies behind the Gospels and other New Testament sources. Then as now, many aspects of communication are taken for granted, but when they are explicitly mentioned, it gives us an important glimpse of both how the New Testament took shape and how its authors differ from us. The things I mentioned are focused on the head, where the ears are and where the mouth is that says the things that ears hear. It is also the location of the brain, which processes the things heard. People in the era of the New Testament did not know this last point yet. Some thought the brain was the seat of cognition. Others thought the heart was. Paul sided with the latter, consistently talking of the heart as believing and thinking but never mentioning the brain. We have no trouble accepting that language metaphorically, even though Paul may have meant it somewhat more literally. The same is true for other New Testament authors. In Ephesians 1:18 we encounter a prayer that light will shine on the eyes of the hearts of readers. The author probably did not think that the heart literally has eyes, but the metaphor nonetheless reflects how ancient people understood both sight and cognition. We encounter it most explicitly in Matthew 6:22, which says that the eye is the lamp of the body. The ancient Greeks believed that vision worked through a process of the eye emitting light and then receiving it back again. Yet just as one doesn't need to know how the eye works in order to see, how the ear works in order to hear, or how the vocal cords work in order to speak, the fact that we know more about certain biological and social processes related to communication doesn't change the fact that ancient people did these things and did them effectively. Yet they did them differently, and thought and talked about them differently, which makes it all the more important for us to closely consider what early Christian communication entailed and how it affects the New Testament both explicitly and implicitly.

Whether one is discussing oral tradition or the copying of manuscripts, sooner or later someone will make an analogy to the telephone game. Did you play it as a child? The teacher lines students up, the first one is told something in their ear, and then each successive student has one chance to repeat it to the next in line. This is a truly unhelpful and misleading analogy for how information circulated in ancient Christianity. People were connected to and communicated within complex social networks. Their communication did not take place in linear fashion with them all lined up single file. Nor did one normally have only one opportunity to say or hear something. Social networking in the modern sense is simply the use of technology to facilitate what people have done in every era. Thinking specifically about the case of Paul, he wrote to the churches in Galatia precisely because other people showed up there and challenged some of what he had said. We don't know that they disagreed with anything that he had passed on about the life and teaching of Jesus. They undoubtedly confirmed much of what Paul had said in that regard. As far as we know, their only disagreement with Paul was about whether gentile Christians needed to convert to Judaism, undergoing circumcision and following the rest of the Torah.

There are two extreme opposing viewpoints that one may encounter in discussions of oral tradition and memory in early Christianity. One emphasizes the fallibility of human memory, the capacity for even eyewitness testimony to be wrong, and countless other things that will make us pessimistic that we can know anything at all about what anyone in the past said. The other emphasizes the remarkable ability not just of rare individuals but of cultures and schools to foster memorization and preserve information accurately across time. Both are correct, and so the issue is not which of these extremes to pick but how to tell where a particular saying of Jesus or tidbit of information falls on the spectrum. A false rumor can be started soon after an event occurs and then persist for generations despite the pleas of eyewitnesses and skeptical investigators. The same legends about places can be found in texts separated by centuries with nothing but an ongoing tradition of local lore and storytelling to bridge the gap. A powerful experience can sear itself on our memories so that even years later the memory seems crisp and clear. The key thing to note is that the people who knew Jesus did not simply vanish after they passed on their stories. A community was involved in the process, remembering and retelling stories. The historian is dependent on what people remembered and what people wrote down, and must always carefully evaluate the information provided.

In a context in which most communication was oral and few things were written down, most of the time it would be impossible to tell whether someone was repeating something verbatim. Of course, people memorize things word for word all the time. However, you need a written text that you can read repeatedly in order to make this happen. If you ever memorized a poem, or have learned a song by heart, think about the process in your own experience. You had the chance to repeat it word for word thanks to something written or recorded that you could read or listen to over and over again. Without a written text or recording to facilitate memorization and check the accuracy of a person's recall, the notion of "word for word" becomes meaningless. The early Christians focused on conveying the sense, the gist, the main point of the message. This may make you feel better about reading the Bible in translation, which seeks to achieve the same thing. The most recent research in historical study has taken to heart what we have learned about human memory and focuses on the gist as well. The variations between the gospels show us that even when one author used what another had written, reproducing their wording precisely was not the aim nor anyone's expectation.

Occasionally, even when the gospels show the same kinds of variations typical of oral performance and recall from memory, they agree precisely on particular words or even a complete phrase. Jokes provide a useful analogy. There is almost never a need to memorize a joke word for word, but it is typically necessary to get certain key words just right and perhaps word the punchline in a particular way, otherwise the joke will not be funny. This is because the humor often depends on a pun or a double entendre (a word that can have more than one meaning). We have already seen that Jesus made puns, and it isn't surprising that those were remembered. The gospels also attribute other kinds of wordplay to him. The Gospel of John features more than one story that involves Jesus using a phrase that can have more than one meaning. The person he is speaking with understands it one way; then Jesus explains that he is talking about something else. We get this in the story about Nicodemus in chapter 3, the Greek word *anōthen* meaning both "again" and "from above." Nicodemus thinks Jesus means that he must be born again, but Jesus explains that he is talking about a birth from above. Likewise, in the story about the Samaritan woman at the well in John 4, Jesus uses the expression "living water," which is the Aramaic way of saying "flowing water." The woman naturally understands him to mean that, since they had been talking about water. Jesus, however, turns the conversation in a different direction using the symbolism of water to talk about something spiritual.

Serial Translators?

Another thing that I hear surprisingly often is that in the Bible we only have "translations of translations of translations." That is not at all the case. When people say this, they seem to imagine that the Bible was translated from Hebrew into Greek, then from Greek into Latin, then from Latin into German, and maybe then from German into English. That is not what is involved in making a translation of the Bible. Bible translations are, as a rule, made directly from the original languages. There certainly have been a few cases in which a modern paraphrase was made by starting with an English translation and then working from there. A paraphrase differs from a translation inasmuch as it prioritizes making sense in the target language even if it means playing fast and loose with the original wording and meaning. There is no sharp line between the two, since all translation involves expressing things in a new language and thus in a new way. Just as translations are not "translations of translations of translations," there is no such thing as a "literal translation" or "the most literal translation." When people ask, "What is the most literal translation of the Bible?" it is clear that they don't really understand translation. As we have seen many times throughout this book, there are places where one translation may stick more closely to the wording or phrasing in the Greek. That doesn't necessarily mean it conveys the meaning clearly, and sometimes the result is the opposite. We have also seen that there are words that have two meanings or a range of meanings in Greek for which there is no equivalent English word with precisely the same range of meanings or connotations. In Greek you use the definite article (i.e., the word "the") in places where you would not in English. Having "the" in an English translation every place one finds its Greek equivalent would not make the translation "more literal." It would just make it a worse translation. Different languages work differently, and to convey the same basic idea in a different language you may have to say something quite different.

When it comes to the words of Jesus, we *do* have most of them only in translation. The Gospels, written in Greek, rarely tell us what Jesus said in Aramaic. In that sense your English translation is indeed a translation of a translation of the words of Jesus. But it is a translation from the original languages in which these texts were written. The New Testament authors show a range of fluency and education in the Greek language. Some were native speakers. Some appear to have been bilingual. The author of Revelation struggled a bit with Greek. Yet it would be inaccurate to say (as people sometimes do) that he "thought in Aramaic but wrote in Greek." If you speak two languages, you know that isn't the way language works. What *does* happen is that the grammar, vocabulary, and idioms of your native language influence how you express yourself in your second language, even when you think in that second language and speak it quite fluently.

When it comes to manuscripts, we do only have copies of copies, but that is something different. The scribe in most instances sought to make an exact copy of the text in front of them. If something in the text they were copying didn't seem right, they might try to fix it. Sometimes in the process they took what the text originally said and changed it. Whether that made it better is another question (anyone who has experience with autocorrect knows that a "correction" doesn't always make what you wrote correct, nor better). When Matthew and Luke used Mark as a source, they clearly felt free to adjust and adapt what they found in it. Some scribes making new copies of a work approached what they did in a similar way. Copying was initially a linear process, inasmuch as a scribe tended to have one copy of a work and made a new copy of it. As time went on, however, libraries and monasteries that carried out the task of copying New Testament texts ended up with multiple copies in their possession. At least sometimes they do appear to have consulted more than one copy and sought to choose what seemed to be the most correct reading from among them. Your English translation is almost never a translation of one particular ancient manuscript. Instead, translators use a critical edition of the Greek New Testament as the basis of their work. That means that they work with an eclectic edition. To produce such an edition, a team of scholars consult all the known manuscripts, and each time there is a difference between them, they discuss which of the options most likely represents what the text originally said.

Hopefully if you hear anyone say that today's New Testaments are translations of translations of translations, you'll gently tell them they're wrong, and explain that they are translations of critical editions of the Greek texts themselves, throwing in as many other details about the process as you can remember. We talked about memory and exact wording earlier in the chapter. When you share information you learned in this book as things like this come up in conversation, you'll rarely remember the exact words you read. But I hope you'll remember the gist.

Talk to My Agent

As I mentioned in a previous chapter, in the time before telephones, faxes, emails, texts, and countless other options for communicating across long distances, the only way to get your will done or your voice heard in a distant place was to utilize an agent, someone to represent you. Call them an emissary if you wish. If you are a ruler, you might prefer to call them your ambassador. The relevant Greek and Hebrew terms both mean someone who has been sent. The Greek word is probably familiar to you, coming into English through transliteration as *apostle*. All four of the gospels show awareness of the key principles of agency. Someone who was appointed to represent you could speak and act with your full authority. Matthew 10:40 (parallel Luke 10:16) says that whoever receives the one Jesus sends out in fact receives him, and so too the one who receives him in fact receives God, who sent him. This is the core principle of agency in a nutshell. John 20:21 expresses the parallel in terms of the Father sending Jesus and Jesus sending his apostles in the same way (see also Mark 9:37; Luke 9:48; 10:16; John 5:23-24; 13:20).

There were no telephones in the first century, and so it shouldn't be surprising that the telephone game is a poor analogy for oral and manuscript tradition in early Christianity. On the other hand, chains of transmission of a message and authority were indeed crucially important. That is why so much attention is given to representatives who speak with authority on behalf of another, whether it be Jesus understood as the emissary of God or individuals like Peter and Paul who understood themselves as emissaries of Jesus.

For Further Reading

Allison, Dale C. *Constructing Jesus: Memory, Imagination, and History.* Grand Rapids: Baker Academic, 2010.
Dunn, James D. G. *Jesus Remembered.* Christianity in the Making 1. Grand Rapids: Eerdmans, 2003.

Ehrman, Bart D. *Misquoting Jesus: The Story behind Who Changed the Bible and Why.* New York: HarperCollins, 2009.

Eve, Eric. *Behind the Gospels: Understanding the Oral Tradition.* Minneapolis: Fortress, 2014.

Viljoen, Francois P. "A Contextualised Reading of Matthew 6:22–23: 'Your Eye Is the Lamp of Your Body.'" *HTS Theological Studies* 65, no. 1 (2009), http://ref.scielo.org/bx3mdn.

U

Unmentionables

It is much easier to notice what is in a text than to notice what is missing.

Acts 11:26 mentions that those who were part the movement centered on Jesus were first referred to as "Christians" in Antioch. It says this as a parenthetical aside, so we ought not to assume that the author is connecting the origin of the nickname with precisely the time or the people that he mentions. Acts 11 tells of the good news reaching Antioch and indicates that this location witnessed one of the earliest crossings of this Jewish faith into contact with non-Jews. That would make sense as the context for the nickname arising. As we explore in another chapter, the use of the Greek word for anointing, transliterated into English as "Christ," would have puzzled non-Jewish Greek speakers. The use of the term would have led naturally to a nickname. Even if the term only caught on much later, it would have been natural for the author of Acts to say, "Hey, this moment here, it eventually led to us having the name you now know us by." That process may have taken a while.

It is easy to miss that when Paul writes to the groups of Jesus-followers that he founded, he doesn't call them "Christians," nor does he refer to "Christianity." This is worth noting because we can learn a lot by considering what this movement represented before it ever had a clear nickname. In Acts we regularly find the movement connected with Jesus referred to as "the Way." I capitalized that since it seems like it could be a title, but it might also be shorthand for "the way of Jesus," this particular way that I am talking about as opposed to others. At first, what came to be called Christianity was one of the variety of ways that Jews pursued the observance of their ancestral religion. Of course, as we discussed in an earlier chapter, "religion" is another modern word that doesn't quite correspond to the way people spoke and thought in Paul's time. James 1:26–27 uses the Greek word *thrēskeia*, which perhaps comes closest to the meaning of the English word "religion." Yet the infrequency of that term in the New Testament illustrates well the fact that even this term did not function the way "religion" does in English, since one can scarcely talk about early Christianity or ancient Judaism without the word "religion" occurring more frequently than it does in the Bible. In Colossians 2:18 that same word is more often translated as "worship." The word also appears in Acts 26:5, where the NRSV translates it as "religion." Yet the NRSV also has the word "religion" in Acts 25:19, where the Greek word is a different one, *deisidaimonias*, which means something like "fear of the gods/spirits" when used positively and "superstition" when used negatively. One could be forgiven for thinking that Luke's terminology might justify after all the saying, "Christianity isn't a religion; it's a way of life." However, Luke clearly views the "way" of the "Christians" as a way of following what we would call the Jewish religion. As such, that way was not necessarily incompatible with other ways or sects of Judaism. For instance, Paul declares himself to still be of the Pharisaic school of thought in Acts 23:6. That surprises a lot of modern readers, both because they think of Jesus's way as inherently opposed to that of the Pharisees and because the word "Pharisee" has itself become a negative epithet that people apply as an insult to groups they disagree with. The word "Pharisee" didn't mean "hypocrite" in Jesus's time. Indeed, the word "hypocrite" didn't mean "hypocrite" either. The English word is derived from the Greek word *hypocritēs*, which means an actor in the sense of someone who performed in theater. When Jesus applied this word to the Pharisees, was he focused on their "play acting," their "putting on a show," the difference between the real person and the character they depicted, the fact that Greek theater regularly featured the wearing of masks, some or all of the above, or something else?

Jesus taught us to put ourselves in the shoes of others and treat others the way we want to be treated. Ancient people stereotyped to a much greater extent than is today considered acceptable, and just as the hashtag #notallchristians appears regularly today, those who empathize with the sentiment should also equally affirm #notallpharisees as well. Just as Christians today are not all the same, the Pharisees as a movement in the first century were by no means uniform.

Pharisees: a first-century branch of Judaism focused on developing and transmitting a body of case law applying scriptural teaching to their time. They were distinguished by their belief in an afterlife involving bodily resurrection, as well as by their concern for matters of ritual purity.

The Rabbinic literature of later centuries (works like the Mishnah and Talmud) preserve debates, discussions, and disagreements galore. These include significant disagreements between two teachers who were contemporaries of Jesus, Hillel and Shammai. When Matthew 19:3 depicts Pharisees asking Jesus whether it is lawful for a man to divorce his wife for any reason, he was referring to one of the many points of disagreement between the schools of Hillel and Shammai. One of the most famous sayings attributed to Hillel is often compared with the similar point Jesus emphasized not much later. Hillel said, "What is hateful to you, do not do to your fellow" (b. Shabbat 31a). It may help you to treat the Pharisees the same way you'd want any group you are part of to be treated when you know that one of the most revered and influential Pharisees is famous for making much the same point.

Rabbinic literature tends not to call these figures "Pharisees." Instead, they are referred to as "Sages." The Aramaic term behind the English word "Pharisee" most likely means "separated." Being separated can be a positive or a negative thing. Just like the name "Christians," the label "Pharisees" may have started as a nickname used by others, perhaps conveying something like the English word "separatists." At least some to whom the label was applied may have been willing to embrace or at least live with it, likely because avoiding sin and uncleanness were positive forms of separation. In Luke 13:31 it is Pharisees who warn Jesus of a threat to his life. Not only were the Pharisees not "in charge" in Jesus's time and thus not the ones responsible for his execution, but some actively tried to help him avoid apprehension by authorities. It is important to emphasize this not only in the interest of understanding the New Testament in its context but also because of the way Christians imagine the Pharisees and generalize about them contributes to an ongoing problem of anti-Semitism in churches. (What is said about another, much smaller group, the Sadducees, is even worse, as you'll know if your Sunday school teacher ever explained their name by saying, "They were sad, you see." Please don't continue to make that joke, not only because it unfairly caricatures a group that we only know about from the writings of people who disagreed with them, but also because the joke is so old and well known that it simply isn't funny anymore, if it ever was.)

We've all heard of sibling rivalry even if we haven't experienced it directly. Often it is hardest to get along with those closest to and most similar to us. Jesus and some of the Pharisees had so many disagreements because they agreed about so much, and yet also disagreed on a few key matters. Jesus held the Pharisaic view of the afterlife, envisaging bodily resurrection. For the early Christians, resurrection was not something they believed happened to Jesus and him alone, but something they expected for every person who ever lived. It is not surprising that Paul might still think of himself as a Pharisee over against the Sadducees, who did not embrace this relatively new idea that God would raise the dead at the end of time.

People are often surprised that although the word "convert" appears in the New Testament, it is never used of Paul, even though today it is quite common for people to speak of Paul having "converted to Christianity." The New Testament only uses the term to refer to gentiles converting, whether to Judaism or Christianity. As we will explore further below, Paul understood himself to have experienced a radical reversal with respect to the question of whether Jesus was the Messiah. That did not involve him thinking he was now something other than Jewish, and may not have involved him thinking that he was any less a Pharisee either. This is relevant to how we understand the message Paul proclaimed to non-Jews as well. Christianity was not at this time a world religion, much less one that stood over against Judaism. Paul was inviting gentiles to become part of Israel, even while removing obstacles such as circumcision. That is a noteworthy development, and it can be easy to miss the significance of it (at least for those who have never faced the prospect of having their foreskin surgically removed in order to join a religious movement). The first major debate in the early church, which according to Acts 15 led to the first church council drawing representatives from many communities to discuss the matter, was about circumcision and observance of kosher food laws by Christians. This is an important event for a number of reasons, and not just for the way it set the stage for Christianity becoming a major religion among non-Jews. The decision that people could be part of the covenant with Abraham and yet not be circumcised was hugely significant and reveals a lot about how these early Christians understood scripture.

We could elaborate on many more things that the New Testament doesn't say, and on words that did not necessarily have the same connotations they have today. We hear nothing of individual leaders of congregations called "priests" or "pastors." Whether "bishops" and "deacons" resembled the roles played by bearers of those titles in our time is a subject that could fill a chapter of its own. There are no mentions of church buildings; the Greek word translated as "church," just like the word rendered "synagogue," meant a congregation, a gathering of people, and only by extension a place where those meetings occurred. When Paul wrote to churches, he didn't instruct them to engage in evangelism. That raises another key question it is always important to ask about letters. Letters in the New Testament are written to deal with specific issues and are not introductions to the Christian faith. That is why they don't contain stories about Jesus, either. It is not because Paul didn't want people in churches he planted to know about Jesus, but because he told them in person when proclaiming his message and instructing those who responded positively to it. What is emphasized in a letter is not always what would be important to that individual in general in the absence of some pressing concern. Likewise, what is not mentioned in a letter was not necessarily unimportant to them. Things may be left unsaid because they are so foundational as not to require mention.

*The words translated "**church**" and "**synagogue**" both denoted a congregation, an assembly of people, and only with time came to denote a building used for such meetings.*

Other things do not get a mention because they never on any occasion crossed the mind of the ancient author we are reading. Becoming familiar with their ancient context is the only way to figure out which is which.

Sometimes it may be perfectly fine to use a term that an ancient author does not use when discussing what they wrote. It is much easier to refer to Paul and the churches he brought into being as "Christian" than to write each time that they belonged to the movement that would eventually come to be known as Christianity. The key thing is that, if you use the label "Christian" for Paul even though he does not, you keep in mind that he understood himself to be proclaiming the good news that gentiles were being welcomed into the people of God, Israel, through Israel's Messiah. That is directly connected to the fact that most scholars avoid referring to Paul's reversal of attitude toward Jesus and the movement focused on him as a "conversion." The reason is not only that Paul does not use the term. We tend to use the word "conversion" when someone leaves one religion for another. We are less likely to do so if someone switches churches or even moves between Protestant denominations. You would talk about a Christian converting to Buddhism but might not say that a Presbyterian converted to Methodism. For Paul, his turnaround was not a departure from one religion for another. He went from rejecting the claim that Jesus was the Messiah to accepting it and proclaiming it. It was a radical reversal, to be sure, but one that is easy for today's Christians to misunderstand and misconstrue. And unless we understand it in a way that is sensitive to Paul's own sense of his identity and mission, we may turn him into a promoter of a new religion that supplants Judaism, when in fact he understood himself to be a proponent of the God of the Jews, inviting non-Jews into relationship with the same God he had sought to worship throughout his life.

For Further Reading

Botha, Pieter J. J. "History and Point of View: Understanding the Sadducees." *Neotestamentica* 30, no. 2 (1996): 235–80.

Eisenbaum, Pamela. *Paul Was Not a Christian: The Original Message of a Misunderstood Apostle.* New York: HarperOne, 2009.

Sievers, Joseph, and Amy-Jill Levine, eds. *The Pharisees.* Grand Rapids: Eerdmans, 2021.

Viviano, Benedict T., and Justin Taylor. "Sadducees, Angels, and Resurrection (Acts 23:8–9)." *Journal of Biblical Literature* 111, no. 3 (1992): 496–98.

V

Variations and Variants

One of the first things I discuss in my one-semester course on the Bible is that there is no such thing as "the Bible." There are only Bibles, and they are not all the same. As I have already explained in this book, Protestant, Catholic, Eastern Orthodox, and Ethiopian Orthodox canons are different with respect to the works included in their Old Testament. It would be easy to simply breathe a sigh of relief on learning that these churches all have the same New Testament. It was a long and complex process getting there, but despite debates and reservations we discussed in previous chapters, Christians around the world have ended up with the same table of contents in their New Testament, a very different state of affairs than in the case of the Old Testament. Yet while that is true as far as the table of contents of the New Testament is concerned, even so not all English Bibles have precisely the same contents within those same books. This chapter explains why.

You might be wondering how the *contents* can be different if the *table of contents* is identical. The reason is that not all manuscripts of the works included in the New Testament are identical. As with almost all ancient literature, we do not have the originals of these works. Our earliest copies are, more often than not, incomplete, and in some cases they are relatively small fragments. When we compare the manuscripts, we encounter differences. The effort to compare manuscripts with a view to reconstructing the likely original form is called "textual criticism." When there are significant differences, most modern English translations will include a footnote indicating this. Sometimes a verse or passage had a long history of inclusion in Bibles, yet, as earlier manuscripts came to light, it turned out that the passage was absent from them. When text critics have judged it most likely that those words were a later addition to the original form, modern English translations will typically place them in brackets to indicate this. That they leave them in the main body of the text at all indicates something important, namely that Bible translators and publishers feel an obligation to give readers of the Bible and churches what they want, at least to a very significant extent. This is also one reason why archaic language sometimes persists even in modern translations. People get upset if you tamper too much with the wording of one of their favorite scriptures, even if you are making its meaning clearer by doing so.

Textual criticism is the effort to reconstruct the original form of a text whose originals no longer exist, by comparing existing copies to one another.

What are some of these more major differences between our earliest copies and later ones that are reflected in differences between Bibles in English? One famous one is the story of the woman who is brought before Jesus and accused of committing adultery. It is found in John 8 in most of our New Testament manuscripts, but not in our earliest copies. In some manuscripts of John it is placed elsewhere, sometimes at the end of the gospel as a sort of appendix. It is also found in the Gospel of Luke in some manuscripts. Some of our earliest post–New Testament authors like Origen and Tertullian do not include it when they comment on the Gospel of John. The Didascalia Apostolorum, a work from the third century, appears to be the first to mention it unambiguously, and yet it does so in a way that leaves unclear whether the author knew the story in precisely the form in which it ended up in the Gospel of John. In the fourth century several authors mention it, including Didymus the Blind, Jerome, and Augustine. Since then discussions have rarely if ever ceased about the status of the story as part of the New Testament canon. Textual criticism and the definition of a canon are inseparable. When you have more than one version of a work in circulation, saying the work is canonical leaves significant ambiguity. If you're a Star Wars fan, you'll know that no one could possibly deny that the first Star Wars film ever made is canon within the franchise. Yet those who agree on this may still disagree about whether Han shot first. (You can look that up if you don't know what I'm talking about.) In the same way, Christians who agree about the canonical status of the Gospel of John disagree about the canonicity of this story. Note as well that the question of a story's canonical status is separate from the question of whether it depicts an event that actually happened. The Gospel of John tells us that Jesus did many more things than could be included in that book, or indeed any number of books (John 20:30; 21:25). The story about the woman accused of adultery may be about an actual event in the life of Jesus, even if it is judged not to be canonical—that is, if it was not originally part of one of the New Testament gospels.

Other substantial manuscript variants serve as classic examples in textbooks and courses on textual criticism. One is the ending of the Gospel of Mark. In our earliest manuscripts the story ends with the statement that the women "said nothing to anyone, for they were afraid" (Mark 16:8). We can tell that it was not a satisfying ending for ancient readers. Scribes confronted with it added several different endings in manuscripts of Mark in an attempt to fix what they felt was wrong. The Gospels of Matthew and Luke (and perhaps others) also indicate dissatisfaction with Mark's ending, since they used Mark as a source and yet felt the story needed to continue further. The key narrative problem is that we as readers are being told about the experience of the women at the tomb, and yet the grand finale in the earliest manuscripts says that they did not tell anyone about that experience. If they told no one, how can the author be telling us about it? Some interpreters today suggest that the gospel is "open ended," challenging us to go spread the word in contrast with the women who failed to. That does not solve the problem. Can you imagine if the final words of Mark were tagged onto the end of Matthew? "Go therefore and make disciples of all nations. . . . But they said nothing to anyone, for they were afraid." That wouldn't be an open ending. In that context, at least, we would recognize it for what it is: an awkwardly abrupt closure. One possible explanation for why Mark ends so abruptly is that the original ending of Mark was lost early on. Even modern books and magazines can break so that sections are lost despite more advanced binding techniques. We have plenty of evidence for the frequency with which this happened to ancient codices. Many of our ancient manuscripts are incomplete, and it is particularly common for the beginning and ending to have become lost. There is thus nothing unlikely about this scenario. Of course, Mark is not known for its literary flair, and so one can hardly rule out the possibility that the author failed to provide a satisfying ending. Nor can we exclude the possibility that the author was interrupted while writing by events that prevented him from finishing his gospel. All we have are the manuscripts. We must judge which explanation seems most probable given the evidence, and in this case it can be genuinely hard to decide. What is clear, however, is that the earliest form of the Gospel of Mark ended at 16:8.

In 1 John 5:7 in the King James Version you will find the statement that "there are three that bear record in heaven, the Father, the Word, and the Holy Ghost: and these three are one." Most modern English translations leave those words out, and with good reason: they appear in no Greek manuscript of the New Testament prior to the fourteenth century, although they were included in Latin versions much earlier. Similar phrases can be found in some of the church fathers, and so it may be that the statement began life as a statement in a sermon, was added as a marginal comment in a Latin Bible, and eventually in the process of copying a diglot of 1 John (i.e., a manuscript that had Greek on one page and Latin on the opposite) a copyist harmonized the Greek with the Latin. You have presumably seen heavily annotated Bibles, whether in your own home, your church Bible study, or a charity store. Ancient owners of Bibles and scribes did not have highlighters and pens such as those used today. That's perhaps just as well, since highlighting doesn't help us learn and remember things the way many today assume. Be that as it may, the custom of making marginal notes is ancient and has never ceased down the ages.

If you ever have the opportunity to work with Greek manuscripts of the New Testament, even if only in digital form via the internet, you may find yourself very grateful to past owners or curators of manuscripts who added chapter numbers in the margins, which help you find a passage you are looking for much more quickly than you might have otherwise. It was only in the thirteenth century that chapter divisions were added to make it easier to refer to a particular section of a work in the Bible. Verse divisions were added later still. Chapter and verse are thus another example of something that is bound to be in your Bible, and yet isn't in the Bible if one is referring to the original texts. The margins of manuscripts are places where all of these things we've mentioned first came to be found: numbers for reference; quotes from a sermon that relate to the biblical passage; commentary. Scribes also sometimes inserted in the margin things that they realized they had inadvertently omitted while copying, perhaps because their eye jumped to the same word on another line. (Don't judge them harshly, as though this has never happened to you!) The hope was that the next scribe to copy the manuscript would put those words back where they belong. You can see how confusion could arise, and how a marginal comment with words from a sermon could have found their way into 1 John 5:7 without any deliberate intent to tamper with the Bible.

Many of the long passages that appear only in later manuscripts have been given Latin names that are still used to refer to them, such as the Comma Johanneum *(the short clause in John, referring to 1 John 5:7) and the* Pericope Adulterae *(the passage/selection concerning adultery in John 8).*

This isn't to say that deliberate tampering never happened. It is only to say that most manuscript variations are not best explained in that way. Even deliberate changes were most often motivated by a desire to "fix" the text when scribes found themselves copying something that did not make sense to them or did not mesh with the doctrines they had been taught. Even when modern Bible-readers do not tamper with the text in the same way, they may simply ignore what it says, or find convoluted ways of interpreting it to mean something other than what it appears to. Is that really so different? The end result seems to be the same.

We have looked at examples involving whole verses or longer passages, in which the matter is rather clear-cut because our oldest manuscripts are consistent in omitting them. These are the exception rather than the rule. Most of the differences between manuscripts are more minor, involving slight variations in wording, spelling, or order. If you are wondering how texts that are now viewed as sacred scripture could be subject to copying errors, to say nothing of deliberate alterations, the simple answer is that initially none of these writings was part of a "New Testament" or a "Bible," and while they were valued, preserving their exact wording was not. This is more likely to disturb someone concerned with maintaining a doctrine of biblical inerrancy than it will someone interested in historical investigation of early Christianity and its literature. For the latter, uncertainty is par for the course. For the inerrantist, what good does it do to say the Bible is inerrant if its precise contents are ambiguous? There is a simple solution to this problem: don't subscribe to a doctrine of biblical inerrancy. After all, unlike the stories and passages we have discussed here, a doctrine of inerrancy is something you won't find in *any* Bible.

For Further Reading

Ehrman, Bart D. *The Orthodox Corruption of Scripture: The Effect of Early Christological Controversies on the Text of the New Testament*. New York: Oxford University Press, 1996.

Epp, Eldon Jay, and Gordon D. Fee. *Studies in the Theory and Method of New Testament Textual Criticism*. Grand Rapids: Eerdmans, 1993.

Knust, Jennifer. "The Woman Caught in Adultery (John 8:1–11)." Bible Odyssey, https://www.bibleodyssey.org/en/passages/main-articles/woman-caught-in-adultery.

McGrath, James F. "Mark's Missing Ending: Clues from the Gospel of John and the Gospel of Peter." *Bible and Interpretation*, February 2011, https://bibleinterp.arizona.edu/articles/mcg.

———. *What Jesus Learned from Women*. Eugene, OR: Cascade, 2021.

W

Women with Authority

This book focuses on things scholars know so well that we might neglect to mention them, thus never communicating that important information about the New Testament to Christians who aren't scholars. There is one thing, however, that most people think they know about scholars: we make things complicated that are in fact simple. Yes, scholars know that people think this about us. One reason for this impression is our failure to explain certain aspects of what we do and about what happens "behind the scenes" of producing a translation of the Bible. Few readers of the New Testament would be happy if their English translation contained lots of parenthetical remarks emphasizing how truly puzzling a passage is in Greek and explaining how much the translation committee debated how to render particular words and ideas in English before deciding. If you look at the footnotes, or consult commentaries, you will catch glimpses of those things. In the text of a Bible translation, however, all you encounter is one rendering that seems clear enough. That can mislead you into thinking that the Greek text being translated is equally clear, and that the pages and pages full of scholarly debates about the meaning of the passage are a waste of time, an exercise in scholarly hair-splitting. If you were to speak with the translators, you would find that they consulted and talked about those lengthy scholarly articles, that they evaluated evidence and debated what to put in the text. Your translation is a result of that scholarly work combined with the desire of translators to make your life easier as a reader.

A good example of this is in Paul's discussion of head coverings in 1 Corinthians 11:2–16. That passage is largely ignored in the English-speaking world, while the passage adjacent to it about the Lord's Supper is famous. In other parts of the world, women covering their heads is a live issue. This in itself is a very good reason to take a close look at it. There are ongoing debates about women's leadership in some denominations, while others consider the matter settled one way or another. Most of those who reject or dispute the appropriateness of women having authority in churches do not care if women's heads are covered nor what exactly they do with their hair (although in some churches dying one's hair green would be a no-no even though the Bible says nothing on that topic). Why these diverse stances? Why such inconsistency in applying texts that relate to women's roles in churches and other spheres? The underlying issue about how, if at all, to *apply* texts to one's own time is in theory distinct from the question of how to *interpret* the text in relation to its original setting in history and culture. In practice the two are not so easily separable. Another thing academics know is that we do not read texts, nor apply them, with a God's-eye view of things that is free from human presuppositions and assumptions. If we assume that women are equal to men in every respect, it will affect how we interpret the text. If we assume they are not, the same holds true. Both interpreters may assume that their assumptions reflect the Bible's teaching and thus do not distort their perception of the meaning of the text. But how can one know, when the assumptions are already in place before a close look is taken at any text related to this topic? We cannot set aside our presuppositions, our culture and upbringing. The best we can do is to seek out interpreters with assumptions different from our own and listen in an open-minded way to what they have to say. Unless we do that, we may not even become *aware* of our assumptions, much less find ourselves in a position to examine and perhaps even rethink them.

Taking It from the Top

Where should one begin an attempt to make sense of a difficult or confusing passage? Starting at the beginning is the best approach to understanding almost anything, as a rule. But if the beginning of a passage is unclear and what follows less so, starting at the beginning might lead us to misunderstand, which may in turn distort our understanding of what follows. Here, if we take it from the top (a musical idiom for beginning once again at the start of the piece), we immediately face several potential issues in our passage from Corinthians. One is that Paul indicates that he is discussing traditions that he passed on to the Corinthian Christians previously. They are apparently holding fast to them, and yet if that was all there was to it, Paul would not take this time to discuss what he does. In 1 Corinthians 7:1 he indicated that he was turning his attention to matters about which the Corinthian church had written to him. He may still be doing so in chapter 11. There are places where he seems to be quoting the Corinthians. He might even at times be quoting the Corinthians quoting him, which can be seen, for instance, where the NIV places several phrases in chapter 8 in quotation marks: "we all possess knowledge," "an idol is nothing at all in the world," and "there is no God but one." These may indeed be quotes from the letter *from* the Corinthians. But the Corinthians might have been quoting things

Paul had said previously and yet applying them in ways that Paul did not approve of. In short, we might need quotation marks within quotation marks for this one. Ancient Greek, as you'll recall, didn't have quotation marks at all. In a letter, you don't need them the same way you do in other forms of writing. If you and I exchange letters, if I used a phrase that you used when writing to me, you may recognize it as such even if I didn't put it in quotation marks. Someone else reading our mail may not grasp the origin and significance of the phrase. When we read Paul's letters to ancient Christians, we are indeed reading someone else's mail. I don't think Paul would mind—although I suspect that the Corinthians might have preferred that their reputation in future centuries not be based on their correspondence with Paul.

When Paul says that the head of every woman is man, the head of every man is Christ, and the head of Christ is God, we might quickly leap to conclusions about what it means for someone to be someone else's "head." We might also not consider that "man" and "woman" could equally mean "husband" and "wife." Greek, like Hebrew, did not distinguish. Is this Paul articulating his own viewpoint, Paul quoting the Corinthians, or Paul quoting the Corinthians quoting him? If we press on, we encounter other ambiguities. The phrase in 1 Corinthians 11:4 typically rendered as something like "with their head covered" is literally "having down the head," which could mean having a veil hanging down over their head, hair hanging downward, garment pulled over their head, and even "each one" (as in "by head count"). The ancient Greek translation of Esther 6:12 used the same expression as Paul to indicate that Haman covered his head in shame, presumably by pulling his garment over it. We have no reason to believe that Haman used a veil or headscarf. It also isn't self-evident to many today that men or women dishonor themselves or anyone else by what they do with their heads when praying. In some churches today women will not be allowed to pray out loud even if their heads are covered, and in many denominations if *anyone* prophecies, it will cause a stir, no matter the individual's gender.

So what is clear in the passage? Toward the end, Paul says that a woman (or wife) ought to have authority over her head (1 Cor 11:10). Despite the words having a clear meaning, you will find some translations rendering it as "a sign of authority" or even "a sign of her submission to authority." The New Living Translation renders it "a woman should wear a covering on her head to show she is under authority." The New King James and New American Standard Bibles insert "a symbol of" to turn the woman's authority into a sign of submission, and even the Amplified Bible (an expansive paraphrase) does this. In the Greek there is no "symbol" or "sign," just women with authority over their heads (which, given the preceding metaphorical use of the word, could just as conceivably mean their husbands).

The whole second half of the passage has Paul emphasizing not only that women have authority but that in Christ men and women are not independent and all things come from God. Please don't ask me what that has to do with angels. What's that? If I didn't want you to ask, I shouldn't have mentioned it? Oh well, I guess we had better tackle it then. The short answer is that no one is entirely sure what Paul meant when he said, "For this reason a woman ought to have authority over her head, because of the angels." One suggestion you may encounter in commentaries is that there was a concern about angels looking lustfully at the Corinthian women (which apparently veils would somehow deter). Another is that the concern was for messengers coming from other places who might have different cultural assumptions about hair and head coverings. One idea that occurred to me is that Paul might be alluding to the teaching of Jesus about

THE A TO Z OF THE NEW TESTAMENT

there being no marriage in the age to come. Since women and men will be like the angels, they should have authority over their heads even in the present. I'm not sure that's the right solution. Just like other academics, I keep trying to come up with new possibilities because no previous suggestion seems self-evidently correct. That is what scholars do. In some instances we are dealing with texts whose meaning is clear as long as one knows the relevant ancient language and cultural-historical context. All we need to do is translate and explain. In other cases our effort is to try to make sense of something that seems puzzling. That may be because the author did not express their idea clearly. It may be because they assumed knowledge that their intended readers had but which we today lack. Quite often we cannot even figure out why the text is so puzzling. All we know is that it is.

It is also important to be aware that the symbolic value of the head differs between cultures. English speakers today assume that it has to do with being in charge because the brain is in the head. Paul, however, did not know what brains do. When he talks about thinking and the mind, he refers to the heart, indicating that he shared the view held by most of his contemporaries that the heart was the locus of human cognition. "Head" could also serve as a metaphor for "source." Interestingly, no meaning of "head" meshes well with the doctrines most Christians hold and the creeds they subscribe to when it is applied to the relationship between Jesus and God. Some, however, have been so certain that Paul is emphasizing the subordination of women that they have preferred to challenge traditional Christology and emphasize Christ's eternal subordination to the Father, rather than rethink their understanding of gender roles. In principle it is appropriate to rethink doctrine in light of scripture. Whether that is being done consistently in this particular instance is another matter. Exploring that question would take us far from our task here of explaining what Paul meant in 1 Corinthians 11. So let's stick with the topic of hair in Corinth, a topic on which Acts has some information that may be relevant.

Paul's Long Hair

According to the book of Acts, just after a long stay in Corinth, when he was at the nearby port city of Cenchreae, Paul cut his hair because of a vow (Acts 18:18; see also Acts 21:22–24). This seems to refer to a Nazirite vow. People sometimes think Jesus had long hair because they confuse "Nazarene" (someone from Nazareth) with "Nazirite," which is unrelated. Confusion often results as well from the fact that most people only know of one Nazirite, Samson, and don't realize that he was an unusual case in *never* cutting his hair. (They forget about Samuel, another unusual case of a lifelong Nazirite, because his hair was not as famous as Samson's, not being associated with unusual physical strength. See Judg 13:4–5; 1 Sam 1:11.) A vow was normally made just for the period until the vow was fulfilled, the promise kept, and then it ended. (Think of the *Friends* episode in which Phoebe says that her friend Marjorie will shower when Tibet is free.) Jesus's vow not to drink of the fruit of the vine again until after the kingdom had come (Mark 14:25 and parallels) also sounds like a Nazirite vow.

We don't know the details of what Paul had vowed, but if one accepts the historicity of the information in Acts, then Paul's hair while in Corinth was longer than it usually was. How long? To know that, we'd have to know how long before this he had made the vow. We cannot answer that question, but noting the likelihood that Paul's hair was longer than usual when he was in Corinth is surely relevant to his comment in 1 Corinthians 11:14 about what nature might have been expected to teach the Corinthians. Since there are no punctuation marks in ancient Greek, Paul could be asking a question, "Doesn't nature teach you . . . ?" or he could be making a statement, "Nature doesn't teach you . . ." It seems odd to envisage Paul telling people in Corinth, where he refrained from cutting his hair in the way he otherwise would, that nature teaches them that men should not let their hair grow. Stranger still from our perspective is the reference to nature. For us today as speakers of English, "nature" denotes what happens through natural processes. From that perspective hair growing is by definition natural, and anything we do to interfere with it is by definition unnatural or contrary to nature. For speakers of ancient Greek like Paul, however, "nature" denoted the way things were supposed to be, including things that we would label with English words such as "culture" or "custom" rather than "nature."

Introducing Phoebe: Translations Matter

Your impression of women mentioned in the New Testament may very well have been influenced by the translations you have read. All translation involves interpretation, just as the act of reading a text does, whatever language you read it in. Compare what these different translations convey about two women mentioned in Romans 16, Phoebe and Junia:

Romans 16:1
NIV: I commend to you our sister Phoebe, a deacon of the church in Cenchreae.
ESV: I commend to you our sister Phoebe, a servant of the church at Cenchreae

Romans 16:7
NIV: Greet Andronicus and Junia, my fellow Jews who have been in prison with me. They are outstanding among the apostles, and they were in Christ before I was.

ESV: Greet Andronicus and Junia, my kinsmen and my fellow
   prisoners. They are well known to the apostles, and they
   were in Christ before me.

ASV: Salute Andronicus and Junias, my kinsmen, and my
   fellow-prisoners, who are of note among the apostles,
   who also have been in Christ before me.

Just as an aside, Cenchreae is the place where Acts says
Paul had his hair cut because of a vow, meaning that Phoebe
is likely one of the people who saw Paul with his hair longer
than usual. The term "deacon" in English is a transliteration
of the Greek word that appears in Romans 16:1. It does indeed mean "servant," but because Jesus taught his followers
that anyone who wants to lead must become a servant (Matt
20:26), the term came to be used by Christians as a title. So
too in Romans 16:7, to be "highly regarded among the apostles" can indicate that someone is an apostle who is highly
regarded, or that the person in question is not an apostle but
the apostles hold that person in high regard. Since there is
no reason for Paul to indicate in this context that other apostles hold Andronicus and Junia in high regard, the former
meaning is more likely. Yet the latter is not impossible. The
main point to take away from the above examples is not that
translation X is consistently "good" or translation Y is "bad"
but that all translation involves interpretation, and often one
can detect what assumptions are at work, or what point of
view regarding a particular matter of doctrine was important to the translators or the sponsors of the translation. If
you are not reading texts in the original languages, then the
next best thing is to make sure you consult multiple translations, and not just any different translations but ones that
reflect different religious traditions or different approaches
to translation. This should in many instances alert you that
a text can be understood in more than one way. Then you
can look into the matter further, consulting commentaries

and other academic resources. Otherwise, you might read the text in one translation and go away thinking you know "what the Bible says," when in fact you know one possible understanding of "what the Bible says."

Perhaps Phoebe being a deacon fits perfectly in the context of your understanding of church leadership. (You might prefer to say "deaconess," but there is no separate Greek word, and so the word "deaconess" should probably be made to go the way of "stewardess," "waitress," and "actress.") You may, on the other hand, be sure that neither Junia nor Andronicus can be *apostles* since Jesus appointed only twelve of those. That objection won't work when you consider that we have been talking throughout this chapter about letters from Paul, who describes himself as an apostle even though he was not one of the Twelve. If Andronicus and Junia are called apostles in Romans, it isn't because they are being added to the list of the Twelve. An apostle was someone who was sent. Jesus sent out larger numbers of people. The core group of twelve probably had a special status, to be sure. Even then, the New Testament evidence suggests that once people got beyond the most famous ones on the list, they often struggled to remember exactly who was part of that group (compare Matt 10:2-4; Mark 3:16-19; Luke 6:14-16). Perhaps what was significant, however, was not so much the Twelve's special authority or inside knowledge as the symbolism of there being a group of twelve. This number conveyed that Jesus's activity was connected with the hope for a restoration and regathering of the tribes of Israel. Either way, there is no reason that Junia could not have been an emissary, whether of Jesus or of her local church or both. Let me also mention the intriguing possibility that Junia might be the same person as Joanna mentioned in Luke 8:3 and 24:10. Saul of Tarsus was by no means the only person who had another name to use when outside an Aramaic-speaking Jewish setting (in his case, Paul). Many Jews had a Greek or Roman name that would be more readily recognizable to people who were not Jewish. Joanna certainly fits what Paul says of Junia: prominent among the apostles and in Christ before him. Even if not the same person, Joanna was a sponsor of Jesus's mission, one of several wealthy and independent women who made what he did possible, and so she too provides an important example of the leading role of women in this movement.

This is perhaps a good point at which to emphasize the importance of not mistakenly referring to Jesus having "twelve disciples." Jesus had many disciples, that term meaning students or apprentices. Apostles, on the other hand, were emissaries, ambassadors, appointed agents who represented the one who sent them. One could certainly commission a disciple as one's representative, and so the point is not that the same person could not be both disciple and apostle. The point is that Jesus appointed a special or symbolic group of twelve apostles, likely

> *A **disciple** is an apprentice or student. An **apostle** is an agent, an emissary, someone appointed with full authority to represent one's interests in another location.*

chosen from among his many disciples, and when people say that Jesus had twelve disciples, either they are confused about what a disciple is or they think that Jesus had only twelve students. According to Luke 10, Jesus sent out more than twelve emissaries at one time. Especially when we compare that passage, about a group of seventy or seventy-two who were sent out, with what Matthew 10 says about the Twelve, it becomes clear that the larger group was a group of apostles. Understanding that apostle did not mean "authoritative leader" but "appointed representative" is important for making sense of how Paul, Junia, and others could be apostles.

But Doesn't Paul Also Say . . . ?!

Often when someone reads the list of women who were Paul's coworkers in ministry in Romans 16, they think immediately of other places where Paul seems to preclude the possibility of women playing such roles. One is 1 Corinthians 14:34–35, which says that it is shameful for women to speak in the assembly (sometimes translated as "church"). The relevant words are found in different places in different manuscripts, as you can see if you consult the critical apparatus in a Greek New Testament or the treatment of this passage in a commentary or article. This has led some scholars to conclude that the statement is an interpolation. If it was written by Paul, it would seem to contradict what he said in chapter 11 of the same letter. If women cannot speak when Christians gather, then they cannot pray or prophesy, which would mean the discussion of the need for them to cover their heads when doing those things was a moot point. This means that if you conclude that the saying is *not* an interpolation, it should be understood in a manner that does not contradict what Paul says elsewhere (unless you adopt the stance that Paul was incoherent and contradicted himself, which people sometimes do, but it seems best to give writers like Paul the benefit of the doubt whenever possible). Perhaps some specific issue in Corinth was being addressed. Perhaps Paul had heard that women, having previously been denied access to education, now found themselves unable to follow the sermon and so asked one another about puzzling aspects of what was said while the sermon was still being delivered. This chatter while someone was delivering a sermon or teaching a lesson, even if done quietly, might still have been judged too distracting. If that was what was going on, Paul might have asked wives to leave their questions until they got home. Perhaps some readers of 1 Corinthians have mistaken advice about a specific situation for a blanket rule that applied in every situation.

First Timothy 2:11–15 is another passage that seems to be at odds with the authority that women mentioned in Romans 16 had. As has already been discussed, the majority of scholars do not think that Paul wrote this letter, nor the other

Pastoral Epistles (2 Timothy and Titus). Pseudepigraphy
(writing in someone else's name) was not uncommon in ancient times, nor is it today. These are by no means the only
works in the New Testament about which scholars reach this
conclusion. There is nearly universal agreement about some
works, while there is significant disagreement in the case of
others. When it comes to the Pastoral Epistles, it isn't just the
apparent difference regarding the role of women in churches
that raised doubts about authorship. The vocabulary and
style are different from the other letters
attributed to Paul and are more similar
to Christian writings from the second
century. At times it seems as though the
Pastoral Epistles could be in direct conversation with works like the Acts of
Paul and Thecla, which tells the story of
a woman who becomes a Christian, renounces marriage, and proclaims her
faith boldly, leading to her martyrdom.

*The **critical apparatus** in a
critical edition of the Greek
New Testament consists of
footnotes that indicate the
differences among manuscripts. An **interpolation** is
something inserted into a text
after it was completed.*

One solution to the apparent contradiction between 1 Timothy 2:11-15 and Paul's indication that women were his coworkers, as well as deacons and prophets in local churches,
is therefore to view 1 Timothy as written by someone other
than Paul. While we should not be too hasty to posit interpolations or forgery as a way of resolving tensions, in both
1 Corinthians 14 and 1 Timothy 2 there is evidence besides the
contents (in the case of the former, manuscript evidence; in
the case of the latter, quantifiable data regarding differences
of vocabulary and even grammar).

What options are available if someone remains persuaded
that Paul wrote 1 Timothy? A close reading of 2:11-15 offers
a possible solution, just as in 1 Corinthians 14 we saw that
there are options other than excision to deal with the seeming contradiction with what Paul wrote elsewhere. Let us
recall once again that few women in the Roman world were

given the opportunity for formal education. This doesn't mean that most men had that sort of education, but only that the relatively few people in total who had an opportunity to study were men. What jumps out at us today in 1 Timothy 2 is the prohibition of women teaching, but in its ancient context the striking thing would more likely have been the indication that women should learn. Perhaps the aim of the passage was to counter women who were insisting that they could and should teach since in Christ "there is no longer male and female" (Gal 3:28). The letter insists that first they must learn. In this way, the moral character of Eve's daughters will lead to her restoration. That would make sense of the otherwise puzzling reference to being "saved through childbearing" (1 Tim 2:15). She (Eve, singular) will be rescued and restored if they (plural, referring to women in the author's time, Eve's descendants) "continue in faith and love and holiness, with self-control." Just as proved to be the case in 1 Corinthians 14, here too the passage can be read as something other than a blanket statement intended to be applied to all circumstances for all times.

Many interpreters of the Bible have given up talking about authorial intention. This is understandable, since we have no way of asking the authors for clarification. Even when it comes to books published in our own time, there can be a divergence between what readers understand and what authors insist in interviews that they meant. Yet although we cannot know for certain what an author intended, that does not make it inappropriate to ask. The key point is to recognize that readers play a role in making meaning. When it comes to texts like the ones discussed in this chapter, interpreters may agree on who the author was but disagree on what they intended to say. They may agree on what the author meant but not on who the author was. They may agree on both points yet disagree on how, if at all, the texts should be applied to the present day. They may agree about the meaning of the words and yet place them against the backdrop of different specific ancient contexts, which affects the connotations and scope of the words. As a reader, you cannot escape the ethical responsibility of exploring the different ways texts have been interpreted and applied and choosing from among the possibilities. Whether you are a male or female reader of the text, you have that authority.

For Further Reading

Bond, Helen, and Joan Taylor. *Women Remembered: Jesus' Female Disciples*. London: Hodder & Stoughton, 2023.

Clark-Soles, Jaime. *Women in the Bible*. Interpretation. Louisville: Westminster John Knox, 2020.

Gooder, Paula. "Apostles, Deacons, Patrons, Co-workers, and Heads of Household: Women Leaders in the Pauline Communities." Pages 163–75 in *Bible Interpretation and Method: Essays in Honour of John Barton*. Edited by Paul Joyce and Katherine Dell. Oxford: Oxford University Press, 2013.

Padgett, Alan. "Paul on Women in the Church: The Contradictions of Coiffure in 1 Corinthians 11.2–16." *Journal for the Study of the New Testament* 6, no. 20 (1984): 69–86.

Payne, Philip Barton. *Man and Woman, One in Christ: An Exegetical and Theological Study of Paul's Letters*. Grand Rapids: Zondervan, 2015.

Peppiatt, Lucy. *Rediscovering Scripture's Vision for Women: Fresh Perspectives on Disputed Texts*. Downers Grove, IL: IVP Academic, 2019.

X

X Marks the Spot

When I teach a course on the Bible and music, I explore with students the way that dramatized versions of New Testament stories have to fill in details. In the Gospels we aren't told so many things that a filmmaker has to think about. When Jesus and Nicodemus talk about the Spirit, are they on the roof and is the wind blowing? When Nicodemus arrives, does Jesus look suspiciously down the stairs past him to see if he has brought others with him? Both of those scenarios are depicted in film versions of the Gospel of John. The respective cinematic portrayals also differ in the mood of conversation between Jesus and Nicodemus. Scholars working on the Gospel of John likewise disagree about whether Nicodemus was a sympathizer who eventually became a disciple, or an antagonist who failed right up until the end to understand who Jesus was. Watching multiple on-screen portrayals of scenes from the New Testament can help us notice just how much is left unsaid in these narratives. This isn't something unique to early Christian literature by any means. No story describes every single person, place, and thing that is mentioned in detail. Filmmakers always have to make artistic decisions when turning a novel or even a script into a movie. The same is true of us as readers, although we may be less conscious of the process because our minds fill in the scenery instinctively. For those who pursue academic study of the Bible, becoming aware of how we fill in the gaps between things that are said, how we set the stage as a backdrop for the words in the New Testament, is a crucial step to becoming wise and skillful interpreters.

Were Crosses Cross-Shaped?

The word "cross" has become associated with a particular shape in English, and this can be seen even across regional variations. What Americans call "tic-tac-toe" the British call "noughts and crosses" (i.e., Os and Xs). In both forms of English you will encounter abbreviations, such as in signs for trains or pedestrians (or ducks or bears) "x-ing" and the train station King's X (London's King's Cross railway station). Yet the word "cross" stems from the Latin word *crux*, which denoted a torture stake without specifying the shape. Interestingly, "crux" has come into English as a word in its own right. Originally it meant the most difficult problem, on the solution of which everything else depends. From there its meaning has broadened to denote what is central. I explain this lest anyone who reads what I wrote above assume that when they read about the "crux" of a particular scholar's argument, it means the part that inflicts the most pain—although on some occasions this may be true.

Cross now means an X or + shape. It derives from the Latin word crux, which refers to any means of impalement. The English word "crux" denotes the central problem needing to be solved.

So how do we know what shape the cross of Jesus was? It is easy to miss the fact that the Gospels do not provide us with this information, at least not explicitly. Readers of the Gospels have seen so many artistic depictions of the crucifixion that we do not even realize that our minds are using this to fill in what the New Testament leaves unstated. (It is the same process that has sometimes led young children who are familiar with only one meaning of the English word "drive" to envisage God in the front seat of a car and two people in the back when they hear that "God drove Adam and Eve out of Eden.") We do have some important evidence from outside the Bible regarding the shape of crosses in general and the cross of Jesus in particular. The evidence includes a jasper amulet in the British Museum that depicts Jesus on a T-shaped cross, a graffito making fun of a Christian named Alexamenos by depicting him worshiping a man with the head of a donkey who is hanging on a T- or t-shaped cross, and another graffito of an unspecified individual being crucified on a T-shaped cross. Ancient authors mention the variety of forms that crosses could take, including a simple vertical stake to which a person was affixed as well as the shape of a T with the victim's arms outstretched. Our New Testament sources do provide some clues but ultimately do not specify the precise shape of the cross as they envisaged it. For instance, Matthew 27:37 says that the accusation for which Jesus was being executed was placed above his head. This is not as unambiguous as it might first appear, since a placard could be attached above the head on a simple vertical stake or a T-shaped one and not only if the cross of Jesus had the form that has become traditional. John 20:25 refers to nails that went through his hands, which is often taken as proof that there was a crossbeam, yet affixing hands to a vertical stake could also involve or even require more than one nail. Clearer evidence is provided by the fact that Jesus is said to carry his cross to Golgotha. The vertical stakes were normally left in place for repeated use, and so, unlike most traditional depictions of Jesus on the Via Dolorosa, Jesus would most likely only have carried the crossbeam. In one movie depiction of the crucifixion, historical information and church tradition are combined so that Jesus carries the complete t-shaped cross while the others to be executed carry only their crossbeams!

Archaeologists found the heel bone of a crucifixion victim named Yehohanan in Givat ha-Mivtar in Israel with the nail still piercing it. This is an extremely rare find, the only other instance of a bone with a nail still through it being found in Italy. The reason for the rarity is that nails were usually pulled out and reused. As a general rule in the ancient world, those who were impaled, whether after being killed or as part of the process, were denied any kind of proper burial. Leaving the body exposed to the elements and scavengers was part of the punishment. Burial was extremely important in the ancient world in general. In Judaism, however, it was a matter of law as well as a core cultural value. Deuteronomy 21:23 explicitly forbids leaving a body hanging on a pole overnight. The first-century historian Flavius Josephus emphasizes the importance of this to Jews in his time, writing in *Jewish War* 4.5 that they even bury victims of crucifixion. It is because of this that Joseph of Arimathea, according to our earliest account in Mark 15:43–47, ensured that Jesus had the bare minimum done for him, wrapping him in a sheet and placing him in a tomb. Mark's story of Jesus being "anointed beforehand for burial" (Mark 14:8) and of women going to the tomb to anoint Jesus's body even after he was already buried (Mark 16:1) together indicate that Jesus was not given the honor of anointing at the time of his burial (contrary to what John 19:38–42 would later depict).

The nail through Yehohanan's ankle reveals something further, namely that each foot or ankle was nailed separately. The length of the nail was not sufficient to pierce two feet or legs as well as the wood. Whether this was typical or not we cannot say. The osteological (i.e., bone) evidence for how the arms or hands were affixed to a cross is much less conclusive.

Some have argued that nails would have been driven through wrists or forearms rather than hands since otherwise the weight of the body might cause the hand to tear. Others envisage ropes being used to support the weight of the person being crucified, whether instead of or in addition to nails. We do not have ancient descriptions or visual depictions that provide a sense of what may have been the "normal procedure" in the case of crucifixions. The evidence we do have suggests that there was no one standard way, and thus it becomes impossible to be very specific about what was likely to have been done to Jesus.

Even if the gospels provided highly detailed descriptions, that would not provide us with historical certainty. After all, the authors of the gospels might have done precisely what modern readers do. They might simply have been told that Jesus was crucified and made assumptions about the shape on the basis of what they had seen. Alas, crucifixions were all too common in the Roman world. That is the main reason why the gospel authors did not feel the need to describe the process in greater detail. They and their earliest readers knew much more about Roman crucifixion practices than we do.

Bone Boxes (Ossuaries)

The Jewish custom in Jesus's time was for a body to be placed in a tomb and allowed to decompose. After a year the bones of the individual would be gathered up and placed in an ossuary, a stone box made for this purpose. Many ossuaries have names on them. You may have encountered reports about some of these. A tomb in the Talpiot neighborhood of Jerusalem contained an ossuary belonging to someone named Jesus son of Joseph, another belonging to a Judas son of Jesus, and several more. While this made headlines (and sometimes causes visitors to the Israel Museum who see them to stand there staring in disbelief), this is not the first authentic ancient ossuary to be discovered that has the name Jesus son of Joseph on it. The fact that the name Jesus is reserved for one individual in English can cause confusion. Jesus of Nazareth had the common Jewish name Joshua. Statistically speaking, there would likely have been quite a few individuals in Jesus's time who, like him, were Josh son of Joe.

Ossuary: a stone box for bones, used in secondary burial. Patina: the chemically altered outer layer of an old object. Provenance: the documented origin and ownership of an object.

Another ossuary that made international news has the inscription "James, son of Joseph, brother of Jesus." There is little doubt that this refers to *that* Jesus, James, and Joseph. It is unusual to mention who someone's brother is on an ossuary. Clearly this individual named James had a brother who was so well known as to make reference to him appropriate. However, rather than being found *in situ* (i.e., in the original place), the ossuary showed up on the antiquities market. In other words, someone who was not a professional archaeologist said they found it and wanted to sell it. Even when an object of that sort can eventually be authenticated, valuable historical information is lost, since an individual object on its own tells us less than a variety of objects found together in a particular place. You'll thus find that many scholars of history are not fans of Indiana Jones and Lara Croft. Tomb raiding is a real thing, and it is a problem. Sure, the movies can be fun, but it is hard to enjoy fictional films when one knows the real-life harm caused by those who plunder artifacts (as well as by those who go looking for objects like the ark of the covenant, even when they fail to find them). In the case of the James ossuary, the object itself is ancient, but the inscription seems to have been added to it more recently, in order to turn a common object of little value into something that a museum or private collector might pay a large sum of money for.

How can archaeologists tell when an inscription has been added relatively recently to an ancient object? The surface of an object made of limestone (and a number of other types of stone and metal) undergoes chemical changes over time as it is exposed to air or water, developing an outer layer that is known as a patina. The patina is largely lacking in the grooves of the inscription on the James ossuary. The would-be seller claimed that this was due to his having cleaned it, but most scholars do not find this explanation persuasive. More likely is that the inscription was added recently, cutting through the patina in the process. You can see why the antiquities trade frustrates scholars. Time is wasted attempting to verify the authenticity of objects. In many instances it proves impossible to do so. When the provenance of an object (i.e., its origin and chain of ownership) cannot be verified, the suspicion arises that it has been acquired in unethical ways. While some scholars consider the potential historical value of such objects, if they turn out to be authentic, to be the highest priority, most refuse to deal with unprovenanced antiquities as a matter of principle.

Lest you be disheartened by the above story, let's turn our attention to one last ossuary, an authentic ancient one. This one is extremely ornate, decorated with patterns that show it belonged to someone of wealth and status. Today it resides in the Israel Museum in Jerusalem. The name on it is Joseph son of Caiaphas. Since Flavius Josephus records that the high priest known from the New Testament simply as Caiaphas was in fact more properly Joseph Caiaphas, it seems that we have the ossuary of this contemporary of Jesus. The ossuary was found in 1990, and scholars took time to carefully study and verify many aspects of the find before publishing about it. This is preferable to what sometimes happens, which is that news of a find breaks almost immediately, before there has been a chance for scientific, linguistic, and other forms of analysis to take place. The public often does not know how to make sense of the fact that a sensational headline appears, only to be followed later by one claiming the first one was wrong. How much better for the scholarly process to be allowed to proceed at the pace it needs to. Historical study does not provide certainty, but its tools are very good at getting beyond first impressions to a fuller and more accurate understanding of what we are dealing with.

The Burial of Jesus

Having moved from crucifixion to burial practices, let us ask about the place where Jesus was buried and the kind of tomb. This is another subject about which art, photography, and even pilgrimage may influence one's perception of the gospel narratives. To a large extent artwork is helpful here. Let's be honest, if someone comes to the gospel narrative about the resurrection and the only "stone" they associate with burial is a gravestone, their understanding of the stone being rolled away is going to be very different than if they've seen a visual depiction of a first-century tomb. Caves were often used to create tombs that served multiple generations of a family. A large, round stone would be used to cover the entrance whenever possible. It would be removed when another family member died and needed to be buried. In places where the bedrock is close to the surface and the dirt is shallow, digging trench graves would be arduous if possible at all. It is easy to understand the preference for adapting caves into tombs. The creation of rock-cut tombs, if more labor-intensive initially than digging a trench, saved time and effort in the long run.

Visiting the places where stories about Jesus are set can be helpful, but also misleading. Many tour guides will point to a spot and confidently tell tourists and pilgrims that it is the place where a certain event occurred. The presence of a church on the spot may suggest that this represents long-standing knowledge vouchsafed by ancient tradition. Yet in a great many instances the identification of a site as significant occurred long after the events. You do not have to be particularly cynical to think that ancient Christians living in Palestine in the fourth century might simply have seized the opportunity when Helena, mother of the emperor Constantine, showed up asking about places where events in the life of Jesus occurred, with a view to building churches on those sites. Be honest—would you have told her, "Sorry, nothing that we're aware of," or would you have directed her to what you considered the best spot for the building of a new church? You can see why we have reason to be skeptical of claims about traditional sites.

However, in some instances there is reason to think that a traditional site does indeed represent the correct location. The Church of the Holy Sepulcher in Jerusalem provides an excellent example. Historians are obviously going to be skeptical of a claim that Jesus delivered the Sermon on the Mount in a particular place, when that sermon appears to be Matthew's thematic arrangement of some of Jesus's teaching into a block. The sites of the crucifixion and resurrection, however, are precisely the sorts of things we'd expect local Christians in Jerusalem to remember and pass on. A number of pieces of evidence point toward the authenticity of the site. One is the fact that, in the time the church was first built, the location lay inside the walls of the city. The local Christians had no explanation for this, and it was only later that archaeologists showed that a new city wall built by Herod Agrippa not long after the time of Jesus changed this site from being outside the city walls to being within them. Had the Christians in the fourth century invented a location, they

The Church of the Holy Sepulcher stands over the traditional site of Golgotha/Calvary, the "place of the skull," where Jesus was crucified and buried.

would have placed it beyond the city walls of their own time to match the description in the gospels. In the fourth century this location was under a platform that was part of the complex of a temple of Aphrodite. When they removed the temple, they found tombs. They identified one of them confidently as the place where Jesus had been buried. It is likely that, even as one can see on the walls of the church today, in ancient times some pilgrims added a mark on the wall to indicate they had visited. Once they were convinced they had found the correct place, workmen carved away surrounding rock to turn that one tomb into a chapel (called the edicule) and built a church over it. The location had been a limestone quarry in the time of Jesus. That might perhaps be what led the early Christians to find Psalm 118:22 so meaningful. It says, "The stone that the builders rejected has become the chief cornerstone," and is quoted multiple times in the New Testament (Matt 21:42; Mark 12:10; Luke 20:17; Acts 4:11; 1 Pet 2:7). Inside the church, one goes up a flight of stairs to the place that would have been the hill known as Golgotha (Calvary). The white rock sticking out of the ground may have been the reason for its nickname, which means "skull."

You may be familiar with another site that some claim to be the place where Jesus died and was buried, known as the Garden Tomb. This site was identified by British general Charles Gordon, who thought the rock looked like a skull or face. It is thus also referred to as Gordon's Calvary. There is no ancient tradition connecting this location with Jesus, and the tomb itself dates from many centuries before his time. These facts do not prevent hundreds of thousands of people from flocking there. This may be a sobering thought for you if you are considering or pursuing a career in biblical studies. You may do research that brings the truth into sharper focus, but that doesn't mean the knowledge you offer will reach a wide audience and be embraced by the general public. It is easy to understand why tourists, especially Protestants, prefer the Garden Tomb to the Church of the Holy Sepulcher. The latter has icons and incense and no tomb of Jesus in sight. The former has a garden and a visible tomb. The experience of being able to imagine oneself back into a biblical narrative is what some visitors are seeking when they travel to this part of the world. Imagination plays a helpful, positive role in the scholarship of historical investigation and reconstruction. It can also play a negative one and be an impediment as we seek to bring the past into clearer focus.

What Did Jesus (and Paul and Others) Look Like?

We started this chapter thinking about what ancient Roman crosses could look like, and the fact that the New Testament does not specify the shape of the cross on which Jesus was crucified. The location of Jesus's crucifixion is also not specified, except in vague terms, yet we have seen in that case as well that traditions from outside the Bible may at times usefully inform our understanding of the New Testament.

Let us end with something else we are not told in the New Testament: what Jesus looked like. We are not told what *anyone* looked like, except for details that are not particularly descriptive. Zacchaeus was short, but how short? (Apparently I would not have been as far below average height in Jesus's time as I am today.) The nickname Thomas means "twin," and that might help us figure out what at least one of the disciples of Jesus looked like—if only we had a description of his brother. New Testament scholar Joan Taylor has written an entire book exploring the topic of what Jesus looked like. Not only historians but also several artists have sought to provide images of Jesus that are more like what a first-century Jewish male might have looked like, and less like the stereotypical depictions influenced by European art. The assumptions of artists not only about skin tone but also about clothing can be seen in painting after painting. Even when we do not have a new discovery that lets us say Jesus looked like this rather than that, further study of the ancient world and increased awareness of our own biases and assumptions can still help us get closer to an accurate understanding. We do not need to discover an eyewitness description of Jesus to know that he would have looked more like a first-century Mediterranean Jew than a modern individual from northern Europe.

One ancient text from outside the New Testament does offer a description of one of the major figures in early Christianity: the apostle Paul. The Acts of Paul and Thecla, which we have already mentioned, provides a description of Paul in its story. In the translation by M. R. James, Paul was "a man little of stature, thin-haired upon the head, crooked in the legs, of good state of body, with eyebrows joining, and nose somewhat hooked, full of grace: for sometimes he appeared like a man, and sometimes he had the face of an angel." If you are a small person with thinning hair, as I am, you may take comfort in the fact that your eyebrows do not meet above your nose. But even if they do, this text indicates that this need not mean your appearance cannot be like that of an angel. More seriously, scholars have wondered what to make of this description. Some have argued that it's likely to be historical, since it seems to us unflattering, and there is little reason why an author who admired Paul would be anything other than complimentary. More recent research has shown that once again our modern assumptions mislead us. We are exposed to images on a daily basis that deliberately seek to define beauty for us in particular ways. Advertising, movies, and other sources express and at the same time influence our values. We must turn to ancient sources to guide us not only when it comes to the shape of crosses but also when it comes to the human features that are considered attractive. People in the ancient Greco-Roman world subscribed to the idea of physiognomy, the now discredited belief that outward appearance indicated something of people's inner character. In describing Paul this way, the author of the Acts of Paul and Thecla would have meant the reader to have the sense that Paul was admirable both in his appearance and as an apostle.

If your appearance mirrors that of Paul the apostle as described in this ancient text, you may find it useful to carry this book with you and show it to anyone who finds your appearance anything other than ideal.

For Further Reading

Arav, Rami. *Jesus and His World: An Archaeological and Cultural Dictionary.* Minneapolis: Fortress, 1995.

Chapman, David W. *Ancient Jewish and Christian Perceptions of Crucifixion.* Grand Rapids: Baker Academic, 2008.

Fisk, Bruce N. *A Hitchhiker's Guide to Jesus: Reading the Gospels on the Ground.* Grand Rapids: Baker Academic, 2011.

Grant, Robert M. "The Description of Paul in the Acts of Paul and Thecla." *Vigiliae Christianae* 36, no. 1 (1982): 1–4.

Hengel, Martin. *Crucifixion in the Ancient World and the Folly of the Message of the Cross.* Minneapolis: Fortress, 1977.

Lawler, Andrew. *Under Jerusalem: The Buried History of the World's Most Contested City.* New York: Doubleday, 2021.

Magness, Jodi. "The Burial of Jesus in Light of Archaeology and the Gospels." *Eretz-Israel* 28 (2007): 1–7.

Malherbe, Abraham J. "A Physical Description of Paul." *Harvard Theological Review* 79, no. 1/3 (1986): 170–75.

Omerzu, Heike. "The Portrayal of Paul's Outer Appearance in the Acts of Paul and Thecla. Re-considering the Correspondence between Body and Personality in Ancient Literature." *Religion and Theology* 15 (2008): 252–79.

Samuelsson, Gunnar. *Crucifixion in Antiquity: An Inquiry into the Background and Significance of the New Testament Terminology of Crucifixion.* Tübingen: Mohr Siebeck, 2013.

Taylor, Joan. *What Did Jesus Look Like?* London: T&T Clark, 2018.

Tzaferis, Vassilios. "Crucifixion—the Archaeological Evidence." *Biblical Archaeology Review* 11, no. 1 (1985): 44-53.

Wingerden, Ruben van. "Crucifixion Practices: How to Attach a *patibulum* to a *stipes.*" *Novum Testamentum* 64, no. 3 (2022): 269-76.

Zias, Joseph, and Eliezer Sekeles. "The Crucified Man from Giv'at Ha-Mivtar: A Reappraisal." *Israel Exploration Journal* 35, no. 1 (1985): 22-27.

Y

Y Chromosome?

As we get close to the end of this book, we are tackling some more difficult topics. That is by design. Often people with radically different viewpoints agree on one thing, namely that the way to decide who is correct is to look at the Bible, find a clear answer, and quote it as proof. Having read this far, you are now aware (if you weren't previously) that the situation is far more complex. The Bible contains diverse works from different authors who did not always see eye to eye. There is often no one thing that the Bible says on a particular topic, but many things. Even if all the biblical authors appear to agree on a matter, there are still questions about the meaning of words, ancient cultural contexts, and other things that must be considered before you assume that what you understand these ancient authors to have meant is in fact precisely what they meant. You are a reader of an English translation of ancient texts from a very different historical and cultural context than your own. If people communicating across cultural difference today can misunderstand each other, how much more when there is a distance in time and no opportunity to ask follow-up questions that might clarify things? It is also appropriate to challenge the assumption that simply finding what the Bible says indicates what should be done in our time. Doing the "same thing" in our own different context may be the same on one level and yet have the opposite meaning and connotation on another level.

Virgin Birth

Let's tackle one of the New Testament topics that has generated substantial debate in the modern era: the virginal conception of Jesus narrated in the infancy stories in the early chapters of the Gospels of Matthew and Luke. We began with the infancy stories, and so returning to them here makes for a nice bookend. A lot of things about this subject remain uncertain and unclear. One thing, however, can be said definitely and without any ambiguity or hesitation: you should not ever, under any circumstances, call Jesus's virginal conception the "immaculate conception." That phrase refers to the Roman Catholic doctrine that Mary was conceived without original sin (sin inherited from Adam). The idea is that she had to have been conceived this way in order for Jesus not to inherit original sin from her. That phrase does not mean the miraculous conception of Jesus. While distinguishing immaculate conception from the virgin birth, we have an opportunity to notice that the idea of original sin is not found in the New Testament, yet it is clearly a major influence on the development of the Catholic doctrine about Mary's conception, which is itself an effort to distance Jesus from sin. It is but one of many ideas that has been introduced in the process of formulating Christian theology, felt by some to be either implicit in the New Testament or required in order to make sense of what it says.

I have sometimes heard people say that it is crucial to accept the virginal conception either to distance Jesus from sin or to safeguard his divinity. The New Testament passages about Jesus's miraculous conception are concerned with neither of these things. Matthew and Luke do not depict Jesus as the incarnation of a preexistent divine person, while the Gospel of John does so without any mention of a miraculous conception. No gospel connects Jesus's miraculous conception with avoidance of the taint of original sin. Often contemporary theological views, at least in their popular form, are a hodgepodge of snippets from the New Testament mixed with modern ideas that the ancient authors of these works did not have in mind. Hence the title of this chapter. If Jesus had no human father, did he have a Y chromosome? If so, was it borrowed from Joseph, miraculously created, or something else? If Jesus only inherited chromosomes from his mother, he would be biologically female, having two X chromosomes. If we ask about Jesus's chromosomes, we are asking questions the New Testament authors do not answer. Yet as people who know about chromosomes, we cannot completely set aside that knowledge when we read ancient texts.

Same-Sex Sex

You may have seen internet memes claiming that the New Testament does not mention homosexuality. You may also have read the New Testament and seen the word right there on the page in front of you. By this point you should know that the appropriate next step is to look into what the underlying Greek words are. That doesn't mean looking at *Strong's Exhaustive Concordance* but consulting a resource like one of Liddell and Scott's Greek lexicons, available online in searchable form. Even doing that, however, you may not notice that ancient Greek had terminology for those who engaged in same-sex intercourse. This practice was *very* common in ancient Greece, not as an alternative to what we might call heterosexual marriage, but as a form of eroticism that existed alongside that practice. It almost always involved older men and younger men or boys. It is thus obviously *not* what today's advocates and defenders of same-sex marriage are talking about. Ancient marriage was about procreating to produce legitimate offspring who could be the heirs of the male in question, without question. Men in Greek and Roman society often had a range of other options for sexual satisfaction that were considered both legal and moral, most of which are at odds not just with Christian views of marriage but with modern secular notions of fidelity and marriage of an egalitarian sort. The difference between ancient and modern views of gender, sex, and marriage absolutely needs to be part of any discussion of what the New Testament meant in its original context, which has to be the precursor to any discussion of how one might apply it today.

I remember hearing someone say "Read Romans 1" in a discussion about same-sex relationships. There are a lot of ironies in that. First, there is the fact that when Paul wrote his letter, it had no chapter divisions. In most instances that is mere trivia, but here it is crucially important because it has become the custom for people to read the Bible either as isolated verses or at most a chapter at a time. Yet it is only in Romans 2 that we learn the meaning of Romans 1. In the first chapter, Paul emulates the way Jewish authors wrote about gentiles (in particular he emulates the text known as the Wisdom of Solomon, which we've mentioned elsewhere in this book). He does this not as an end in itself but so that, like the prophet Nathan confronting David, he can turn on those who join in the condemnation of others and tell them that in so doing they have condemned themselves. Hopefully you can see the irony now if you hadn't previously. The point of Romans 1 is to allow Paul to turn to the gentile-condemning Jews in his audience in the church in Rome and say in chapter 2, "If you talk this way and condemn others, whoever you are, you are without excuse." Anyone who uses Romans 1 as a weapon to condemn others has missed the point entirely. If they read just a few more lines, they would realize that in so doing they have condemned themselves.

There are too many detailed questions related to this topic to try to tackle them all here. The key thing is that you now have the tools you need to research it and figure out what you think. You know that the terminology used by the New Testament authors is not the more obvious terminology that would have denoted same-sex intercourse to people in this time. You know that Greek culture valued pederasty, sexual feelings and relationships between older men and adolescent males. Since that was the typical same-sex relationship in Paul's time, and marriage was a union aimed at producing legitimate heirs to inherit one's property, that means our whole framework with regard to sex and marriage today is different from Paul's. What some today call "biblical marriage" is rarely akin to what is described or treated as normative in the Bible. To be clear, fidelity between two people is a wonderful lived expression of core principles articulated in the New Testament, but it was not the norm of marriage as an institution that existed in New Testament times. Thus even today's secular monogamous marriages owe something to the influence of an ideal portrait of marriage that is emphasized in the New Testament precisely because it was anything but the norm in that era.

Passages and Principles

When broaching a subject that is controversial for some Christians, whether it be same-sex relationships, ordination of women, or equality in marriage, I regularly turn first to the subject of slavery. It is a good place to begin precisely because most people today consider it a settled matter, something clear rather than a topic of controversy. Yet this was not always the case. Not by a long shot. Some of today's denominations in the United States exist precisely as a result of splits that happened over the issue of slavery. There were strong advocates for abolition among Christians, but there were also staunch defenders of slavery. Some of the key elements of the doctrine of biblical inerrancy emerged out of these controversies. A key accusation of those who defended slavery was that abolitionists make the biblical texts out to be fallible at best, and at worst make their authors promoters of sin. If slavery is evil and the laws in the Pentateuch and the household codes in the New Testament letters fail to challenge it, then where does that leave us? It leaves us with human writings that one cannot simply cite as though they provide a definitive answer concerning moral matters that will seem adequate in every age and for all time. Yet despite the claims of the inerrantists, this does not mean that the choice is between being faithful to the Bible or abandoning its authority. Many abolitionists appealed to the Bible to support their stance. They just used the Bible differently than their opponents. While the defenders of slavery pointed to many specific passages, abolitionists often focused more attention on principles. The Golden Rule ("do to others what you would want them to do to you") makes the matter seem simple to resolve. Would you want to be someone else's property? No? Then don't make someone else your property. Simple—but not a conclusion that the authors of the Pentateuch, Colossians, Ephesians, 1 Timothy, or Titus drew. This approach makes central what Jesus and the Gospels emphasize as central, yet it does so in a way that reveals that the early Christians who produced the New Testament were fallible as we are. They had many of the same principles we do, but they did not always implement them consistently. Neither do we. And like them, we can do no better than to take the teaching of Jesus and seek to apply its core principles to our own time. There is a long history of Christians deciding that, in order to follow Jesus faithfully in our time, we will need to do something different than his followers in the past did.

Some will object that the issue of slavery is not the same as the issues of same-sex marriage, ordination of women, or gender equality. Of course they aren't the same. No two issues are identical, and just because one was addressed in the past, it does not mean we can bypass debates and difficult conversations in the present, or in the future for that matter. My point is that the same approach to the Bible that was used to justify slavery is often visible in justifying patriarchy and other stances. As we saw earlier in the book, the early churches that welcomed uncircumcised gentiles as full members in their movement were at odds with what Genesis said plainly and unambiguously. Being aware of this fact doesn't offer us a clear-cut, simple answer to any contemporary issue, neatly served on a platter. What it tells us is that those who say "the Bible clearly says" and point to specific passages may seem with hindsight to be either courageous defenders of the Bible and traditional values, or conservative traditionalists who stood in the way of a new thing that God was doing. The Bible won't tell us which. This book hasn't given you the answers to today's pressing moral issues, nor can it offer you a glimpse of how today's debates will look when viewed with hindsight from future centuries. But hopefully this book has prepared you to wrestle with issues in the best way possible, precisely because you know that the Bible will provide principles but not simple answers, and it is up to Christian communities today to work out how to put them into practice.

The New Testament doesn't answer questions about things like chromosomes because no human being in that time was aware such things existed. The same is true of countless other topics. The exegetical study of the New Testament focuses on placing it in its ancient context, making sense of words within their original cultural and historical setting. It is not immediately obvious how to get from there to present-day application. Finding that challenging is a *good* thing. The biggest problem in our time is not that applying the New Testament is difficult and time-consuming. The biggest problem is rather that so many people think or pretend that this is something easy. If the result of your reading this book is that you consider this a genuinely daunting task, writing it has been worthwhile, and you are better off as a result of reading it. Things that are worth doing and likely to be rewarding are rarely quick, simple, or easy.

For Further Reading

Dunning, Benjamin H. *The Oxford Handbook of New Testament, Gender, and Sexuality.* New York: Oxford University Press, 2019.

Horsley, Richard A., ed. *Paul and Politics: Ekklesia, Israel, Imperium, Interpretation.* Philadelphia: Trinity Press International, 2000.

Lewis, Lloyd Alexander. "An African American Appraisal of the Philemon-Paul-Onesimus Triangle." Pages 232–46 in *Stony the Road We Trod: African American Biblical Interpretation.* Edited by C. H. Felder. Minneapolis: Fortress, 2021.

Lincoln, Andrew. *Born of a Virgin? Reconceiving Jesus in the Bible, Tradition, and Theology.* Grand Rapids: Eerdmans, 2013.

Loader, William. *The New Testament on Sexuality.* Grand Rapids: Eerdmans, 2012.

Meeks, Wayne A. "The 'Haustafeln' and American Slavery: A Hermeneutical Challenge." Pages 234–53 in *Theology and Ethics in Paul and His Interpreters: Essays in Honor of Victor Paul Furnish.* Edited by Eugene H. Lovering Jr. and Jerry L. Sumney. Nashville: Abingdon, 1996.

Roberts, Kyle. *A Complicated Pregnancy: Whether Mary Was a Virgin and Why It Matters.* Minneapolis: Fortress, 2017.

Scroggs, Robin. *The New Testament and Homosexuality: Contextual Background for Contemporary Debate.* Minneapolis: Fortress, 1983.

Shanks, Hershel. "The Dispute about Slavery in America." Pages 203–16 in *Biblical Studies Alternatively: An Introductory Reader.* Edited by Susanne Scholz. Upper Saddle River, NJ: Prentice Hall, 2003.

Z

Zacchaeus, Zebedee, Zebulun, Zechariah

There is no way to cover absolutely everything it might be important to know about the New Testament in *any* book, much less one this size. This book is intended as an introduction to this field of study. It covers the ABCs but in the process meanders casually through "the weeds," as some might put it, and eventually takes you from A through Z, covering a lot of genuinely challenging topics on the journey, hopefully without making anyone feel overwhelmed in the process. If you take a course on this subject, you will typically get something called a syllabus. If you are a typical student, you won't read it and at some point in the semester will annoy your professor by asking a question that was answered on it even before the first day of class. It seems I have finally learned my lesson after several decades of teaching. I did not tell you in the introduction what you would learn as you make your way through this book. If I had, you might have stopped reading, just as some who do read a syllabus may realize just in the nick of time that a particular course is not for them. If this book had been called *Antipas to Zebulun*, you would never have purchased it.

If you are one of the very tiny number of people on this planet who might have read a book by that title, then you are probably also genuinely hoping that in this chapter I'll finally dig into a lot of detail about Zacchaeus, Zebedee, Zebulun, and Zechariah. I'm sorry to disappoint you—the title of this chapter is mainly intended as an amusing way to indicate that you've reached the end. But I'll say a little, and in fact a little has already been said about most of these individuals at some point earlier in this book. (If this sounds like a snoozefest, skip this chapter and catch some Zs of a different sort.)

We said a little about Zacchaeus being little. The only story that mentions him, in Luke 19:1-10, tells us that he was a chief tax collector in Jericho. You will guess that it's a safe assumption that tax collectors were not more popular in the past than they are today, but thanks to your reading this book you'll also know that the amount and methods of taxation in the past are bound to have been different, and that it is important to look into this if you want to understand exactly why tax collectors were disliked. Briefly, a chief tax collector would likely have been someone who paid Rome the amount they were owed for a particular territory and in return was granted the right to collect the taxes owed, and to add whatever they saw fit on top of that so that they earned a profit. While a government employee deserves to earn a living, as you can probably imagine the Roman system left a lot of room for people to make themselves wealthy at the expense of others in ways that were unjust and unfair. Was that the case with Zacchaeus? In Luke 19:8 Zacchaeus tells Jesus what he is doing for the poor and those he may have defrauded. Although he uses present tenses, which would normally mean that it is his current practice to give half of his wealth to the poor and pay back anyone he inadvertently defrauds four times the amount, the reference to salvation coming to his household (Luke 19:9-10) suggests that this is a new commitment in response to his encounter with

Jesus. The way the society and its economy worked is crucial background information, something everyone reading
Luke would know—which you now at least know you need
to investigate when reading a story like this one. You have
also learned about the importance of comparing translations
and reading commentaries and articles so that you become
aware of things that might not be immediately obvious from
reading one English translation, such as the tenses used and
different possible interpretations that result.

We also said a bit about Zechariah, mostly the fact that Jesus's saying about martyrs from Abel to Zechariah probably
didn't refer to the father of John the Baptist, although later
Christian literature assumed he did and developed stories
of his martyrdom. We also covered how Zechariah 9:9 is interpreted in the New Testament, especially Matthew 21:1-7.
Zebedee has gotten attention in this book, and I hinted that
his fishing business might have been something much more
elaborate than a family catching fish to feed themselves. If he
was part of the fishing industry, what kind of education could
he provide for his children? Even the little we are told about
Zebedee and his family allows us to draw on what we know
about this era, its society and economy, to fill in information
that these texts do not tell us because that information was
taken for granted by the author and earliest readers.

As for Zebulun (which I didn't mention until this chapter, but it's a Z-word so let's not skip it), that is the name of
one of the tribes of Israel, and Matthew mentions it twice
(Matt 4:13, 15). Were Jesus and some of his Galilean followers
descendants of Zebulun or other tribes in the northern parts
of ancient Israel? The northern tribes are largely neglected by
Christians, yet not only Samaria but also Galilee represents
their historic homeland. The fact that Zebulun is mentioned
at all in the New Testament is noteworthy. So is the fact that
it is mentioned so infrequently. Why was the connection of

Galilee with the northern tribes largely ignored in the literature we have from this era? Did local people living there nonetheless remember this aspect of their Israelite heritage? How does this relate to Jesus's symbolic appointment of the Twelve, which we discussed earlier in the book? These are all things that someone may or may not notice reading by themselves in isolation. This book has shown you the benefit of reading in conversation with others and letting both modern scholars and ancient authors from in and around New Testament times be part of your reading group. There is much we don't know, but you'll find your reading of the New Testament enriched, not because you always find answers to your questions, but because the questions you've begun to ask are more insightful, more penetrating, and better informed.

Most of us experience in childhood that learning can be fun. It does not have to be dull or tedious. There are many children's shows that teach the literal ABCs, but the children who watch them don't realize they are learning the alphabet—they are just enjoying the show. In that same spirit I didn't tell you that you'd be wrestling with differences between the gospels and with texts that have played a role in anti-Semitism. There was no warning that the history of the Hasmoneans and the Herodians would feature. I hope that neither those few who came looking for such things, nor the majority who might have been put off by making reference to them too early, were disappointed with what they found in these pages. If you're reading this, either you made it this far on your own or a professor has required you to do so. (If the latter, please send me an email and let me know how they made sure you did the reading.)

The key things that I hope you will take away with you from reading this book have already been said, and in most instances said more than once. The way the book revisits topics from different angles and in slightly different ways has been intentional. The same issues of interpretation come up in relation to many different passages, and different methods prove relevant to the same passages. No system of organizing content can avoid having to cross-reference between chapters. Each time we have had occasion to return to a text or topic we touched on previously, we have brought some additional aspect into the picture or drawn connections that we could not when the subject first came up. The repetition, adding depth and detail each time, will have cemented key information and concepts in your memory.

Grouping material in the order of the New Testament texts or by interpretive method makes sense in some contexts, but let's just say that it might take a significant dose of self-motivation to read a book of that sort. This book has sought to communicate the same key information as is found in a standard textbook or introductory course, but to do so in a readable way that is useful to anyone, perhaps especially those who did not know when they started reading what exactly they needed to learn. The book has focused on methods, issues, and examples but does not include the things that you can most easily look up. Looking things up will continue to be necessary no matter what one learns in an introduction to the New Testament. Now that you've read this book, it is much more likely that you'll find what you need when you look things up and that you'll wisely interpret the information you find.

This book is an introduction. It offers the core things that New Testament scholars know about the New Testament that absolutely anyone interested in the New Testament ought to know. Scholars build on that foundation and dig into the specific details in ways that go beyond what is covered here. You now have the tools and the core knowledge you need to do the same. As you return to your reading of the New Testament, you won't find that all the mysteries and puzzles are now resolved. Rather, you'll find yourself noticing more of them than you ever did before. Perhaps you'll be the one to come up with a definitive solution to a question that I'm still wondering about. Scholarship is a conversation. I hope this book warmly welcomed you into it as a participant. I look forward to hearing *your* voice as part of the conversation in the future.

For Further Reading

Jeffers, James S. *The Greco-Roman World of the New Testament Era: Exploring the Background of Early Christianity.* Downers Grove, IL: InterVarsity, 1999.

Millard, Allan. *Reading and Writing in the Time of Jesus.* London: Bloomsbury Academic, 2005.

Staples, Jason A. *The Idea of Israel in Second Temple Judaism: A New Theory of People, Exile, and Israelite Identity.* New York: Cambridge University Press, 2021.

Tobolowsky, Andrew. *The Myth of the Twelve Tribes of Israel: New Identities across Time and Space.* New York: Cambridge University Press, 2022.

Acknowledgments

In a book for a general audience it seemed best to place the thank-yous and other such things at the end, since the majority of readers skip them while those who read everything within a book will not overlook them here. It also provides the nice symbolism that once we think we are done, having reached Z, we circle around to find that there are new discoveries to be made in the things that we began with. Even with all the information that was undoubtedly new to readers, most things in this book can be explored at even greater depths and with far more detail. I promise that there is more to be learned and that these texts have not finished unlocking their mysteries. I hope you will view the end of the book as the beginning of a journey. After the Z comes a new and richer A.

I am grateful to my editor at Eerdmans, Trevor Thompson, for the invitation to write this book. I am grateful to him, Laurel Draper, and Kristine Nelson and to all his colleagues at Eerdmans for the encouragement to channel my decades of teaching and blogging into a book of this sort, and to Ryan Davis for copyediting the book. Most of my teaching experience has been at Butler University in Indianapolis, where

I have offered introductory classes in the core curriculum
as well as upper-level classes open to everyone and not only
majors and minors in religious studies. Thus in no class could
I assume that students already knew anything in particular,
or found it interesting. That, coupled with my blogging in
an effort to convey the fruits of New Testament research to
a general audience, has resulted in an approach that is hopefully accessible to and enjoyable by anyone. I am grateful to
my wife, Elena, who read my book thoroughly and spotted all
kinds of little issues that could be improved. She also literally
laughed out loud and told me how much she enjoyed reading
it and how much she learned from it. Since she has studied
the New Testament and, what's worse, has lived with me and
put up with hearing me talk about these things for decades, if
she could find what I wrote fresh and interesting, it gave me
some hope that others might too. I am also grateful to those
in my Sunday school class at Crooked Creek Baptist Church
who have provided an opportunity to reflect weekly on what
my work as a New Testament scholar has to say to Christians. They have never allowed me to just find these things
interesting as an intellectual exercise without asking about
relevance and application. I thank them all, and in particular
Rev. Dr. Don Scott and Rev. Joy Amick, who expressed interest in reading the manuscript even before publication.

I am grateful to my many Butler students and blog readers. This book is dedicated to one in particular, Kelly Lewis-
Walls Porter, that rare student who didn't merely say they'd
stay in touch after graduation but actually did so. When her
health deteriorated so that work and many other things became impossible, she told me she'd like to record at least one
of my books as an audiobook, just because she enjoyed them
and wanted to do so. I was thrilled. Unfortunately her health
prevented her from doing so, and sadly as the book you are

reading was nearing completion she died. At the celebration of life for Kelly, her husband shared with me that by my name in her phone she didn't have "Butler University" or "professor" or even "friend," but instead had labeled my contact "writer extraordinaire." I was deeply moved, and it seemed fitting to take the opportunity of this book's publication to repay the compliment as well as to lament the fact that I will not get a call from her telling me what she thought of it.

Index of Names and Subjects

Index of Scripture and Other Ancient Texts